Protestant and Roman Catholic

Prospects for Rapprochement

Protestant and Roman Catholic

James M. Gustafson

The University of Chicago Press

Chicago and London

The University of Chicago Press, Chicago 60637
The University of Chicago Press, Ltd., London

© 1978 by The University of Chicago
All rights reserved. Published 1978
Printed in the United States of America
83 82 81 80 79 78   9 8 7 6 5 4 3 2 1

Library of Congress Cataloging in Publication Data

Gustafson, James M.
    Protestant and Roman Catholic ethics.

    Includes bibliographical references and index.
    1. Christian ethics—Comparative studies—
Addresses, essays, lectures. I.   Title.
BJ1251.G877   241   77-21421
ISBN 0-226-31107-4

JAMES M. GUSTAFSON is University Professor of
Theological Ethics at the University of Chicago
Divinity School. He is the author of numerous
books, including *Theology and Christian Ethics*
and *Christ and the Moral Life*.

Contents

Preface

My study of Roman Catholic ethics extends back to my years as a student. I first became interested in the social encyclicals of Pope Leo XIII and Pope Pius XI; from them I have gradually been expanding the range of my knowledge and clarification of issues. In the mid-fifties at what was called "The Institute of Ethics and Politics" at Wesleyan University in Connecticut I participated in seminars led by the late Kenneth W. Underwood in which Roman Catholic political ethics was a major topic; difficult as it is to believe at the present time, our academic Roman Catholic representation was limited to a layman who taught political science at Wesleyan. During and since Vatican II, as every reader of this page knows, the opportunities for common exploration of issues have expanded greatly. My first public lectures on the topic of this book were delivered in April 1964, at the United Theological Seminary of the Twin Cities, New Brighton, Minnesota. A summer session course at Union Theological Seminary, New York, in 1966 was particularly exciting; I had announced the general area of this book as my topic for six weeks, only to find (much to my astonishment) that most of the members of my seminar were Roman Catholic theologians and philosophers of considerable intellectual maturity. During the following summer at Loyola University, Montreal, I participated in a week of intensive discussion with Robert Johann, Bernard Häring, and John C. Bennett as principals and scores of teachers of theology and ethics as secondary participants. In my seminars and lectures for twenty years I have used Roman Catholic materials when they have been relevant to the topics under discussion; frequently I have used them as a basis for critically exploring deficiencies in Protestant theological ethics. All this is by way of saying that what is here offered expresses a long-standing and deep interest.

The flush of ecumenical enthusiasm is gone; we are in for a long haul of harder and more careful work; there is not the same eager population waiting to hear from us that there was a decade ago. I have come through these years with a deep conviction, expressed in this book, that Roman Catholic and Protestant theologians can begin to delineate fundamental questions inherent in our field of competence, to explore answers to them with critical reference to both traditions, and to propose some small increments in solutions that these questions demand. Thus the subject matter and the agenda of questions arise out of the bibliography, out of the texts, whether Roman Catholic or Protestant. The task is to formulate the important questions and find the most adequate and coherent answers; it is not to find the least common denominator to which both traditions can give allegiance. I believe I can honestly say that I care not one whit whether a position or an argument has been historically identified with one or the other tradition, and by implication whether one or the other tradition can take pride in giving a more satisfactory answer. I do care, very deeply, about Christian theological ethics. I care about the intellectual cogency of the field; I care about the quality of intellectual life of the Christian community, tempted as it is to find its strength solely in popular pieties and/or in its utility to individuals and society; I care about the mission of the Christian community in these decades, and thus about the quality of thought that provides reasons for and direction to its activities.

All this does not mean that I do not care about the ethos of modern society, the oppression of groups of peoples in various societies, the terrorizing loneliness and hopelessness of individuals, the strategies for social change. It does not mean that I do not know that my work is relative to a culture and to a society, that it is tinged by the interests of a theologian whose professional environment has always been very secular universities, that "praxis" (as we have learned to call it) is a matrix of theory, that social and historical changes must be taken into account in explaining changes in ideas. It does mean, however, that nothing can substitute for intellectual honesty and for the best achievable cogency in thought about Christian faith and morality, Christian theology and ethics. This is to claim that the task undertaken in this book is important; the extent of success in fulfilling it is a matter about which I, indeed, have good reasons to be modest. If its effect is only to stimulate critical rejoinders, or to prompt colleagues to take the discussion a step or two further, I shall be satisfied.

Acknowledgments

The contributions of four close friends and professional colleagues are far greater than footnote references indicate. Richard A. McCormick, S.J., has been my mentor in person and through his writings for many years and made significant suggestions about Chapters 2, 3, and 4 when they were first prepared for public lectures. Charles E. Curran has also been a conversation partner in voice and print on many occasions through the years; his academic agenda has breadth comparable to my own, and I continually learn from his frequent publications. David Tracy responded thoughtfully to the middle chapters after their first public hearing in lecture form and, as a coinstructor in seminars and a conversation partner, has been encouraging and critically helpful. Paul Ramsey has for longer than the others been a major stimulus to my thinking and writing; while he had nothing specific to do with this book, in general he has had a lot to do with it and many of my other writings.

Rabbi Hanina is often quoted, "Much have I learned from my teachers, and more from my comrades than from my teachers, and from my disciples the most." In the pejorative sense, I hope I have no "disciples," but I do wish to acknowledge my indebtedness to my students, past and present, especially those who have been members of my graduate seminars on theological ethics.

Special acknowledgment is due to those Roman Catholic theologians whose dissertations were written with my counsel: Albert R. Jonsen, James F. Bresnahan, S.J., Margaret Farley, R.S.M., Richard R. Roach, S.J., and Lisa S. Cahill. They symbolize others, Protestants and Catholics, who have made those seminars the most satisfying aspect of my professional life.

An invitation to deliver the William Henry Hoover Lectures on Christian Unity in January 1973, from the late Dean W. Barnett Blakemore of the Disciples Divinity House at the University of Chicago, crystallized the first development of the middle three chapters of this book. This lectureship was endowed in 1928 by Mr. Hoover to provide an opportunity to discuss "the problems of Christian unity and make a positive contribution toward the closer cooperation of the many Christian denominations and the ultimate unity of the Church of Christ." These lectures, delivered annually, are sponsored by the Disciples Divinity House, and planned by representatives of the theological schools in the Hyde Park area of Chicago.

John Carroll University sponsored a program in the same month· in which the Touhy Lectures were given on Roman Catholic ethics by Charles E. Curran, on Jewish ethics by Lou Silberman, on Buddhist ethics by Frank Reynolds, and on Protestant ethics by me. The first chapter of this book is drawn from my Touhy Lectures. President Prescott Williams and the faculty of Austin Presbyterian Seminary subsequently invited me to deliver the Currie Lectures. A version of this book was delivered there in February 1975. The second chapter was also used, in an earlier form, for a lecture in a series on Christian ethics, sponsored by the Fordham University Department of Theology. The first draft of the final chapter was read at the meeting of the American Society for Christian Ethics in January 1976.

Since the present book is significantly different from any of the sponsored lectures, and since I have enjoyed the support and hospitality of four institutions in developing this book, it is not published under the name of any of the lectureships. I do, however, desire to record my indebtedness and thanks to the sponsors of each and especially to the committee on the Hoover Lectures because of the decisive role they had for me.

To my dean, Joseph M. Kitagawa, and to the University of Chicago for its remarkably stimulating intellectual environment, "general thanksgiving" is offered.

Historic Divergences

Current convergences and divergences between Roman Catholic and Protestant ethics can be understood more clearly if some historic characteristics of each are kept in mind. Surprisingly, there is little significant historical scholarship dealing with either, or with the history of their relations to each other.[1] The first chapter of this book does not pretend to be a historical study. In it, my modest intention is to draw some plausible generalizations about salient historical characteristics of each in order to render the following chapters more intelligible.

Ecclesiastical Functions

The ecclesiastical function of writings in ethics or moral theology has been radically different in the Protestant and Roman Catholic traditions. Failure to recognize that Catholic moral theology developed in the service of the priestly role in the sacrament of penance has led to a great deal of misunderstanding and to misplaced criticisms by Protestant theologians. Protestants misread moral theology if they do not remember that, like canon law, it has functioned not only pedagogically but also "juridically" in Catholic Christian life. Writings in moral theology are used not only to teach persons what principles ought to guide their conduct and what actions are judged morally illicit; they also provide the priest whose vocation is to administer the sacrament of penance with criteria by which he can enumerate and judge the seriousness of various sinful acts in order to assign the appropriate penance. In a way not dissimilar to that of a judge in a civil court, the priest must determine the severity of the penitent's moral guilt; to do this he is trained to grade actions according to the seriousness of their sinfulness. The distinction between mortal and venial sins, for example, provides a principle by which sinful acts can be clearly classified both by the faithful who confess and by the priests who hear their confessions.

It is not unreasonable to suggest that this role of the priest is more similar historically to one aspect of the office of the rabbi in traditional Judaism than it is to the role of the Protestant minister. Both the priest and the rabbi function as teachers of morality. They are the instructors of their congregations in the requirements of morality and, indeed, of moral law. The rabbi is a scholar in Torah, and much of the activity of the synagogue has been the study of Torah by the faithful. While the rabbi does not have the power to grant absolution that the priest does, he has functioned as a judge in disputed claims made in accordance with the *halakhah*. To be a wise judge he must know the law, just as the priest must know the moral and canon law to be a sound and wise confessor. To make judgments, both the priest and the rabbi exercise their capacities to reason—granted, in quite different ways. For both, however, a body of law (or quasi-legal moral theology) is necessary if they are to function in their professional roles.

Indeed, it is worthwhile to note that the *halakhic* tradition in Judaism has significant similarities to the development of moral theology and canon law in Catholicism. Morality and law have a similar centrality in the two traditions; only the Anglican tradition has come close to these in Reformed Christianity. Torah is the foundation of the moral and religious life of the Jewish community. Moral and religious guidance is provided through its interpretations in the Talmud, in classic biblical commentaries, in the great codifications by Maimonides and by Rabbi Karo in the *Shulhan Arukh*, and in the *responsa* of learned rabbis. As in the Catholic tradition of canon law and moral theology, in the Jewish tradition there is heavy emphasis on precision in interpretation of law, and there is a continuous body of literature to which reference is made. Rabbinic rationality and logic are parallel in function to the rationality of canon lawyers and moral theologians. Law, on the whole, has not had a similar centrality in Protestant history.

Consequently, seldom in Protestant church life has such a juridical role existed. The closest kin to Catholic moral theological literature to be found in Protestant Christianity is in Anglican moral theology and in Puritan texts on "cases of conscience."[2] In those parts and periods of Anglican history that have emphasized examination of conscience and private confession there is significant continuity with the Roman Catholic tradition. Puritanism also required an examination of conscience as a part of the Christian life, though the Puritan clergy did not have "priestly" authority. For the most part, however, the sacrament of penance quickly atrophied or was in principle discarded in Protestant life. There is an irony to be noted; in Lutheranism and Calvinism the emphasis on man's sinfulness was greater than it was in Catholic theology, yet in Catholicism the criteria for judging sins were clearer and more precise. The irony is resolved, as we shall see shortly, when the way in which sin was understood in Protestantism is made clear. But the liturgical practice has been that of a general confession of sin: "general" in two references, (a) the congregation confesses together, and (b) it is more a general state of sin than specific sins that is confessed. The Protestant pastor has not needed the refined case-oriented literature that Catholic moral theology provides because he has not been the examiner of conscience and the judge of conduct in the same way. He has not needed manuals to assist him in adjudicating, for example, whether masturbation is a more serious infraction of the moral law than is fornication, since he has not had to make such a judgment.[3] He has not had to assign penitential acts (there are exceptions, for examples, the use of the "shunning" in Anabaptist communities and the denial of a person's right to take communion in Puritan congregations) but has read to the penitent congregation "the comforting words" of forgiveness.

The function of writings in ethics in Protestantism has consequently been more diffuse and ambiguous, but that it has been more pedagogical than juridical is clear. Subsequently, attention will be given to the theological deterrents to the kind of precision that has characterized Catholic ethics. I know of no Protestant text, for example, whose author felt compelled to ask, as did St. Thomas, "Whether a man ought, out of charity, to love his children more than his father?"[4] Among the reasons for not asking is that there have been no, or very few, occasions in Protestantism's moral history and ethos or in its ecclesiastical practice on which a pastor would ever have had to answer such a question. There are no prayers of general confession, to the best of my knowledge, which read, "We confess, O God, that we have loved our fathers more than our children," or "our children more than our fathers." Even as teachers of morality, Protestant theologians have seldom attended to an issue as specific as this. Indeed, as teachers, Protestant theologians have with few exceptions written ethics that are more theologically than morally oriented,[5] and there has normally not been an ecclesiastical role that directs the work of the theologian either to the pastor or to the laity in an authoritative way. In the Lutheran tradition, particularly, the dread of "legalism" has deterred ethical precisions; to state specific expectations of moral conduct is deemed to invite Christian people to justify themselves before God by their moral righteousness rather than to rely upon God's gracious favor for their salvation. In Calvinism the primacy of the "third use" of the law, to inform and goad Christians, provides a foundation for greater ethical specification. Some of the theological reasons for the difference in ecclesiastical functions of ethics will be noted subsequently.

In addition to the correlation between the sacrament of penance and the way in which ethical writings developed in Catholicism, another ecclesiological factor has been decisive in its consequence for the development of ethical thought. Catholic moral theology is done in the context of the magisterial, or teaching, authority of the church. The church makes a theological claim to authority not only to determine the proper dogmas and doctrines to be adhered to, not only to determine the proper inferences to be drawn from Scripture, but also to determine the correct interpretations and applications of the natural moral law.[6] An old joke from the "equal time" circuit of Catholic, Jewish, and Protestant speeches makes the point in an exaggerated but illuminating way. Asked to address a common specific moral issue, the priest begins his reply, "The church teaches that . . ." The rabbi begins, "The tradition teaches that...." And the Protestant pastor begins, "Well, now I think that...." The three opening remarks suggest three patterns of religious authority in moral matters.

Protestant ethics has never been developed in a setting in which there is a supreme court of appeals to adjudicate what is morally right and wrong. Nor have Protestant theologians customarily worked under conditions which have so strongly required loyalty to specific moral teachings and doctrines. (Theological restrictions have been more frequent.) Since the time of the Great Sanhedrin in Jerusalem, Judaism has also developed without a "supreme court," though in some settings the "chief rabbi" has great authority. While the Bible has frequently been a basis for authority in Protestant ethics, and the Torah and Talmud have been in Jewish law and ethics, the criteria for determining what is "authoritative" moral teaching in both of these traditions is much more complex than in the Catholic tradition.[7]

Non-Catholics, as well as many Roman Catholics, often presume that the Catholic church's teaching authority is clearer and simpler than it actually is either in principle or in practice. The current discussion, which is addressed in Chapter 4, indicates that the range of "infallibility" and of authority to determine the rightness of particular acts, has been frequently overextended. For example, Pope Pius XII was especially interested in medical moral questions and spoke about them often. His "allocutions" in these matters are not infallible; yet they were received as having almost infallible authority by many Catholic physicians and hospitals. The authority of an encyclical, as the discussion of *Humanae Vitae* has made apparent, is not absolutely clear; at least there are serious differences of opinion about it, as the religiously literate world knows. What is beyond dispute, however, is that the church has had a teaching authority in morals that is foreign to Protestant experience.

The major consequence of this is a much greater diversity in the history of Protestant ethics than in that of Roman Catholic moral theology. On particular moral matters such as war or abortion, until the modern period Protestants have largely accepted the dominant Western Christian cultural stance; the Protestant pacifist movements are the exception. When such issues become more problematic and controversial, however, there is no institutional way that permits the inquirer to find out "the Protestant tradition."[8] Diversity has occurred not only on particular moral issues; the theological diversity within Protestantism since the time of the Reformation has had the consequence of sustaining diverse ways of doing ethical thinking. In contrast, by tacitly and finally officially approving a general Thomism in theology and ethics, the Catholic history has been a more cohesive one. As shall be noted, the use of both the concept and the substance of "law" in Protestant tradition has been different for theological reasons; in turn "styles" of ethics are very different. There has been no Protestant magisterial authority to restrain diversity, though specific Protestant traditions have retained certain characteristic concepts (like the "two realms" in Lutheranism, and "discipleship" in Anabaptism) for many generations.

For the Protestant theologian the absence of magisterial authority established a climate of greater freedom within which to work in all areas of research including the ethical. The Protestant has had his contemporary peers judging his work; he has had the complex and rich Bible as a charter document; he has had the giants in his tradition looking over his shoulder. He has not, however, been as subject to institutional censure in the writing of ethics as has been the venturesome Catholic moral theologian. This climate of greater freedom has nourished a greater variety of flowers and weeds than has the climate of Catholicism.

Theological and Religious Context: Sin

Conventional wisdom and scholarship state that one basic difference between Roman Catholic and Protestant theology and ethics is located in the interpretations of human sinfulness. This factor has already been suggested in the above discussion of the significance of the sacrament of penance, but some amplification is required.

While it is unfair to claim that Catholicism has not perceived immoral acts, or sins, to be rooted and grounded in a more fundamental human fault, or sin, the basic morphology of Catholic theology and ethics made immoral actions a deterrent to salvation, and moral actions an asset to salvation, in a way that the great Reformers, Luther particularly, found to be in error.

That morphology in outline is well known. Western Catholic

theology and ethics from the time of Augustine have with remarkable continuity retained a neo-Platonic pattern of all things coming from God and returning to God, *exitus et reditus*. This teleological theme embraces and grounds a theological pattern: all things have their proper ends toward which they are oriented by their natures. When humans are properly oriented toward the end for which they have a natural inclination, when they are directed by and toward their real (but not always apparent) good, they are rightly ordered morally and on the right course spiritually (though faith is also necessary). The ultimate end of humans is God; it is contemplation of God, or spiritual communion or friendship (as Thomas Aquinas used the term) with God. Humans are also naturally inclined toward their natural end or good; thus there is a ground for a natural morality available to the knowledge of all rational persons. This ground, theologically interpreted, comes from God; it is graciously given in his creation. The ultimate end and the natural end are continuous in an important way. Not to be oriented by and toward God leads to a moral disorder in personal life and in social arrangements. To be properly oriented toward the natural good is one dimension of being properly oriented toward God. Thus a frame is set in which specific infractions of the natural moral order, specific sins, are salvifically deleterious, and right moral acts (in accord with the natural moral order) are salvifically beneficial.

Thus, for example, in the love of (for) God tradition, grounded so cogently in Augustine's thought, humans have a natural desire or love for God. When other objects of human desire or love take undue preeminence or significance, God is displaced. The consequent moral disorder, both in specific infractions of a proper natural order and a general disorientation toward the ultimate object of desire, is a threat to salvation. Conversely, a preeminent love for God has the effect of reordering human life in its individual and collective aspects in a way that is morally salutory.

With the interposition of metaphysics and ethics informed by Aristotle into this pattern, the criteria for very precise determinations of morally right and wrong acts, morally good and evil ends, were extensively developed. Not only *sin*, a basic disorientation toward the ultimate good, but *sins*, specific infractions of the proper moral order of nature, could be determined with precision. Clear and precise judgments about actions could be made, and reasons based both on natural law and on revelation could be given for them. St. Thomas' *Summa Theologica*, II-II, abounds with examples.[9]

The historic fate of this morphology, due to many other factors than its intellectual foundations, was in part that *sins* tended theologically and practically to receive more attention than *sin*. The view of the *telos* was dimmed by the attention given to formulation of precise rules of conduct and to the infractions committed against them. A reward and punishment mode of thought gained practical ascendancy; for a violation specific penitential disciplines are required, for a good act specific indulgences or other marks of merit are conferred. Salvation was always the highest stake, but the preoccupation with the precise deterrents to it or the precise merits for it frequently usurped the attention of clergy and laity alike.[10]

The theology of sin, as it differed from Protestant emphases, and the extent of corruption, which is the subject of standard theological discussions, are involved in this. I do not treat directly the issue of the extent of corruption here because I wish to get at the theological issues by the route of ethics.

To Luther, as it has to many Protestants since the time of the Reformation, this preoccupation with avoiding sins for the sake of salvation sounded like "works-righteousness." It sounded as if salvation is earned on the basis of meritorious works rather than received as a free gift of God's grace. For Luther the human fault was judged to be more basic than immoral acts. Its locus was in human *sin*, a matter of the "first table" of the Decalogue, of which particular sins are the fruits. To be sure, the Roman Catholic tradition had a fundamental fault: not being oriented toward the true natural and supernatural good. But the morphology of the relation of humans to God was conceived differently by Luther. It was not so much persons inclined toward God as their end, as persons trusting or not trusting in him. There was what now is commonly called a shift in paradigm. The *exitus et reditus* is dropped, as is to a large extent the metaphysics and ethics that gave precise patterns to created life. Philip Melanchthon, in his Apology for the Augsburg Confession, 1531, makes clear the difference between Lutherans and "the scholastics" over the understanding of sin.

> Thus when they [the scholastics] talk about original sin, they do not mention the more serious faults of human nature, namely ignoring God, despising him, lacking fear and trust

in him, hating his judgment and fleeing it, being angry at him, despairing his grace, trusting in temporal things, etc. These evils, which are most contrary to the law of God, the scholastics do not even mention.

We wanted to show that original sin also involves such faults as ignorance of God, contempt of God, lack of the fear of God and of trust in him, inability to love him. These are the chief flaws in human nature, transgressing as they do the first table of the Decalogue.[11]

The effect of this emphasis, and of the replacement of the language of inclination toward an end by the language of trust and mistrust, was an alteration in the significance of morality in relation to salvation, with a consequent difference in the significance and function of ethics within theology. If sin is basically a violation of the "first table" of the Decalogue, it is basically a *religious* problem rather than a moral problem. To be sure, bad trees bear bad fruit, but the answer to the problem of evil moral fruit is a matter of the trees and their roots. Thus if sin is basically a religious problem, its answer had to be basically a religious answer, not a moral answer. If sin is basically unfaith, a lack of trust in God, the antidote had to be faith or trust in God. No moral rectitude could achieve faith; to be properly oriented toward the natural moral good did not set one on a course toward salvation. Faith had to be a response to the free gift of God's grace. Grace was strongly perceived to be mercy, and not so much the rectification, redirection, and fulfillment of nature. To be sure, good trees will bear good fruit (as in Catholic theology virtuous persons are disposed to do good deeds), but the good tree comes fundamentally from grace and faith and not from a morally rigorous adherence to rules of right conduct.

The point can be made by an analogy with civil laws and courts. In Luther's religious and theological context, one's relationship to the judge was more important than one's obedience or disobedience to the laws. One was "made righteous" not by obeying the laws but by the judge's gracious verdict of forgiveness and by responding to him in trust and love. Once one confessed his "unrighteousness," or lack of trust and fear toward the judge, the judge forgave the person. Not only were one's infractions of the law forgiven, but the judge considered the person to be righteous because the person's relation to him was right. The person was declared righteous by the judge's act, not on the basis of his or her moral rectitude.

In this theological and religious context morality and ethics function differently than in the traditional Catholic one. Confession was of the "root" of sin, which was a violation of the religious commands of the first table of the Decalogue. No longer did *sins* have to be numbered and graded, for sins do not get to the heart of the matter, the relation of the person to God. Indeed, as has been noted, when morality was related to salvation in the Catholic manner, when morality had that sort of religious seriousness, a temptation to rely on moral righteousness for approval in God's sight was built in. The disciplines of moral theology and ethics were set in a different context by Luther; on the whole they suffered from benign neglect. Such treatises as St. Thomas' on moral questions were no longer needed, not to mention the continuous publication of moral manuals. The debates over the proper judgments of conscience between the extremes of rigorism and laxism that shaped decades of the history of Catholic moral theology would not occur; to the Protestant observer these debates could be dismissed as legalism. If salvation, the principal concern, comes through God's imputation of righteousness to persons, then the moral life no longer has the same *religious* seriousness. It is serious, but is set in a different religious and theological context. Ethics and moral theology no longer have the same theological significance.

The philosophical and theological underpinnings of Catholic ethics were attacked with vigor equal to the attacks on Catholic practice. To claim that all the vestiges of the natural law tradition were wiped out by Luther, however, would be an error, for in the doctrines of the orders of creation and the two realms there was a view that saw reason as determining what justice and the duties of one's office were. Luther also had confidence in the Golden Rule as a statement of the natural law. I shall return to this in the subsequent discussion of the function of law.

Ethics and morality took on a greater religious seriousness in Calvin and Calvinism than they did in Luther and Lutheranism, but the difference cannot be traced to greatly divergent opinions about sin. For Calvin, as for Luther, sin was basically a matter of the root and tree.

Original sin, therefore, seems to be a hereditary depravity and corruption of our nature, diffused into all parts of the soul, which first makes us liable to God's wrath, then also brings forth in us those works which Scripture calls "works of the flesh" [Gal. 5:19]. And that is properly what Paul often calls sin. The works that come forth from it—such as adulteries, fornications, thefts, hatreds, murders, carousings—he accordingly calls "fruits of sin" [Gal. 5:19-21], although they are commonly called "sins" in Scripture, and even by Paul himself.

Calvin goes on to elaborate this with several metaphors.

This perversity never ceases in us, but continually bears new fruits—the works of the flesh that we have already described —just as a burning furnace gives forth flame and sparks, or water ceaselessly bubbles from a spring.[12]

The antidote must be proportionate to the poison. Thus for Calvin as for Luther the first moment in the salvation of a person is the gracious gift of righteousness given to humans by God. Persons cannot earn salvation on the basis of moral merit. Again it must be noted in fairness that Catholic doctrine in principle did not imply the earning of salvation, but the practical preoccupation with sins as deterrents to union with God created conditions in which the charge had some validity. That morality was a more serious matter for Calvin than for Luther, and thus that ethics had a different role in theology, has been noted. The reason for this, in my judgment, was related to other areas of theology than the doctrine of sin. As Althaus and others have noted, Luther's ethics were developed primarily in relation to his view of justification by faith;[13] Calvin's were developed in relation to his view of sanctification. Both reformers clearly believed that God's grace evoked faith and created a freedom for the person; both clearly believed that God's gift of righteousness had effects on the life and activity of the Christian. In Calvin, however, this sanctifying effect is given greater weight and attention; this is seen in his emphasis on the "third use" of the law.

   In a cursory fashion I have indicated that a correlation can be made between several factors: (a) the paradigm of the relation of humans to God (e.g., trust/unfaith, orientation/disorientation toward a *telos*); (b) the primary locus of the human fault; (c) though not developed, the efficacy of divine grace (e.g., mercy/ restoration of nature); and (d) the function and procedure of moral theology, or ethics in a theological context.[14] The preoccupation of Catholic moral theology with sins is coherent with the ways these factors are brought together in the tradition; Protestantism's (and particularly Lutheranism's) failure to develop a precise moral theology coheres with its correlation of these factors. To show differences within Protestantism, and to indicate another difference from Catholic tradition, the "uses of the law" can be examined.

Theological and Religious Contexts: The Uses of Law

Law, I believe, provides an illuminating subject matter for disclosing historic divergences between Catholic and Protestant ethics; its locus, authority, purpose, and religious significance open up more general issues. Only in the context of Anglicanism was there a thoroughgoing continuation of the natural law tradition of Thomism; this is most striking in Richard Hooker's *Of the Laws of Ecclesiastical Polity.*[15] Law also provides, as I have noted, a subject matter about which the differences of opinion among Protestant Reformers were crucial; in some respects the distinguishing characteristics of Lutheran, Anabaptist, and Calvinist ethics in post-Reformation developments were established by those opinions. The religious and theological contexts in which law was interpreted were crucial. The present discussion, in keeping with the purpose of this chapter, is brief and general.

Aristotelian metaphysics and ethics, set in the theological context of *exitus et reditus*, of all things coming from and returning to God, provided the grounds for the natural law tradition that the Reformers knew. The natural moral law in that context provided a basis for procedures to make fine discriminations of moral faults, for precise rules of conduct, and for the religious significance of moral conduct. It conceptualized the nature that was in part disoriented by human fault and was properly reoriented by the consequences of grace. It provided a sense of moral certitude that lent weight to the church's claims for moral authority. Until our own point in history the debates about moral questions in the Catholic tradition took place within this frame of reference.

To set the Catholic tradition in the alien context of the Reformation discussions for comparative purposes, one needs to remember the following. The moral law was grounded in creation, and thus was a gift of grace. The moral law in nature

participated in the eternal law in the mind of God. The civil law
and the customary law participated in the natural law. The
revealed moral law in Scripture was a clear expression of the
natural law; it did not establish a different morality. The "new
law," the law of the gospel, is preponderantly "the grace of the
Holy Ghost, which is given through faith in Christ"; it is
primarily an inscription in the heart, and only secondarily a
written law.[16] It is a fulfillment of the old law in three ways: it
explains the true sense of the law, it prescribes the safest way of
complying with the law, and it fulfills the precepts "by adding
some counsels of perfection."[17] Thus, ethically speaking, there is
one moral law; any known exceptions to it occur as a result of
secret commands of God, and the most rigorous counsels of Jesus
apply to those with special vocations.

If one attempts to set this in the context of the Reformation
discussion of the "uses" of the law, how would it look? Luther's
charge seems to be that the principal use in Roman Catholicism
was to assure human consciences that they were pleasing to God
by their obedience to the law, and thus had merit which was
salvific. The quarrel was principally one about the religious
significance of the role of law and obedience to it. Even if
Luther's perception of its principal use in Catholic practice was
correct, it is clear that it had an accusatory use, making persons
conscious of their sins and their need to do penance (repentance
was part of penance). In Luther's eyes, as I have noted, it was
sins, more than sin, that the accusatory use disclosed to persons.
The law in Catholicism clearly had what Luther called a "civic"
use, ordering and preserving life in human society, not only as a
dike against the chaos Luther saw threatening community, but
also as enabling positive common good. It also clearly had
Calvin's "third use"—an exhortative and instructional use to
those who had received grace. If these generalizations are correct,
the issues of the Reformation were not basically ethical but
theological and religious. But the theological and religious shifts
had wide implications for ethics. The "uses" of the law were set
in a different theological context.

It is important to recall the shift in paradigm from man
oriented toward God as ultimate *telos* to man trusting or dis-
trusting God. For Luther the primary purpose of the law of
Moses is a theological or spiritual one, not, however, to orient
persons to God but to increase their transgressions to the point

where they despair of their righteousness and are led to a radical trust in God for their salvation. Notice his vivid language: "Therefore the proper and absolute use of the law is to terrify with lightning (as on Mt. Sinai), thunder, and the blare of the trumpets with a thunderbolt to burn and crush that brute which is called the presumption of righteousness. . . . For as long as the presumption of righteousness remains in a man, there remain immense pride, self-trust, smugness, hate of God, contempt of grace and mercy, ignorance of the promises and of Christ."[18] When "the heart is crushed to the point of despair," one is prepared to hear the gospel of the grace and mercy of God.

The law also has a civic use. "God has ordained civic laws, indeed all laws, to restrain transgressions. Therefore every law was given to hinder sins." "When I refrain from killing or from committing adultery or from stealing, or when I abstain from other sins, I do not do this voluntarily or from the love of virtue but because I am afraid of the sword and of the executioner. . . . Therefore, restraint from sins is not righteousness but rather an indication of unrighteousness." Since "the devil reigns in the whole world," God "has ordained magistrates, parents, teachers, laws, shackles, and all civic ordinances" to at least bind his hands and "keep him from raging at will."[19] The corruption of humans and the world is so deep and thorough that the civic use of the law at best preserves the world from falling into chaos; it really cannot be a basis for developing a more positive common good.

Luther's theological and religious context for the law and its uses alters the religious significance of morality and thus sets ethics in a different context. Fulfilling moral requirements leads not to salvation but to the presumption of righteousness before God. Orientation to one's proper natural end by a life of moral virtue and obedience to the law is a hazard to salvation and, given the state of corruption, not really possible in any case. Only out of fear is one moral. The antidote is proportionate to the poison; it is the free gift of imputed righteousness; salvation is by faith alone. Ethics as a subject of thought and writing has to be pursued within this theological and religious context.

The consequence is that there are two aspects of the moral life for Christians, and two distinguishable tasks of ethics. There is moral life under the civic use of the law, or in the orders of creation. One is obliged to obey the moral law, to fulfill duties to one's office (as soldier, magistrate, mother, and so on). Reason must prevail in this aspect; it has a proper role in determining the administration of civil justice and the proper exercise of social roles. An ethics of natural reason (not natural law in the sense that one reasons in the context of a Thomistic ontology) prevails.

There is also moral life under faith, the "ethics of justification" under forgiveness and righteousness imputed to humans by God's grace. Here the agent is central; he or she has a Christian freedom of the inner person. Even while continuing in sin (at the same time justified) the person can freely and even joyously do what the moral law and social roles require. One can go beyond that and be "Christ to one's neighbor," meeting the immediate and deepest needs of the other out of love. Persons act morally out of gratitude for God's gift of grace. Obligations are met, both out of a sense of duty and a sense of freedom and love. Morality is expressive of the state of the agent (justified, but also a sinner). Ethics in this aspect becomes a matter of describing the motives and the dispositions that faith and grace induce, and the pattern (love of neighbor) in which they issue.

In the Anabaptist movement, or the Radical Reformation, the person of Christ and his teachings became a "new law" for Christians. Given the variety of movements that are normally classified as the Radical Reformation, and the continuing scholarly discussions about the extent to which generalizations about it are warranted, brief comments are no doubt hazardous.[20] The Reformers to the left of those whose imprint on history is most striking had a spectrum of ethics that included antinomianism, violent revolution, pacifism, and spiritualistic quietism. Two major documents, however, provide data that sustain a view that assists in locating different views of the law. One is the 1527 "Schleitheim Confession," or the "Brotherly Union of a Number of Children of God Concerning Seven Articles," written by Michael Sattler, perhaps the greatest of the first generation of Anabaptists. The other is a more thorough statement, *Account of Our Religion, Doctrine and Faith*, by Peter Riedemann of the Hutterite community, first published in 1545. For these men and others the Christian community was to be a distinctive and disciplined group which, while its members lived by grace and faith, was called to radical obedience to Jesus as Lord, to a way of nonparticipation in certain "orders of creation," to pacifism, and to the way of the cross. Sattler, for example, wrote to the Strasbourg Reformers a twenty-point declaration of convictions, among which are these: "7. The foreknown and called believers shall be conformed to the image of Christ." "8. Christ is despised in the world, so are also those who are His; He has no kingdom in the world, but that which is of this world is against His kingdom." "9. Believers are chosen out of the world, therefore the world hates them." "15. Christians are fully yielded and have placed their trust in their Father in heaven without any outward or worldly arms."[21] Each point is supported by a New Testament citation. In the confession, the basis of authority for the morality of Christians is clear. "Christ teaches and commands us to learn from Him, for He is meek and lowly of heart and thus we shall find rest for our souls."[22] His words and his life are the law of Christians. Thus Christians may not and should not "use the sword against the wicked for the protection and defense of the good, or for the sake of love." Christians shall not "pass sentence in disputes and strife about worldly matters." "Christ, who teaches the perfection of the law, forbids His [followers] all swearing, whether true nor false. . . . You see, thereby all swearing is forbidden."[23]

Some striking sentences from Riedemann's text also illustrate the new law for Christians grounded in radical obedience to Christ as lord of a spiritual kingdom. "Thus no Christian is a ruler and no ruler is a Christian, for the child of blessing cannot be the servant of wrath." "Therefore a Christian neither wages war nor wields the worldly sword to practice vengeance." Although taxes should be paid because civil government is ordained by God (though "no Christian can rule over the world"), "where taxes are demanded for the special purpose of going to war, massacring and shedding blood, we give nothing." Christians must not go to court and must not take oaths.[24]

Notable in this movement are the following features. The natural moral law tradition has been left behind. Even the civil authority which has legitimacy under God's ordinances (though Christians cannot be rulers) is justified purely on biblical textual evidences. Thus the authority for moral and civil law rests in the confidence that Christian Scripture and particularly Jesus, are authentic and sufficient revelations of God's law as well as of his mercy and grace. A revelational positivism, to use a modern term, has replaced the natural inclination toward the good.

The teachings and life of Jesus have a greater moral and religious seriousness in this view than in Luther's position. Luther also had a notion of conformity to Christ, but it was couched in terms of a general morphology of action; Christians are to meet the needs of the neighbor as Christ has met their needs. The implications of gratitude as a motive are not lost to the Anabaptists, but to have been redeemed by Christ brought a sterner obligation to obey his teachings and to follow his way of life, expecting to be despised and open to the possibility (all too frequently actualized in the barbarism of religious conflicts) of suffering and dying because of this discipleship. No equivocations were justified; the new life in the spirit demanded conformity to a new law. To be a Christian was not only to be disposed to love; Christian ethics was not limited to a *Gesinnungsethik*; it was to be conformed to a pattern in this world that had clear and precise behavioral demands.

Jewish law and ethics are also grounded in the texts of Scripture. In distinction from the Jewish tradition, the Anabaptists went back directly to their biblical source, to obey it without benefit of a tradition of interpretation. There is no body of literature to which they turn which refines and amplifies the meaning of biblical commands. In distinction from Luther and Calvin, there is no engagement with major writings from the time of the closing of the canon to the sixteenth century.

In distinction from Thomas Aquinas and from Calvin (as we shall see) the "new law" is in discontinuity with the "old law." What to Thomas might be counsels of perfection (though poverty and chastity did not take on the same significance) were for the Anabaptists obligations of all Christians. While both Thomas and Calvin emphasized continuities between the natural moral law, the Decalogue, and the "new law" of the Christian Scripture, the Anabaptists seldom cite the Old Testament[25] and emphasize a more radical discontinuity in the conduct expected by the New Testament writers. The Christian community was a new community, distinctive not only in its faith but in its rules of conduct.[26]

Clearly the "third use" of the law has distinctive emphasis in this movement. The law is used not only to exhort and instruct, as in Calvin; it becomes a pattern in the light of which judgments are made about the rectitude of the lives of persons, judgments which lead to the discipline of "banning" offenders from full fellowship.[27] The community undertook a judicial function by examining accused offenders, judging their culpability, and imposing on them a penalty. That Calvin also set up procedures for church discipline is clearly the case, and that there were similarities between Calvin's combination of firmness and mercy (with reconciliation as the end in view) and the purposes of banning in Anabaptism is also true. A major difference, however, was in the rigor of concern for the purity of the church.[28]

Whereas the new law, which it was obligatory for Christians to fulfill, sharply defined a Christian morality and Christian ethics for the Anabaptists, John Calvin stressed in his discussions of law (as has been noted) a continuity between the natural moral law, the Decalogue, and the moral teachings of Jesus. In this respect there are significant similarities to the ethics of the Catholic tradition. But he also shared Luther's conviction that grace—both forgiving and sanctifying—is a gift, and not earned. Since he was, for various reasons, concerned with how the Christian life ought to be lived, for him the principal use of the law was the "third use." He accepted Luther's accusatory and civic uses, but stressed another (which is not clearly articulated by Luther though it is present in a qualified sense, but is articulated by Melanchthon).[29]

> The third and principal use, which pertains more closely to the proper purpose of the law, finds its place among believers in whose hearts the Spirit of God already lives and reigns. For even though they have the law written and engraved upon their hearts by the finger of God, that is, have been so moved and quickened through the directing of the Spirit that they long to obey God, they still profit by the law in two ways.
>
> Here is the best instrument for them to learn more thoroughly each day the nature of the Lord's will to which they aspire, and to confirm them in the understanding it. . . . And not one of us may escape from this necessity. For no man has heretofore attained to such wisdom as to be unable from daily instruction of the law, to make fresh progress toward a purer knowledge of the divine will.
>
> Again, because we need not only teaching but also exhortation, the servant of God will also avail himself of this benefit of the law: by frequent meditation upon it to be aroused to obedience, be strengthened in it, and be drawn back from the slippery path of transgression.[30]

Christians need the law to be instructed and to overcome listlessness. "The law is to the flesh like a whip to an idle and balky ass, to arouse it to work." Progress toward a "purer knowledge" of God's moral will, and the fulfillment of it in the human community was a major enterprise in the individual Christian life. The Christian community, coordinately, had as part of its vocation the development of a proper order in society as well.[31] Morality was to be pursued with religious zeal, and ethics had a high dignity in the theological enterprise.

Thus, in Calvin we have a significant difference from Luther. The continuities with the Catholic tradition are stronger, as are similarities to the Anabaptists. One major difference from the more radical Reformers that accentuates the continuity with Catholic tradition is the interpretation of the "new law" in the moral teachings of Jesus. Like the Anabaptists, Calvin had particular obligations for Christians, indeed "the sum of the Christian life" is the denial of ourselves.[32] But unlike the Anabaptists he claimed that Jesus was "the best interpreter" of the "old law" and not the giver of a new law. As the best interpreter Jesus was able to disclose "the chief point of the law," its "spiritual" point, which had been obscured by the Pharisees. The law "not only demands obedience of soul, mind, and will, but requires an angelic purity, which, cleansed of every pollution of the flesh, savors nothing but the spirit."[33] "Those who did not comprehend these teachings fancied Christ another Moses, the giver of the law of the gospel, which supplied what was lacking in the Mosaic law."[34] In one sense Jesus' teachings were the best interpretation not only of the Mosaic law but also of the natural moral law. This marks a continuity with the Roman Catholic tradition (which, incidentally, suggests that constructive ecumenical ethics done from the perspective of Protestantism might best begin with Calvin).

"Calvin's view of the Commandments as a divinely authorized text expressing the natural law engraved on all hearts is a traditional one," John T. McNeill correctly notes.[35] It is not too strong to affirm that for Calvin, as for the Catholic tradition, there is one moral law, and that it is "written on the consciences" of all persons. "Now that inward law [the natural law],[36] which we have described as written, even engraved, upon the hearts of all, in a sense asserts the very same things that are learned from the Two Tables."[37] The moral law is God's law and, "Whatever he requires of us (because he requires only what is right), we must obey out of natural obligation."[38] God "published" the law because humanity is shrouded in such darkness that we hardly begin to grasp the natural law. Calvin has no treatise on moral law comparable in scope and detail to what Thomas Aquinas has, but Calvin clearly holds the traditional view. Because of human darkness, and because of his Reformation accent on Scripture as the source and ground of Christian theology, however, the explication of the "published" law is dominant. Thus, a biblically based ethics can be an ethics for all, since its ultimate moral referent is "written, even engraved, upon the hearts of all." What distinguishes Calvin most from the Catholic tradition is not his doctrine of natural law but his use of Scripture as a basis for knowing it (in contrast with the more supportive role Scripture takes on in the Catholic tradition) and his view of sin which makes the natural reason less reliable in determining the natural moral law.

What has this overview of the places of moral law yielded? Surely the conclusion that a contrast between Roman Catholic and Protestant ethics can be made in terms of "natural law" and "the ethics of love" is grossly oversimplified.[39] We have seen the significance of certain questions. To attempt to summarize the answers of the traditions would lead to greater redundancy than even a patient reader can bear. The questions, however, continue to be important in contemporary discussion. (1) How is the moral law known? By natural reason? By reading Scripture? (2) What is the law that is known? A basic abstract principle? Specific commands for all persons? Special commands for Christians? (3) What are the purposes of the moral law? I hope I have shown that to understand how these questions were answered in the classic period in which Protestantism emerged requires consciousness of other theological and philosophical motifs. Part of the stage for the playing out of ecumenical ethics in our time is thereby set.

Many themes, such as love, could also be developed on a comparative basis, but with a diminishing rate of return for the reader. Since Protestantism began with an emphasis on *sola scriptura*, Scripture alone, and since that emphasis has had a strong impact on Protestant ethics, special attention must be given to the role of Scripture as an historic issue.

Theological and Religious Contexts:
The Place of Scripture

The Reformation principle, *sola scriptura*, had fateful consequences for the subsequent history of Protestant ethics. It became so deeply embedded in the Protestant tradition that many writers who were uninterested in defending a view of revelation which would support it nonetheless wrote ethics—theological and practical—based on the Bible as the sole, or at least final, source of authority. For example, in the modern period the liberal Christian social-gospel writers, fundamentalist writers, and those called "neo-orthodox" all grounded their ethics basically in Scripture. Just as the theory of a natural moral law set the boundaries within which debates took place in Catholic moral theology, so it is not unfair to claim that the debates within Protestant ethics took place within the boundaries of Scripture. The plurality of opinion was greater in the Protestant tradition; it would be a gross error to claim great uniformity. But when the centrality of the natural moral law in Catholic moral theology is set in contrast to the centrality of Scripture in Protestant ethics, a historic divergence of great proportions is made clear.[40]

The divergence can be illustrated by comparing Catholic and Protestant treatments of any number of subjects. For example, in the United States there were in the same period Catholic and Protestant social reform movements. John A. Ryan (1869-1945) the dominant Catholic theoretician and activist had a role in Catholic life comparable to that of Walter Rauschenbusch (1861-1918) in Protestant life. What these two men had in common is interesting to note; some of it is superficial and some of great significance. Ryan's two major books, *A Living Wage: Its Ethical and Economic Aspects*, and *Distributive Justice: The Right and Wrong of Our Present Distribution of Wealth*, were published in 1906 and 1916, respectively, both by Macmillan.[41] The two books that brought Rauschenbusch to national attention were *Christianity and the Social Order* and *Christianizing the Social Order*, published in 1907 and 1912, respectively, also by Macmillan.[42] Both were seminary professors, Ryan at St. Paul Seminary in Minnesota (and subsequently at the Catholic University of America where he began in the Department of Political Science), Rauschenbusch at Rochester Theological Seminary where he was professor of church history. Both were much influenced by the economist Richard T. Ely of the University of Wisconsin; Ryan's *A Living Wage* is dedicated to Ely, who contributed an Introduction to the book. More significantly, both were responding to the economic and social conditions in American industrial life at that time. Both were critical of American capitalism and conversant with socialism. Rauschenbusch cites Ryan favorably once.[43] I have found no references to Rauschenbusch in Ryan's *Distributive Justice*. Both had an interest in grounding principles of social justice, and in applying them to current circumstances. It is in the grounding authority that Rauschenbusch's biblical heritage appears in sharpest distinction from Ryan's heritage of natural law.

For the purposes of this chapter it it sufficient to make some general comparisons based on the first of the cited books by each author. Rauschenbusch's first three chapters deal with the eighth-century prophets as the "historical roots" of Christianity, with "The Social Aims of Jesus," and with the primitive churches. His interpretations of these elements, all biblical in their sources, provide the theological grounding for his analysis of the predicament of his time and for his proposals for social reform.

Ryan's basic ground is developed in Chapter 3 of *A Living Wage*, "The Basis and Justification of Rights." That his Argument is in the natural law tradition can be seen from the following quotations:

> The thesis to be maintained in this volume is that the laborer's claim to a Living Wage is of the nature of a *right*. This right is personal, not merely social; that is to say, it belongs to the individual as individual, and not as a member of society. . . . Again, it is a natural, not a positive right; for it is born with the individual, derived from his rational nature, not conferred upon him by a positive enactment. In brief, the right to a Living Wage is individual, natural and absolute. . . . Natural rights are the moral means or opportunities by which the individual attains the end appointed to him by nature. . . . Man's natural rights are absolute, not in the sense that they are subject to no limitation—which would be absurd—but in the sense that their validity is not dependent on anyone except the person in whom they inhere. . . . With respect to their natural rights, all men are equal, because all are equal in the rational nature from which such rights are derived. By nature every man is a person, that is, a rational, self-active, independent being. Every man is rational because endowed with the facul-

ties of reason and will. His will impels him to seek the good, the end of his being, and his reason enables him to find and adjust means to this end.[44]

This doctrine of natural law and rights is the basis of what Ely calls "a Roman Catholic system of political economy."[45] Ryan does not disguise the theological principles which provide natural law with another level of justification.

In a word, the supreme earthly goal of conduct is to know in the highest degree the best that is to be known, and to love in the highest degree the best that is to be loved. These highest objects of knowledge and love are God, and, in proportion to the degrees of excellence they possess, His creatures. . . . The ultimate source of the obligation is the will of God; just as the ultimate source of the distinction between the higher and lower faculties, activities, and goods is the Divine Essence; and just as the ultimate source of the intuitions by which we perceive these distinctions is the Divine Reason.[46]

These theological references are clearly a rendition of the Thomist tradition in its philosophical aspect and form. In this chapter, basic to the whole treatise, there is no reference to Scripture, to the prophets, or to Jesus and his "social aim." Indeed I have not found even an allusion to Scripture in the entire book.

Rauschenbusch's appeal was to a history which was normative for him, not to the natural law; that history is found in the Bible. His Introduction gives as much defense of this as is offered.

Its first chapters are historical, for nothing more is needed than a true comprehension of past history if we are to forecast the future correctly and act wisely in the present. I have set forth [in the first three chapters] in order to ascertain what was the original and fundamental purpose of the great Christian movement in history.[47]

The final appeal is to "the original and fundamental purpose" of the historical Christian movement, not to the nature of man. It is an historical appeal, not an appeal to man's being. It requires an interpretation of the Scripture in which that history is portrayed. The normative past history is the basis for interpreting the present, forecasting the future, and "acting wisely."

Both Ryan and Rauschenbusch made recommendations about "what to do." Again, with injustice to the total lifework of both authors, I confine myself to the same two books. Ryan had taken his cue to center on the living wage from the great encyclical *Rerum Novarum*, by Pope Leo XIII. Indeed the whole book can be read as an application of that encyclical to the American situation. This concern leads to a specific recommendation of a living wage which, in Ryan's judgment, meets one of the great injustices of American society. It does not fully realize what distributive justice requires, but a living wage immensely improves adverse social and industrial conditions with less difficulty than other proposals. Using social and economic data available, Ryan calculated the wage required in some detail; he settled on an annual income of $600, or a daily wage of $2.10.[48] Once the ground of the principle was established, and the principle itself fleshed out by a process of reasoning about economic and social data, a clear and precise recommendation could be made. The procedures were clear and cogent once one accepted the premises; there were no intuitive leaps to a practical conclusion.

Rauschenbusch, with his biblical and historical basis, cannot provide the same kind of practical argument; thus his most specific conclusions are not as rationally defensible as are Ryan's. Rauschenbusch's discussion of wages occurs in his chapter "The Present Crisis," which is an account of the problems in American society that he perceived to be most pressing. The method of the chapter could be called "prophetic interpretation"; just as the eighth-century prophets had described conditions from an evaluational stance that was at best briefly stated and often only implied, so Rauschenbusch describes conditions from an evaluational stance informed by his understanding of the prophets, of Jesus' social aims, and of the witness of the primitive church. He has an implied standard of justice, but no theory of justice such as Ryan's.

> But the justice of our system will be proved only if we can show that the wealth, comfort, and security of the average working-man in 1906 is much greater than that of the average working-man in 1760 as the wealth of civilized humanity is now greater than it was in 1760. No one will be bold enough to assert it.
> The bulk of the increase in wealth has gone to a limited class who in various ways have been strong enough to take it. Wages have advanced on foot; profits have taken the Limited Express.[49]

If one is persuaded of the accuracy of the first chapters, then this evaluative description has a defensible basis. Justice is part of the message of the prophets and of Jesus; it is not grounded in a theory of natural right and natural moral law.

The different audiences that, one can conjecture, were intended by the authors explain only in part their differences in approach. Rauschenbusch surely intended to stir the consciences of the Protestant churches and their members. Ryan's argument can be read as directed to a wider public; indeed, interestingly, *A Living Wage* has no *Nihil Obstat* or *Imprimatur* as *Distributive Justice* does a decade later. Symbols and arguments used for practical moral suasion do have to take into account the readers' interests. It is my thesis, however, that Rauschenbusch's biblical way of launching his discussion is largely a legacy from the Reformation, with its principle of Scripture alone, while Ryan's way is a legacy of the natural law tradition of Catholicism.

That Catholic moral theologians perceived the difference between their discipline and Protestant ethics in this way is clear. A manual widely used in the United States, "Koch-Preuss,"[50] states, "Thus Catholics, unlike Protestants, do not regard the Bible as the sole source of knowledge in matters of faith and morals."[51] The Protestant reader of Catholic manuals has good reason to assert that Scripture, when used, was generally cited to proof-text an argument basically derived from natural law. Thomas Slater's discussion of killing the innocent is a good example of this.

> It is never lawful directly to kill the innocent, or, in other words, it is never lawful to kill the innocent when the death is intended in itself, or when it is inflicted as a means of attaining of some other object. Such an act is expressly forbidden by God: "The innocent and just person thou shalt not put to death." [Ex. 23:7.] Reason, too, teaches us the same truth, for if ever it were lawful directly to kill the innocent, it would be so when such a death would be of great advantage to the commonwealth.[52]

The rest of the section is basically a natural law argument applied to abortion and other problems. The structure of Slater's book reinforces the view that the Bible is primarily a source of proof texts; its first three "books" are Thomistic accounts of human acts, conscience, and law. The argument is not developed exegetically; the Exodus citation is not set in the context of a theology of covenant; it is not a rabbinic elucidation of the command. Rather a "divine command" functions to confirm an argument from natural law. The reason this is possible was indicated earlier; both revealed and natural law express God's eternal law.

The legacy of *sola scriptura* left Protestant ethics with two unresolved questions that are as old as Christian theology itself. What is the authority of Scripture for ethics? How is Scripture relevant to, or applied to, practical moral matters? How the first question is answered implies an answer to the second, and vice versa. That Catholic moral theology must answer the same two questions is clear; the questions, however, have not been as important to Catholic moral theology because of the weight given to the natural moral law.

A very generalized overview of the Catholic position will suffice for this chapter. Scripture is of central importance as revelation of knowledge of God, and particularly of God's redemptive work. The way in which God's creative and redeeming work was explicated, however, was not so much by means of biblical exegesis as by the neo-Platonic *exitus et reditus*, with a structure of created life developed from Aristotle, as we have indicated. This theological framework, which has one of its grounds in Scripture, has tremendous implications for ethics, some of which I have indicated and will not repeat here. The major one is that moral theology has two principal sources, reason and "revelation."[53] The existence of two sources, however, does not lead to a view of a double truth, either theologically or ethically.

It is defensible to say that the authority of Scripture for ethics is that of "revelation," but what is revealed in the moral teachings of the Bible can also be known to humans on the basis of reason. Thus, with few exceptions the proper conclusions of reasoning about the natural moral law will not be inconsistent with the ethical teachings and events in the Bible. Given this, it is appropriate, as was illustrated from Slater, to cite a biblical teaching as an independent source of revelation which is confirmed by a conclusion from reason. There are no serious cleavages between the revealed moral will of God and the natural moral law, since both have the same ultimate source.

The application of Scripture, then, to practical moral questions does not have the significance it had for the Protestant *sola scriptura* tradition. In applying the natural moral law by use of reason one is in effect applying nothing different from what one would be using if one used Scripture.

In the discussion of law it was indicated that for Luther the civic use of the law retained a function similar to that of natural law. Thus to know one's duties in one's office, or to administer justice, one did not need to turn to Scripture. Lutheran "social ethics" was based theologically on the ordinances or orders of creation, which in turn were explicated by "natural" (though corrupt) reason. Calvin, it will be recalled, viewed the natural moral law, the revealed law of the Torah, and the moral teachings of Jesus in significant continuity; they all, finally, refer to the same moral law. But Calvinist ethics could become very biblicistic because of the confidence that the Bible revealed the moral law.

Our concern here, however, is with the legacy of *sola scriptura*, and not with further discussion of the sixteenth century. The centrality of the Bible for ethics which was common to much of Protestant ethics did not have the same implications for all theologians and churches.[54] There were differences in answers to the question of authority and to the question of procedures for application. What has been very characteristic, however, is a return to Scripture directly and immediately. As in the Jewish ethical-legal tradition, the ground text is the Bible, and sources have to be cited and used; in distinction from that tradition, there is no normative body of interpretive literature which also must be considered—no Talmud, no authoritative codes.

Generalizations about the different forms of that legacy will have to suffice. If the Bible is authorized by divine verbal inspiration, it is the mandatory source for knowledge both of God and his relations to man, and of the moral requirements of human life. Since the inspiration is definitely confined to the Bible, ethics, like theology, must confine itself to the biblical texts; it cannot take recourse to "tradition." Since tradition is not reliable as a guide to understanding the Bible, its moral teachings in the context of its theology must be directly applied verbally to a current moral issue. That this approach bristles with problems of interpretation is clear. A favorite example of mine will show how this view of *sola scriptura* works out.

Jacob J. Vallenga deals with capital punishment from this perspective. He quotes the standard references in Torah used to defend capital punishment: Genesis 9:6, "Whoever sheds the blood of man, by man shall his blood be shed, for God made man in his own image"; Exodus 21:12, 14, "Whoever strikes a man so that he dies shall be put to death. . . . If a man wilfully attacks another to kill him treacherously, you shall take him from my altar that he may die";[55] and so forth. In a key transition, Vallenga states, "The teachings of the New Testament are in harmony with the Old Testament. Christ came to fulfill the law, not to destroy the basic principles of law and order, righteousness and justice." One wonders, if this is the case, how the narrative found in John 8:3-11 about the woman caught in adultery would be interpreted. "Teacher, this woman has been caught in the act of adultery. Now in the law Moses commanded us to stone such. What do you say about her?" "He ... said to them, 'Let him who is without sin among you be the first to throw a stone at her.'" Vallenga, however, does not consider this story. Rather, he takes a saying from the Sermon on the Mount, and interprets it as follows: "The Christ speaks of hate and murder: 'You have heard that it was said to the men of old, You shall not kill; and whoever kills shall be liable to judgment [capital punishment].' But I say to you that everyone who is angry with his brother shall be liable to judgment [capital punishment] (Mt. 5:21-22)." Vallenga comments, "It is evident that Jesus was not condemning the established law of capital punishment, but was actually saying that hate deserved capital punishment."[56]

The Bible can be claimed to contain the revelation of God's creative, sustaining, and redeeming work without recourse to divine verbal inspiration. Its primary significance is theological, not ethical. Some theological judgment must be introduced to form the principles which in turn provide the order of significance of various aspects of Scripture. The theological judgments and principles that are salient for a particular theologian or tradition set the terms for the import of the Bible for ethics, and for the import of the distinctively moral teachings of the Bible. Protestant history is replete with many different patterns of this general sort. As we saw, Luther's judgment that justification by grace and faith is central to the biblical theology had consequences for his understanding of the uses of the moral law found in Scripture. Similarly Calvin's "third use" of the law coheres with his ordering of the significance of doctrines which he found central to Scripture. The Anabaptists' emphasis on being called to radical discipleship (as central to a New Testament theology) led to their way of using the Sermon on the Mount. In the modern period other theological emphases (grounded in the Bible) lead to their particular thrusts in ethical reflection and in how the moral teachings of the Bible are used.[57]

The problematics of Protestant ethics, with the legacy of *sola scriptura* adapted in one way or another, can be summarized in a series of questions. If one holds to "verbal inspiration," how does one resolve, theologically and ethically, discrepancies within the Bible? If one has a looser view of the authority of the Bible, how does one determine which theological and ethical principles will be the central ones for interpreting the texts? If one uses biblical theological themes, like hope or liberation, to interpret the moral and religious significance of current events, does one only come to the threshold of ethical reflection, and, if so, how is an appropriate course of action determined? If one uses moral teachings of the New Testament, how are these nearly two-thousand-year-old teachings applicable to the twentieth century? How can one claim for teachings "revealed" in a Hellenistic Jewish culture a validity in a modern secular culture? How can the beliefs and teachings developed by a then insignificant and powerless minority community be applied in a cosmopolitan world by Christians who are frequently strongly identified with the culture of that world? *Sola scriptura*, adhered to strictly or loosely, does not answer these questions.

To Catholic moral theology these questions do not pose the same critical threat. Protestant ethical writings have bent and stretched the principle of *sola scriptura*; they have gone beyond it sometimes with conscious awareness (and sometimes with a biblical justification for doing so). It remains fair to say, however, that a major difference in the two traditions historically has been in the place of Scripture in ethical thought. Indeed, this has been *the* major difference.

Many other aspects of theology and ethics could be developed to highlight historic differences, but a point of diminishing returns from such exposition has been reached with reference to the purpose of this book. The next three chapters attempt to analyze convergences and divergences in our contemporary period. To do so, alas, will require further historical references, but the ordering issues for the analysis are different from those used in this chapter. They are procedures of practical moral reasoning, underlying philosophical assumptions, and basic theological convictions.

2

Practical Moral Reasoning

The principal purpose of this book is not to describe the issues between Roman Catholic and Protestant ethics from the sixteenth century to the present, but to determine what, in the light of very recent developments in both traditions, the prospects for ecumenical Christian ethics are. Our primary concern is with the contemporary context of discussion.

Several persons have noted that many socially and theologically radical Catholics relate well to their Protestant counterparts, that moderate Catholic theologians relate well to moderate Protestant theologians, and that the most conservative Catholic and Protestant theologians do not relate to each other at all. In the United States, for example, the Berrigan brothers had their congenial associates among William Sloane Coffin and others, but they were not in serious theological conversation with moderate Catholic moral theologians such as Charles E. Curran and Richard A. McCormick, S.J. These theologians have been, however, in consistently serious interaction with Paul Ramsey (who to many Protestants is "conservative" morally if not theologically) and other moderate Protestants. [1] The theologians who support the arguments for *Humanae Vitae* are not very congenial to any of these persons but are not in theological conversation

with Carl F. H. Henry and other conservative Protestant theologians either.

The point of this is to indicate the limitations of the range of
materials that are most carefully considered in this book. I do not
take into account in any systematic way the developments in "political theology" as this is represented by Roman Catholic theologians such as J. B. Metz, Gustavo Gutierrez, J. L. Segundo,
Rosemary Ruether, and others, and by Protestants such as Jürgen
Moltmann, Paul Lehmann, Frederick Herzog, Dorothee Soelle,
and others. One reason is that "political theology," which has
vivid and illuminating powers to interpret the significance of
general historical trends and movements through the use of
biblical symbols, on the whole comes only to the threshold of
ethics in a more limited sense.[2] Such theology sometimes sees the
writings I am concerned with, to use a remark heard fairly
frequently, as an activity like that of rearranging the deck chairs
on the Titanic. (I suppose the alternative, to be equally pejorative, is that of pushing the icebergs away.) I firmly believe that
one aspect of systematic theological ethics is the interpretation of
history from a theological point of view, and thus by not treating
"political theology" here I do not intend to dismiss it as invalid. It
is, however, incomplete, just as exclusive focus on moral theology, in its usual terms, is incomplete. Primary attention is given
here to a middle range of Catholic and Protestant theologians
now writing in ethics because I believe they are more concerned
with classic questions of ethics in the context of theology in a
rigorous and promising way.

The thesis of this chapter can be stated in general terms. The
strength that traditional Roman Catholic moral theology brought
to the contemporary scene is this: there was an ordered pattern of
moral thinking, based upon rather clear philosophical and
theological principles with positive moral substance. With both
method and substance, moral theologians could come to precise
and clear judgments about a variety of current moral issues: war,
living wage, abortion, and so forth. It provided a high degree of
moral certitude about practical moral judgments and decisions.
The weakness of traditional Catholic moral theology in the
contemporary scene is this: the method and the substance tend to
be rigid and closed; when developments in various areas of
human experience become complex and morally problematic,

when empirical data about various moral problems pose new ways of predicting and understanding the consequences of certain actions and policies, and when the philosophical and theological grounding of the substance and the method is questioned, moral theology is in grave difficulty. Put very generally, traditional moral theology has a rather tight and closed system which needs loosening and opening to come to grips with modern moral and social problems.

The strength that traditional and especially contemporary Protestant theological ethics brought to the modern scene is this: it provided a theology and an ethics that has a looseness and an openness which is responsive to modernity as the context in which the Christian community has to find fresh and relevant ways to counsel and to act. The methods are loose and open: one has to hear the command of God in the particular set of circumstances in which he or she acts, for God is free, and in his freedom he commands anew each day (Barth). Or, in the life of faith, and in the love of neighbor engendered and sustained by that faith, one knows what he ought to do, almost in an intuitive sense (Bultmann). The substance also is loose and open: while there has to be some coherence with the biblical witness, and while one has to be informed about contemporary circumstances and events in which action is called for, the churches do not burden themselves and their members with a historic legacy of particularized moral teachings. Such certitude as Protestant theological ethics can provide is that of promising the forgiveness of sins if what one believed to be the morally right thing to do turned out to be wrong. The weakness of Protestant ethics in the contemporary scene is this: the method and the substance tend to be excessively open-ended. When asked for a theological and ethical reason to justify particular decisions and actions, this theology takes recourse to extraordinarily elusive sources: individual conscience, sensitivity to what God is doing in the world, eschatological impatience with contemporary institutions and patterns of action, hearing God's command, or reading the *New York Times* in one hand and the Scripture in the other. Put very generally, Protestant ethics has a rather loose and open character which needs some tightening and closing to come to grips critically with modern moral and social problems.

Thus at the level of practical moral reasoning, Catholic moral theology and Protestant ethics share in common a very serious question, namely, how can the Christian community and its members make moral decisions and moral judgments which are both responsive and responsible: responsive to problems emerging in contemporary science and technology, political and social institutions, and interpersonal life; responsible not only for the consequences of actions in new circumstances, but responsible also to the moral values, the moral principles, that are grounded in the faith and life of the Christian community, and to the moral values and principles that are grounded in our common humanity. In the light of this shared question, Protestant and Catholic theologians are learning from each other and from various moral philosophers at the level of practical moral reasoning. In the remainder of this chapter, I present evidences that make this claim plausible, not denying divergences and noting convergences.

Protestantism:
A "Wasteland of Relativism"

The main stream of Protestant ethics in America and in Europe has been charged by evangelical Protestants with being excessively relativistic in its teaching.[3] The popular term "situation ethics," the use of which was widespread in the 1960s, captured all that was to be feared about Protestantism's drift from absolute moral principles and values.[4] The accusers, however, were not limited to those who accepted a stronger doctrine of the authority of the Bible for morality. In 1961 Paul Ramsey accused Protestant ethics of being in the "wastelands of utility" in his study of the ethics of war. In *War and the Christian Conscience*, Ramsey carried on a two-front debate: one about the substance of Christian ethics of war, and one about the methods appropriate to thinking about war or any other moral problem.[5] Interestingly, both substance and method, as Ramsey formulated them constructively, came from the just-war tradition which had been largely a legacy of Catholicism and of international law in the modern world. In the time of the Vietnam War, Ramsey's considerable defense of American involvement made him look to some persons like a "relativist" on the matters of substance; his concern for greater rational rigor in formulating judgments, however, had continuing and wider impact. I believe his 1961 book sparked a new interest in a more rigorous philosophical and theological approach to practical moral questions among American Protestant thinkers.[6] This concern is increasingly reflected in works by Protestant theologians now living on the North American continent.

Without engaging in a careful interpretation of Ramsey's work, one can indicate the import of his concerns, and some of the reasons why they are shared by other Protestant theologians as well. Part of Ramsey's charge was that Protestant practical ethics had become almost exclusively an "ethics of consequences." Two issues emerge from this observation. First, does the position imply that there are no intrinsically immoral acts, that is, acts which are morally wrong even though some beneficial consequences follow from them? Second, does the position take cognizance of the difficulties in predicting consequences and in judging their moral value?

It is clear that the best of Protestant practical ethics, done with admirable and widespread effectiveness by a person like Reinhold Niebuhr, were almost exclusively an "ethics of consequences." That good reasons can be given for doing theological ethics this way, and that the fruits of so doing practical moral reasoning can be beneficial, are clear. That there are critical problems in this approach was often overlooked. With creative genius as much akin to that of the insightful literary artist as to that of the rigorous philosopher Reinhold Niebuhr was able to interpret political, economic, and social life in the light of convictions about power, the human condition, and love and justice in such a way that certain "immoral" features were brought to sharp focus. The dark side of human nature as well as its positive possibilities had to be taken into account in interpreting the moral significance of past history and events, in analyzing present ones, and in forecasting potential consequences of various courses of action for individuals and communities. The valuation was consistently of consequences.

In a sense, Ramsey was suggesting that the results of such brilliant work were better than the method used to achieve them. For example, the major questions of traditional just-war theory (Is the cause just? Is the war conducted justly?) were implicit in the writings of Niebuhr and others during the late 1930s and 1940s, but little or no attention was given to the theory. The contention would be that these two questions and the principles developed historically to ascertain a proper answer to them can establish a clearer, more logically rigorous way of thinking about the matter. Indeed, one can read Protestant literature during that period and see in it implicit use of distinctions from the tradition. The notion of choosing the "lesser evil" implied some conception of a "principle of double effect" (or triple or quadruple effects) and a procedure of "proportionate reason" in determining which course of action would be morally preferable. The underlying judgment is that to be explicit, clear, and articulate in a highly rational way about one's methods and procedures of practical moral reasoning is "better" than to rely upon creative insight. Or, at least, it is "better" to be able to give explicit, clear, and articulate rational justification for one's insights than not to be able to do so. The relativism that Ramsey objected to was in part lack of self-consciousness and clarity about procedures of moral reasoning. The presumption is not that the penetrating insights of a moral genius are wrong, but that they can be given a more rational justification. Also presumed is that persons of lesser insight will be more likely to avoid serious moral mistakes if their methods for making moral choices are "rational." More thoroughgoing theories about reason, man, and the moral order might be offered to sustain these presumptions, but that argument is not a matter for this chapter.

Few persons would argue that Christian ethics ought not to calculate the consequences of various possible courses of action. Among major American theologians only Ramsey has claimed that Christian ethics is deontological, that is, an ethics of right conduct determined by obedience to or compliance with principles of conduct defined in terms of imperative or "ought" statements.[7] Ramsey is also concerned about consequences, though this is modified by another concern, namely, that certain acts are intrinsically morally evil and thus wrong even if the consequences would be of some benefit. But what has come under question in Protestant practical moral reasoning is principally these two matters: the extent to which consequences of a course of action are predictable (which can be turned back on the moral subject in the question of whether the agent is morally accountable for not only foreseen but unintended consequences, but also for unforeseen consequences caused); the extent to which beneficial and deleterious consequences are convertible to some common terms so that the comparative evaluation can be reasonably made (e.g., how can the benefits and costs be calculated to a community on limited rations that chooses to take the lives of innocent infants and other nonproductive persons?). The difficulties, the slipperiness of this enterprise has become increasingly clear to a number of Protestant theologians. These difficulties are similar to, if not formally the same as, those in the utilitarian tradition in moral philosophy.

An illustration frequently used, namely, "promise keeping" will indicate more precisely the difficulties. The strongest deontological statement would be, "You have an unconditioned and unconditional obligation to keep your promise." If someone has made a promise, by breaking it he or she has committed a morally wrong act. It is morally wrong to break a promise whether or not keeping it is inconvenient, requires extraordinary effort, or creates adverse consequences to oneself or to others. Conduct is morally right if it is in compliance with the rule. Quite another approach is that a person should judge whether there is an obligation to keep a promise in the light of the consequences of doing so. Thus, if one might do more "good" by breaking a promise than by keeping it, he or she is released from the obligation, and ought to do that which achieves the greatest good. If the latter approach is taken, how accurately can one predict all the consequences of breaking a promise, and of the alternative course of action? How can one judge qualitatively and quantitatively the harms and benefits of keeping or breaking a promise so that potential consequences can be weighed? If the deontological approach is taken, the person more concerned for consequences can ask how long one is obligated to keep a promise, if keeping it is destructive to persons immediately involved, and to others. (Was the United States obligated to "keep its commitment" to the Saigon government in the light of the harms entailed? Is a couple obligated to keep their marriage vows when the relationship is "destroying" one or both partners?)[8]

Protestant ethics had, for various reasons, slipped into an ethics of consequences without sufficient self-consciousness of the philosophical and theological grounds for doing so, or for not doing so. Three popular words in Protestant theology and ethics can be used to sustain the point: loving, humanizing, and liberating. On the theological level there is some clarity about the authorization of these adjectives. God is loving, and his activity in the world is loving; God is engaged in humanizing work in the world; God is engaged in liberating work in the world. (While it is not our purpose here to analyze theologies, it is fair to note that each of these has, in effect, become a thematic unitarianism, a simplification of the richness of the tradition; liberating, yes, but also ordering and limiting, for example.) The moral implications are that human activity in obedience or response to God should effect loving, or humanizing, or liberating consequences. (A thematic theological unitarianism implies a thematic ethical unitarianism.) One ethical problem, which has always plagued religious and secular minds, is how to determine what the "good" consequences are; indeed these three terms can be understood to be specifications of "good." Another is how, in view of the limitations of the control of consequences of any act, an agent can predict consequences and effect them. What consequences, and for whom, are to be approved as loving, humanizing, and liberating? How can one be certain that intentions to achieve these consequences will actually effect them?

The problems that Protestant ethics of consequences face are old ones. Not only do they exist in the utilitarian tradition, but in the classic teleological tradition as well. In both of these traditions they were faced more squarely than in Protestant ethics. I limit my remarks to the classic teleological position. Human agents were to do good and to avoid evil. Good and evil to a large extent meant good or evil consequences. For such an ethic some clear specifications were necessary. Answers were given with considerable precision (though some inherent ambiguities remained) to questions such as the following. What is the human good? (Happiness, blessedness.) How is that good known? (By analysis of the nature of human life.) How do individuals or communities know their own good? (First, by knowing their inclinations; second, by reflecting on the experience of the human race. But they often perceive only their apparent good and not their real good, and thus err.) How is the knowledge of the good effected in good consequences? (When the will is governed by the proper moral intentions.) There are unintended consequences as well (the principle of double effect and other procedures clarify the ambiguity), and so forth. On the whole Protestant ethical thought has not had the philosophical drive which could provide the rational structure in the light of which ethics of consequences could function with comparable precision. Humanizing, for example, has functioned more as a rhetorically eloquent term with immediate affective appeal than it has as a concept. The operating concept of the human could, to some extent, be formed by inferences from the ways that "humanizing" is used, but this task is, alas, frequently the reader's. My point is, that to judge which consequences are humanizing, one needs a concept of the human, indeed of the normatively human (the "real" and not the apparent "good"). Since there are conflicts about that, it is incumbent on any critical systematic work to give reasons for the concept designed, for its simplicity or its complexity, and for various qualities designated. Such would at least reduce the ambiguities in making judgments about humanizing consequences, although, as utilitarians and classic teleologists have found, it will not eliminate them. The same holds for love, for liberation, and other favorite words. (Joseph Fletcher has, to his credit, faced this with reference to a crucial term in his work, "human.")[9]

Protestant ethical thought has used two procedures to make practical moral judgments. One has been a not very systematic calculation of consequences and a moral judgment of the consequences in the light of seemingly self-evident principles and values. The procedures have been more or less common-sense ones and assume that within the community addressed the principles used and their authority need no elaborate justification. Just as the eighth-century Hebrew prophets could make their moral indictments of social and religious wrongs by assuming that the community knew the law from which the indictments were made and accepted its authority, so also a great deal of Protestant ethical writing has assumed the persuasiveness of its analysis and prescription on the basis of a religious cultural tradition. Few who are basically utilitarian in their procedures have been as explicit about it as was Joseph Fletcher in his widely read and discussed *Situation Ethics*.[10]

In that book Fletcher was addressing primarily a Christian readership; he was clearly writing as a Christian theologian. While he was carrying on a two-front battle, against both legalism and absolutism on the one hand, and against existentialism and antinomianism on the other, his principle debate is with the former. He chose to develop the book around the single theme that has for generations been widely accepted as the distinctive one in Christian ethics, love. The clearest statement of his imperative of calculation of consequences comes in his chapter "Love Justifies Its Means," the principal proposition of which is, "only the end justifies the means; nothing else"; his illustrations throughout the book, however, are framed to support this proposition. In that chapter Fletcher wrote,

> Once we realize and truly accept that only love is good in and of itself, and that no act apart from its foreseeable consequences has any *ethical* meaning whatsoever—only then will we see that the right question to ask is, Does an evil means always nullify a good end? And the answer, on the basis of what is sometimes called "due proportion," must be "*No.*" It always depends on the situation.[11]

Fletcher is concerned with motives and means, but, in my judgment, the weight of his argument falls on the evaluation of consequences—*all* the consequences, as he stresses. While he is not very precise in *Situation Ethics* about how various possible consequences should be compared, partly because of his confidence in love as a motive being able to perceive what the loving consequences are, he has in subsequent articles attempted to develop a set of criteria to be used. These pertain to "humanhood" (he has become less concerned about love) and are worked out with applicability to the ethics of medicine, an area in which he worked long before it attained its current public and academic vogue. As anyone working in the ethics of consequences must do, Fletcher makes value judgments about certain facts, and uses the facts to substantiate the value judgment. (He does not clarify sufficiently his answer to the "is-ought" or "fact-value" question which has been so intensively debated throughout this century.) For example, "Any individual of the species *homo sapiens* who falls below the I.Q. 40-mark in a standard Stanford-Binet test, amplified if you like by other tests, is questionably a person; below the 20-mark, not a person." The reason he offers is as follows. "*Homo* is indeed *sapiens*, in order to be *homo*. The *ratio*, in another turn of speech, is what makes a person of the *vita*. Mere biological life, before minimal intelligence is achieved or after it is lost irretrievably, is without personal status."[12] The practical applicability of this is to be used in judging whether there are obligations to patients; if the patient is not a "person" or will not be a "person" in the light of this and the other criteria developed, there is no moral obligation to him or to her. Thus one is to calculate potential consequences of proposed courses of action, and to judge them by the standards proposed. Fletcher is making specific and objective what many other Protestant writers tended to assume, namely procedures for utilitarian calculus. This is one procedure used to make practical moral judgments in Protestant ethics.

The second procedure used to make practical moral judgments was something like what Maurice Mandelbaum calls "perceptual intuitionism."[13] Considerable latitude must be given to the term "intuitionism" so that it can include the variety of its recent Protestant forms, for proposals vary in complexity and are set in relation to different theological patterns. Very complex is H. Richard Niebuhr's ethics of the "fitting" response.[14] The moral agent is responsive to the events in which he or she is participating, and must act accountably in them. From the theological perspective, God is acting on the agent through the actions of others. For the Christian, then, the practical moral task involves an interpretation of the events and actions in the light of not only such political and other concepts as pertain, but also in the light of religious beliefs and theological principles. Through this interpretative process, one can get insight into God's action and respond in a way that is "fitting." To be sure, the "fitting" response is not exclusively one determined by anticipated consequences, but these are normally a significant aspect of it. What is to be noted here is that utilitarian calculus as a specific procedure is rejected, and its place is taken by a perception of the "fitting."

A different form, I believe, is implied in Rudolph Bultmann's interpretation of the ethics of St. Paul, and one can be quite certain that Bultmann commends the Pauline view as the Christian view.

> Service of Christ realizes itself in actual life as *service to the neighbor*, of whom precisely the man is who is free, and only he, should and can make himself a genuine servant. . . . Such service is the fulfillment of the "law of Christ"; it is "love" which is the fulfillment of the law. . . . Naturally, for one who stands in love, an "ethic" is no longer necessary, however much brotherly admonition, such as Paul himself practices, can point out to another his responsibility and show him what he has to do.[15]

Here, the notion of "fitting" is not used, but it is implied. The agent perceives what action would be fitting to meet the need of the neighbor. The perception, however, is not guided by an interpretation of what the sovereign God is doing in and through the neighbor; it is rather that the agent who is in a condition of Christian freedom, who "stands in love," can know the neighbor's need. It appears that a rational calculation of the neighbor's need, and of the action which will meet that need is not necessary; "an ethic is no longer necessary for one who stands in love." One intuitively, in love, perceives what ought to be done.

Although Karl Barth rejects the label of intuitionism for good theological reasons, from a skeptical philosophical perspective, his view of practical moral judgments surely has affinities with it. Barth's reasons for denying that his ethics are intuitional are grounded in his doctrine of a sovereign, commanding God. Theological ethics "must not believe in the possibility and reality of a general moral inquiry and reply that are originally and ultimately independent of" God's command and God's grace. The objective revelation of God's grace is the basis of practical moral judgments. Theological ethics will regard that revelation "as so true" and its work "as so powerful" that it regards man "as actually determined by God's command, as altogether oriented by it objectively."[16] Clearly, if one grants his theological objectivism, there is no intuition; there is only obedience to the divine command. That command "is given to us at each moment" and "is always and only one possibility in every conceivable particularity of its inner and outer modality."[17] The order of the argument runs something like this: in each moment God commands what is right to do; God is the primary active agent in moral conduct—he discerns what a human ought to do and commands it; the human agent obeys that objective command. If one brackets or qualifies the theology out of a conviction that the role of the human agent is greater, if not primary, this view looks like a perceptual intuitionist view. The agent discerns (an anthropocentrism repugnant to Barth) what he or she ought to do in the particular circumstances. Barth's arguments against the sufficiency of all philosophical ethics—natural law, Kantian, utilitarian, or what have you—lend weight to the charge of intuitionism, though once the arguments have been discarded in favor of theological objectivism they can be annexed by it. But in

Barth's terms, even then they only prepare one to hear the concrete command of God; in nontheological terms they only aid the process of rational intuition.

To Paul Tillich, Barth's ethics would be heteronomous; they involve a command laid down upon the agent by an extrinsic power and authority. His own ethics, grounded in a radically different theology, are, however, equally intuitional at the level of practical moral choices. "The 'Will of God,'" he writes, "for us is our essential being with all its potentialities, our created nature declared us 'very good' by God." It is "manifest in our essential being." The moral demand, then, is "to fulfill one's own nature." Thus for example, one chooses not to destroy oneself in a state of despair because "the silent voice of our own being ... denies us the right to self-destruction."[18] There is a *telos*, or aim, inherent in our being, namely, to become a person within a community of persons; a "centered" person is "the bearer of the spirit, its creativity, and its self-transcendence." The moral aim, then, is to preserve and actualize these created potentialities.[19] While this has similarities to the natural law tradition that informs Catholic practical moral reasoning in that the being of humans has a moral aim toward the realization of potentialities, its application leads to intuitionism rather than to casuistry. The reasons for this lie in Tillich's theology and the view of the human that it informs, and will not be elaborated here. What enables Catholic moral theology to move from a basis similar to Tillich's to casuistry is the specification of its anthropology, as well as its different concept of reason and its functions that requires a more explicit mode of practical moral reasoning. The metaphor of the "silent voice" is utterly inadequate for Catholic moral theology, although this theology also begins with a natural inclination to the good and away from the evil. But Tillich's ethics, I believe, offer no epistemological grounds other than intuitive ones on which to settle conflicts of moral values or duties. This becomes apparent when one attempts to come to a conclusion about specific proposals on the use of human subjects for medical experimentation, on abortion, and on other practical issues.

My last example of Protestant intuitionism is from the writings of Paul Lehmann. Perhaps the following claim for a theonomous conscience is the most intuitive of all. "The *theonomous* conscience is the conscience immediately sensitive to the freedom of God to do in the always changing human situation what his humanizing aims and purposes require."[20] The notion of "immediate sensitivity" intentionally includes the imagination and the affections, as well as the capacity for clear understanding.[21] The view that Lehmann holds plays down the importance of the rational elements that one sees, for example, in H. Richard Niebuhr's process of interpretation. That to which the agent has immediate sensitivity is the "freedom of God," a freedom limited only by confidence that his action always has a humanizing aim and purpose. Humanizing action is that which leads to "maturity," that is, to "the integrity in and through interrelatedness which makes it possible for each individual member of an organic whole to be himself in togetherness, and in togetherness each to be himself."[22] There are no "indicators of humanhood" such as Fletcher has devised to attempt to make the notion of the human available to rational calculation of consequences. In the end, in seeking to know what God is doing in order to be engaged in that activity, one must rely upon a biblically informed interpretation of events to guide one's conscience in its intuitive perception of what ought to be done.[23]

The evaluation of predicted consequences by some rational calculus is difficult; to evaluate them by some sort of "perceptual intuitionism" is even more difficult. This, I believe, was what gave some warrant to Paul Ramsey's critical charge that Protestant ethics was in the wastelands of relativism. It is not that evaluation of consequences is per se dissonant with the ethics of the biblical and subsequent Christian tradition. But the assessment of them, both factual and moral, requires a much more critical method than often is used in Protestant theology. More critical and sophisticated specification of the moral values and moral principles that are to be used in judging consequences is required. Loving, liberating, and humanizing are far too elastic or, to change the metaphor, far too woolly terms to provide clarity in judging benefits and harms. This is not to deny that affectivity and insight have roles in the making of practical moral judgments; it is, however, at least to indicate the need for clearer direction by more objective and rational concepts in that process.

Further, even if the principal reference of Protestant ethics is to consequences rather than to rules and principles by which actions are judged to be morally wrong or right, there are ways to engage in practical moral reasoning which do not eliminate the language of right and wrong. (This has been a particular concern of Paul Ramsey's; his certitude about most judgments usually exceeds my own.) In the first chapter it was noted that a major Reformation, and particularly Lutheran, charge was against "legalism." It was to be avoided not for moral reasons primarily, but for a religious one, namely, that it inherently tempts persons to self-justification in the eyes of God. This charge continues in the work of Karl Barth, Rudolph Bultmann, and others. Insofar as this theological and religious problem has led to the elimination of general moral principles, or of clear concepts of moral values, Protestant theology has gotten into an irrational and morally dangerous ethical position. It has frequently failed to see that general principles and rules and concepts of values are necessary in the Christian life in order to give guidance (if not a sense of moral certitude) to human action.

The weakness of this Protestant openness is apparent when it takes a trivialized form. A Protestant divinity school student in the late sixties told me his view of practical moral reasoning. "I get up in the morning and look out the window to see what God is doing in the world. I read the *New York Times* to find out where he is doing these things today. Then I get with it." He apparently did not find it necessary to read the Bible! The questions are: How does one know what God is doing? How does one know what acts "get with it"? To many contemporary Protestants even the more sophisticated answers of the theologians are too shrouded in mystery, too reliant on crude calculations of consequences, too reliant on momentary intuitions, to be adequate to what moral responsibility requires.

From such a standpoint it is possible to have a fresh appreciation for the tradition of Roman Catholic moral theology. One does not need to subscribe to the warrants that gave much of this moral theology its sense of absolute certitude about cases to appreciate the clarity and rationality of many of the arguments. Nor is it necessary to subscribe to the theological and philosophical principles which validate the rationality of Catholic moral theology to initially appreciate the fact that the writers do have a justification for their method and their particular conclusions. One can appreciate the rigor with which Catholic moral theologians move from theological and philosophical first principles to the choices made, and to the judgments made about particular acts. For example, ask a Catholic moral theologian of the old manualist school whether it is wrong to engage in obliteration bombing during war, and he can give a decisively negative answer and articulate clearly his reasons for doing so, as John C. Ford, S.J., did in his significant article, "The Morality of Obliteration Bombing" before the use of atomic weapons in World War II.[24] Ford had a process for making meaningful moral distinctions; there was substance to the discriminations he made. Even if, in one sense, Ford's arguments could be reduced to saying that obliteration bombing is "inhuman" or "unloving," the character of the argument and the distinctions required provide more practical moral guidance than do those popular Protestant terms or the usual Protestant procedures for making a judgment about a particular act.

From the same frustration with Protestant intuitionism and utilitarianism, has come an appreciation for and absorption of work done recently by British and American moral philosophers. In Paul Ramsey's writings this is most evident in his essay, "Two Concepts of Rules in Christian Ethics" which was inspired and partially guided by John Rawls' famous essay on "Two Concepts of Rules."[25] It is also evident in other of Ramsey's methodological and practical works. A reading of articles and books by Protestant theologians, mostly younger ones, on the topic of ethics through the decade of the 1960s gives clear evidence of the appropriation of the concerns, concepts, and procedures from various British and American moral philosophers that began in that decade. Citations of R. M. Hare, Stuart Hampshire, Iris Murdoch, H. L. A. Hart, Elizabeth Anscombe, Philippa Foot, Henry David Aiken, John Rawls, William Frankena, Roderick Firth, Alan Gewirth, R. S. Peters, Ronald Dworkin, and many others are the external evidence for this observation; the texture of the arguments and analyses is the internal evidence. Some of these writers are named in note 6 in this chapter. Since an account of this openness to a modern philosophical tradition is ancillary to the purpose of this book, I do not elaborate it here. Suffice it to note that a function of this appropriation has been to provide a conceptual rigor and critical self-consciousness that Protestant ethics of previous decades generally lacked and that "political theology" lacks currently. From my point of view undesirable consequences of this interest, which on the whole I support, are a preoccupation with formal analysis of arguments of the work of others, a tendency to focus on practical moral reasoning rather than other "levels" of ethical writings, and particularly a loss of interest in the theological aspects of Christian ethics. These undesirable consequences are not, fortunately, present in all of the work currently being done.

Perhaps the main point of dissatisfaction with much of Protestant practical moral writing can be made rhetorically. Few persons are saints; few persons are moral geniuses or moral virtuosos; few have the theonomous conscience that Lehmann describes; few have heard an unambiguous, immediate command of God; many who live "in faith" and "in love" have not been able to determine clearly what the needs of the near and distant neighbor are; many who are moved to actualize their potentialities for life in the spirit, for creativity and for self-transcendence find that conflicts of moral values are not thereby resolved. Given this state of experience and perhaps even of *being* human, it is both necessary and possible to work out procedures for practical moral reasoning which provide both substantive guidance for moral choices and acts and provide clearer reasons for them. Catholic moral theology has become a conversation partner for Protestant theologians as they seek to bring the openness of Protestant theology and ethics to focus on particular moral and social problems. The just-war tradition is but one example; distributive justice in economic, social, and political life, ethical issues in medical research and care are among others.

During this same period there has been increasing frustration in Roman Catholicism about the rationalistic character of the casuistry of the manuals of moral theology and about the defensive posture taken toward many currents of modern knowledge. Among the interests of the reformers, interestingly, have been the exploration of a more intuitional mode for making choices, and a greater concern for the assessment of consequences of actions.

Catholicism:
The Search for Responsible Openness

Since World War II Catholic moral theology has been in a ferment perhaps unlike any it has had in history. While the historic debates over probabilism were sharp, they took place within a pattern of thought that was in principle accepted by all the parties that became distinctive. Certainly the standard Protestant criticisms of Catholic moral theology assumed a greater unanimity of opinion and procedures than actually existed. Perhaps, for example, only the writers of the poorest manuals, the least nuanced and historically sophisticated, have claimed that the gap between general principles and particular choices and actions could be closed by logic alone, a charge often made indiscriminately by Protestant writers. But since World War II (and thus also prior to the Second Vatican Council) within the Catholic church there have been charges that the traditional way of doing moral theology has led to unresponsiveness to aspects of modern knowledge and contemporary events.

A discussion of "situation ethics" occurred in Catholicism in the 1940s and early 1950s, thus long before the term achieved its currency in American Protestantism. The movement was significant enough to warrant responses from Karl Rahner, Josef Fuchs, John C. Ford and Gerald Kelly, and other major Catholic theologians, and finally was condemned by Pope Pius XII in 1952 and ecclesiastically censured by the Holy Office in 1956.[26] In a vigorous defense of Christian situation ethics first published in 1951 in response to the criticisms of Karl Rahner, Walter Dirks lined out the reasons why the "movement" developed in Catholicism. At a general level, Dirks notes what is really a "paradigm shift" for groups of modern Catholics. "A situation-ethics was possible only when the capacity for dialogue and the historical dimension of man's existence reached the deepest level of his consciousness."[27] This level will receive more attention in the next chapter, but the introduction of the paradigm of dialogue makes possible a view of morality that the analogy of being does not. The invocation of the historical dimensions of human existence alters, if not discards, the traditional preoccupation with human *nature*.

Like many concerns of theory, this one arises also out of the practical state of affairs. Dirks indicates that the traditional casuistry of moral theology relied implicitly on an "objective social framework" that has collapsed, with the result that "the individual is forced to take a position which is more free, more conscious, and more fully responsible."[28] It also assumed a normalcy of human experience that did not include today's extended zones of behavior in recreation, professional life, and modern collective social, economic, and political life. In the complexities of modern life persons perceive "that traditional casuistry does not take into consideration the various new elements of existence and consciousness," that it "has insufficient powers of discrimination" and is "too clumsy a tool" to open the contemporary locks, "too complicated and ambiguous to be easily handled." Thus to be open to situations is to hear "the claims which reach me from reality," reality referring not so much to an ontological structure as to the immediate life-world.[29] Casuistry depersonalizes; it makes every situation a "case"; it makes the norm a being in itself.

Rahner's criticisms warned against the radical extension of situational morality, and Dirks admits such extensions are problematic. But for him situation ethics "is the ethics of a believer," of a partner with God. It seeks to know what God's will is in the situation. Thus situation ethics "does not indicate a collapse of basic norms," but a different way of apprehending them; it does not lead to normlessness, but a more earnest openness to determine "what *I* ought to *do*, whom God has called by name." It is not lawlessness, but recognizes that "the law can make few precise regulations and usually does not go beyond fundamental indications."[30]

The family resemblances between Dirks as an exemplar of Catholic situation ethics and what I have called Protestant intuitionism are apparent. God calls persons to do what he wills in particular circumstances; the language of the relation to God is personalized—speaking and responding, commanding and obeying. The contributions of existential and biblical modes of thought are clear. But particularly to be noted is the implied and explicit criticism of casuistry. Moral theology has created a labyrinth that makes vital history into cases, that encumbers the Christian with unmanageable and not very useful baggage, that intervenes in the human's personal relation to God and to others with an apparatus that does not help despite its claims to hit the moral mark. In other words, moral theology had become too closed to meet relevantly new circumstances, and its rationalistic procedures corrupted the religious sense of personal dialogue with God.

What did this look like to the defenders of traditional moral theology? The instruction of the Holy Office in 1956 states that both succinctly and authoritatively.

> The authors who follow this system hold that the decisive and ultimate norm of conduct is not objective right order, determined by the law of nature, and known with certainty from

that law, but a certain intimate judgment and light of the
mind of each individual, by means of which, in the concrete
situation in which he is placed, he learns what he ought to do.
And so, according to them, this ultimate decision a man
makes is not, as the objective ethics handed down by authors
of great weight teaches, the application of the objective law to
a particular case, taking into account at the same time and
weighing according to the rules of prudence the particular circumstances of the "situation," but that immediate, internal
light and judgment. This judgment, at least in many matters,
is not measured ultimately, is not to be measured, and is not
measurable with regard to its objective correctness and truth,
by any objective norm situated outside man, and independent
of his subjective persuasion, but is entirely sufficient unto
itself.

The description continues, and the judgment is made that
"situation ethics" contradict truth and "the dictates of sound
reason, betray traces of relativism and modernism, and wander
far from the Catholic doctrine handed down through the centuries." Finally, "this Supreme Sacred Congregation of the Holy
Office forbids and prohibits this doctrine of 'Situation Ethics,' by
whatever name it is designated to be taught . . . , or to be
propagated and defended in books . . . or in any other manner
whatsoever."[31]

Happily, to the benefit of theological ethics, this statement did
not terminate the discussion. It did, however, clearly state the
major issue, namely, whether an objective moral order could be
known clearly and whether principles derived from it could be
applied correctly to every set of circumstances. The issues, as
Louis Dupré and others indicated, are both philosophical and
theological. Philosophically, Dupré argued, the principal issue is
the status of human nature, and particularly the radicality of
human freedom and subjectivity; theologically it is the manner of
thinking about God's relation to man, the appropriate paradigm
for that relationship.[32] These concerns are the subject matter of
subsequent chapters. But the "intuitionism" of Catholic situation
ethics was not the only matter to be discussed; moral theologians
have also been concerned to clarify the status of consequences
and their evaluation.

The teleological framework of Catholic theology and ethics has
always set the concern for consequences in a central place in
moral theology. That Catholic moral theology became very

deontological in practice, however, was not a matter of historic accident or intellectual heedlessness. The human good to be realized was not only fulfillment of values, of potentialities; it was also right conduct in relation to others. The properly fulfilled life is one which is conducted rightly. Also, the rules which became the practical focus of attention could be justified in terms of the values of human realization that the rules sought to preserve and sustain. Rules, whether unexceptionable or exceptionable, have a teleological justification. The rule against adultery has validity not only because adultery violates a covenant (a more deonto-logical justification) but also because adultery is harmful to the parties involved, to the values of family life and so forth.

The evaluation of consequences of actions, then, is not novel in moral theology, and, as a number of important contemporary moral theologians argue, can be justified on traditional Catholic principles.[33] I believe, however, that the recent discussion emerges out of serious exposure to some patterns of non-Catholic thought. Both American pragmatism and European existential phenomenology have emphasized the importance of human experience, not only as a basis for knowing consequences, but also as a basis for judging their human and moral worth. Knowledge of what constitutes human realization comes from human experience, and that knowledge is also confirmed by human experience. In addition to these philosophic trends, there has been increasing exposure to the social and behavioral sciences particularly as these have flourished in North America. Writings of scholars in sociology, psychology, and other disciplines have been used to provide data, concepts, and theories about what the human good is. They provide procedures and ideas for analyzing the moral agent and the conditions of personal action, for predicting the effects of interventions in personal life and social processes, and even for formulating moral norms on an inductive rather than a deductive basis.[34]

When the experience-centered philosophies and the behavioral sciences take a more central role, there is a perceptible alteration in practical moral reasoning. Some matters about which unam-biguous moral judgments have been made in the past clearly are perceived to be more complex. Masturbation, for example, was judged to be a serious moral wrong because it was "unnatural." It must now be interpreted, however, in the light of modern knowledge. Thus Charles E. Curran writes, "A more personal approach and better psychological as well as physical knowledge points out that masturbation is ordinarily not that important a matter." Every such act is not equally grave; indeed it is to be viewed as "symptomatic," sometimes of a "deep-seated inversion," or of "an adolescent growing-up process." Curran believes it is wrong, but not for the traditional reason; its wrongness lies in its failure "to integrate sexuality in the service of love."[35] Thus the problem is altered in its moral significance by virtue of what one could call excusing conditions (e.g., the "growing-up process"), and the sanctions against it require revision. It is modern knowledge that gives a different explanation of the act, and that explanation is morally significant. It is modern knowledge which also explains a pathological guilt that the older moral view often engendered, and this also must be taken into account. There is a basic philosophic criticism of the older view—its view of natural law had a "physicalist" bias, but that is a matter for the next chapter. Similar sorts of considerations must be taken into account when homosexuality is the issue. While homosexual acts are wrong, a theology of sin in terms of "modern psychological knowledge indicates that most often homosexual actions do not involve the person in grave or mortal sin." Indeed, in cases where medical science cannot provide therapy, "homosexual acts might not even be wrong," though they are never the goal or ideal. "Homosexual acts . . . , provided there is no harm to other persons, might be the only way in which some degree of humanity and stability can be achieved." A "theology of compromise" is required where the sciences indicate a limitation of accountability for actions and their consequences.[36]

John Giles Milhaven, in a chapter on "Homosexuality and Love," states that "[t]o understand what is good for a person . . . a man of the twentieth century relies exclusively on experience. For him, love knows no *a priori* law, sees only the ones loved and what experience shows is happening to them." Milhaven desires to think about homosexuality as a Christian for whom love, informed by Jesus Christ, is the sole norm. From that perspective the question can be asked, "Would homosexual behavior really be good or bad for myself and the other person?" In discussing answers to the question, he cites the ambiguity of the "prevailing scientific appraisal of homosexuality as the living out of sick and stunted emotions." How this evidence will finally come out should "determine the ethical decision." For Milhaven the odds on the evidence still favor accountability, and thus homosexuality is evil (like alcoholism is evil, wrong, and un-Christian). It is evil not because it abuses a faculty, but because it is a refusal to love, "i.e., to live and let live a full human life." But, implied in the discussion is the judgment that homosexuality is more like alcoholism and "shrewishness"; all are wrong and un-Christian, but that does not make persons who have these faults "great sinners"; it does not assume they are fully free to be otherwise, that they should be excluded from church membership or punished by law.[37] Milhaven's concentration of love, which resembles Joseph Fletcher's, must be appreciated to understand his argument, but in addition to that are the appeals to experience and to the sciences for an understanding of both the agent and the consequences of action. These appeals soften the severity and weaken the certitude of moral judgments; judgments are made not deductively from an objective moral order as in the manuals, but more inductively as informed by experience and science. Indeed, the inability of the rationalistic casuistry to take into account fully the modern knowledge and experience is one reason why it needs to be either revised or abandoned.

The Catholic authors who have moved most explicitly toward the assessment of consequences of actions as the basis for judging them morally vary in the extent of their adherence to the natural law tradition. Among those in the United States who remove themselves a greater distance is Milhaven, who distinguishes two "mentalities," a classic and "other-worldly" one that is characterized by the manualists and a modern one that is "experience-oriented" within the lives in this world of ordinary individuals.

> The modern mind, therefore, sees man and his life, human good and human evil, by focussing principally on: (1) what is revealed in his experience of this world, (2) as the experience would be even if there were no God, (3) as it is shaped, or can be shaped, by man's technological power, (4) as it occurs in the lives of ordinary men, (5) as it is created by the unique self of man, by his on-going self-creation or freedom that is "I," by the creative interaction with "Thou."[38]

This modern mentality relies upon empirical evidence to determine the human good or evil in abortion, homosexuality, or other matters. This theme runs through several of Milhaven's articles; it is clearly indicated when he writes "that it is empirical evidence, not direct insight into what something is, but the observation, correlation, and weighing out of numerous facts, which reveal the value of most human acts; for they show what effect these acts will have in the concrete, existing world on those absolute values a man discerns by immediate insight."[39] The "modern mentality" appears in Milhaven's work to be far removed from the "classical" one. It works inductively from experience and empirical evidence to determine what is the human good. Its norms are not derived from the structure of the natural law, and thus its processes of practical moral reasoning differ from that of traditional casuistry. Indeed, for Milhaven love becomes the norm, or perhaps better the value, to be realized, and no *a priori* system can predetermine a limited and fixed order from which experiences of love are to be assessed. Both Milhaven and Curran are relatively cautious about moving away from traditional judgments about actions such as homosexual ones, but even the reasons for their measure of compliance with them are justified on a distinctively different basis. Curran is, in many writings, more attentive to the natural law tradition; he does not endorse a "modern mentality" uncritically as Milhaven appears to do. Both, however, like others even more closely related to the traditional practical moral reasoning, move into the arena in which the difficulties associated with utilitarianism cannot be avoided.

It is John R. Connery, S.J., who has perceptively chosen to make his criticism of not only Milhaven but also more "traditional" or conservative reformers of moral theology via the problematics of utilitarianism. He does not charge them with violation of the principles of "objective ethics handed down by authors of great weight," as does the Holy Office statement condemning early situation ethics, but rather sees in their work an increasing difficulty in preventing teleological ethics from becoming merely utilitarian ethics.[40] Connery turns his attention to Peter Knauer, S.J., Bruno Schüller, S.J., Joseph Fuchs, S.J., and others, and by implication to the work of his colleague, Richard A. McCormick, S.J. (who has responded regularly to proposals of these and other authors in his "Notes on Moral Theology" and in *Ambiguity in Moral Choice*).[41] Connery acknowledges the importance "of role effects or consequences" in traditional morality as one aspect involved in the determination of the morality of an act; indeed, it is likely that any human action will sooner or later have some bad effects as well as good. In the tradition, however, the role of consequences is but one aspect; consideration has also been given to the object of the act, the end (*telos*) of the act, and the circumstances of the act. This indicates the relation of the concern to the structure of human acts as delineated by Thomas Aquinas, which is itself a part of the conceptualization of the nature of the human. As Connery, with all other persons who take the tradition more seriously than Milhaven, points out, the practical principle that is used to "apply" the concern for consequences to actions without losing a base in the "classical mentality" is that of double effect. Thus it is not surprising that an intensive discussion has been going on about this principle in Europe and North America among contemporary moral theologians and philosophers.

The crucial difference between a crude calculation of consequences in an uncritical popular utilitarianism and the exercise of the principle of double effect is that in the latter the moral judgment about an act remains focussed on the *intention* of its agent, and thus the heart of the issue is the moral accountability of the actor for the effects of an action. Thus, as Richard McCormick indicates, the distinction to be clear about is between the directly voluntary and the indirectly voluntary consequences; this distinction is used to resolve conflicts in which an evil is reluctantly caused as a result of achieving a good (or avoiding another evil). Causing such an evil is justified under a four-fold condition. The act cannot be one that is *intrinsically* evil; such an act is not permitted for the sake of any good. The intention of the agent must be "upright," "that is, the evil effect is sincerely not intended." Both the good and evil effects must be caused with equal immediacy; if this were not the case the evil might be a means to the good, and such is not permissible. And finally, there "must be a proportionately grave reason" for permitting the evil effect to occur.[42] It is clear from this that the scope of actions to which the principle of double effect can be properly applied is restricted. The restrictions are set by four judgments: about whether the act is intrinsically evil, which implies a clear principle for determining that; about the sincerity of the agent's intention, which is an evaluative judgment with empirical dimensions; about the chain of causality, which is an empirical judgment that makes a moral difference; and about the proportionality of the reason which involves three other judgments that fuse evaluative and empirical factors—"a value at least equal to that sacrificed is at stake," "there is no less harmful way of protecting the value here and now," and the way it is now protected "will not undermine it in the long run."[43]

I have elaborated these judgments because the last three (the first requires a deontological ethics) cannot avoid, indeed necessarily entail, empirical factors, and the last, which is the burden of McCormick's own constructive proposal, is sufficiently "slippery" to cause Connery to say that consequentialism "is difficult to establish on the theoretical level and dangerous to apply on the practical level."[44] On issues like abortion, war, experimentation on human subjects, and many more, it does not resolve ambiguity sufficiently to eliminate nervousness on the part of more conservative theologians.

The discussion between proponents of the principle of double effect need not be developed for our purposes. The persistent issue is how to take consequences more seriously than some previous theologians did without surrendering the rational principles of judgment that the conservative reformers value as a heritage from the tradition. Or, to put it in the "vernacular," once the theologian has his feet on the slippery slope of consequences, what restraints can he locate to keep him from sliding all the way to the bottom of an experiential verification in which recourse is taken to the self-evidence of goodness and evil;[45] and from the assumption that the *ought* arises from the *is* in an unambiguous way?

The "situation ethics" of Catholicism, the reliance upon human experience as a source of knowledge about the human good and as a confirmation of moral judgments; the openness to the behavioral sciences as providers of data, concepts, and theory for understanding the moral agent and predicting and judging consequences of action; and the more explicit "consequentialism"—all indicate, in my judgment, efforts to make the traditional patterns of Catholic moral reasoning more adaptable for the sake of responsiveness to modern conditions. More general observations underlie these efforts: there is a new "historical consciousness" abroad in the world; there are philosophical and religious reasons for being more concerned about the uniqueness and richness of personal and interpersonal existence; there is a breakdown of traditional acceptance of ecclesiastical authority; there is a new interest in biblical thought and in Protestant theology. With admirable intellectual self-consciousness, the best among the contemporary Catholic moral theologians do not revise practice without also undertaking to rethink traditional theory; they do not revise fundamental moral theory without also adjusting practice. To be sure there are Catholics who wish to break with the rigorous intellectual tradition of moral theology altogether; some have become as intuitive as radical Protestants. There are also those who are deeply worried that the recent Catholic appreciation of pluralism and other modern trends will lead to an accommodation to modern culture and to majority opinions in society.[46] Nonetheless, a number of moves being made show the possibility of a new convergence between the ethical work of Protestants and Catholics.

Some remarks about Pope Paul's encyclical on birth control, *Humanae Vitae*, and the critical responses it engendered, will illustrate both some of the themes of this chapter and some of the more general philosophical and theological issues to be discussed in the next two chapters. In that historically fateful text, the pope takes cognizance of the altered circumstances which thought about birth control must consider. He notes the rapid growth of population, the economic and educational stresses that many families undergo, the changing roles of women in society, the value "to be attributed to conjugal love in marriage," and the "stupendous progress" man has made in "the domination and rational organization of the forces of nature." He does not attack contraception based on control of sexual drives by acts of will, and he supports the so-called rhythm method. Yet he does judge the use of artificial devices for birth control to be illicit and makes the decisive positive affirmation: "Nonetheless the Church, calling men back to the observance of the norms of the natural law, as interpreted by her constant doctrine, teaches that each and every marriage act must remain open to the transmission of life."[47]

The response to this encyclical has been, as every reader of this book knows, extensive and intense. The encyclical represents, in effect, a reaffirmation of pre-Vatican II moral theology and particularly of Pius XI, *Casti Connubii*.[48] That critical Catholic moral theologians responded to it on bases similar to those used by Protestant ethicians is the important point. Questions of practical moral reasoning as well as of theory arise; revision of practice and theory go hand in hand. From the discussions of

Humanae Vitae, I shall indicate four strands which indicate possible convergence of the two traditions.

The first is what is loosely called "historical consciousness." By tracing the historical development of moral doctrine on contraception (and other issues) one can indicate both the continuities and the alterations. John T. Noonan's massive and brilliant scholarship in *Contraception* indicates that the tradition has not been unilateral and absolutely uniform.[49] Perceptions and concepts are shown to take place in particular historic conditions (significant philosophic ideas, medical knowledge, particular threats to religious practice, and so on) which influenced the views stated. Just as the just-war theory was not formulated from a nonhistorical reading of the moral law of nature,[50] so the teaching about contraception was not. If an interpretation of the historical development is taken seriously, then there are consequences for both moral theory and practical moral reasoning. The theory of natural law must be discarded or, at the very least, be reinterpreted to take into account in some way this factor of change in history. In practical moral reasoning it requires that recognition be given to new knowledge, new conditions of society, and new capacities for control of reproduction. This recognition may lead to different judgments about the morality of contraception.

The second strand is what can be called "personalism," again in a loose sense. A higher valuation of the personal significance of sexual intercourse between married persons, its significance as an expression of human love and as a nurture to that love, has consequences for theory and practice. In moral theory it requires a reassessment of the "nature" of human life so that the personal aspects of human nature ascend in importance and are rethought in relation to the sheer biological aspects of life. It requires an alteration of the understanding of the meanings of marriage so that sexual intercourse can be valued more highly as an act of personal meaning which fulfills relationships, an act that is less a "remedy for sin" and not in every instance a procreative act. Consequently contraception is licit in a way it had not been judged to be; and whether the couple rely upon sterile periods or upon pharmaceutical or mechanical means is a question of little importance.

A third strand is the wider "totality" to be taken into account in thinking about morally responsible marriages. Responsibility is not only to the need to continue the species, it is responsibility for the care and nurture of those whom parents have brought into life. It is, by extension, not only for the next generation but for generations to follow long into the future. It is not only to one's family of procreation but to the human family on the finite planet earth. If there is an extension of the "finality" to be kept in view in the act of sexual intercourse, then there are reasons which justify limitation of birth as an act of moral responsibility. The question of whether that limitation comes by restraint of sexual drives by an act of will, or by other means which are not "intrinsically evil," becomes a matter of less importance. The extension of the totality becomes a matter of revision of theory as well, for if the concept is used it can no longer be restricted to human individuals or even to couples and families.

The fourth strand takes into account the role of the church. The discussion of *Humanae Vitae* has led to intense discussion of the rights of the consciences of individuals, a matter secured in key texts in the tradition but not always respected in practice. The large questions of the authority and role of the church in moral matters and of the right of dissent from its official teachings by informed and conscientious persons have been evoked in a dramatic way. Practically, the import of the discussion has been a wider exercise of the consciences which dissent from authoritative teaching and a new confidence in the moral integrity of informed, conscientious persons. The church, while remaining *magister*, teacher, is not perceived to have the same extent of freedom from error as it has often claimed to have. It is, perhaps, more the fallible teacher with much to learn, even from students, than the authoritative requirer of absolute conformity and subservient obedience. The issues of theory are clear; they pertain to the authority of the church in moral matters and the role of the church in the formation of conscience—both basic ecclesiological issues.

A Protestant theologian can find new bases for serious convergence of thought in each of these four strands; they include appreciation for an intuitive moment in moral choice and a concern for consequences. But the Protestant need not rejoice only in those movements toward his or her own tradition; for anyone in that tradition there is much to be gained by taking seriously the rigor and precision of traditional Catholic moral theology. If one is open to the practical moral reasoning, one

must also be open to consider the theory that justifies and
informs it. That goes both ways, from Protestant to Catholic and
from Catholic to Protestant. The theory is both philosophical and
theological, and these aspects also must cohere with each other.
To these matters we turn in the next two chapters.

5

Philosophical Bases

From the previous chapter it is clear that differences in patterns of practical moral reasoning are grounded implicitly or explicitly in more general philosophical assumptions or principles. Traditional Roman Catholic moral theology, as we have seen, cannot be appreciated and understood without a knowledge of the classical Western philosophies and their use in the development of Catholic doctrine. The neo-Platonic theme of all things coming from and returning to God, *exitus et reditus*, and the use of Aristotelian concepts to delineate the character of nature have been of particular importance. The ethics of the Reformation authors cannot be understood historically without awareness of the impact of the nominalism of late medieval philosophy. Certain forms of Anglican ethics, for example the writings of F. D. Maurice in the nineteenth century, suggest dependence on a generally Platonic pattern of thought. Most modern Protestant ethical thought is inexplicable without recourse to the impact of Kant and various post-Kantian developments in philosophy. My intention is not to develop a historical account but to examine recent discussions in order to indicate the crucial contemporary problematics of each tradition and the ways in which they are and can be related to each other.

In my judgment, the basic questions that Roman Catholic and

Protestant writers share are these. What philosophical foundations are necessary and sufficient to provide conditions under
which theological ethics can do justice both to the historical
particularities of the Christian tradition and to the common
humanity and rationality that religious persons share with all
members of our species? What foundations are necessary and
sufficient to provide conditions under which theological ethics
can do justice both to the persistent temporal continuities of
human experience ("nature") and the historical changes in it
("history")? What foundations are necessary and sufficient to
provide conditions under which theological ethics can do justice
both to the dimensions of human freedom and individual personal existence on the one hand and limitations of freedom and
co-humanity on the other?

The thesis of this chapter can be described in the following
way. Modern Protestant ethics have operated explicitly or implicitly from philosophical presuppositions which are basically
Kantian in historical origin. Two post-Kantian developments
have been particularly influential; both have made it difficult for
Protestant writers to develop universally applicable principles of
morality, for both have led to highly confessional theologies
which radically question the possibility of rational knowledge of a
universal moral order and of universally applicable moral principles. These movements can be roughly labeled historicism and
existentialism. Both have made it difficult, for philosophical
reasons, to develop ethics which are persuasive to persons who do
not share the religious life and presuppositions out of which the
ethics have come. Both have, however, made it possible for
Protestant writers to be very biblical in their ethics, to accept
relational, or even relativistic, interpretations of morality, and to
accept the individuality of the moral agent as important for
ethics. On philosophical grounds Protestantism has been open to
the biblical message and to flexibility in morality relative to the
circumstances in which actions occur, to the agents who act, and
to the moral principles to be applied or human values to be
realized.

Roman Catholic ethics has been grounded in the philosophy of
natural law. This has made the Bible less central to moral
theology but has given that tradition a basis from which to
address "all men of good will" and to argue for the rightness of
particular acts without recourse to religious motives, insights,

and norms, that is, without recourse to "revelation." The form that natural law ethics took, however, led to a very static view of the moral order, to claims for absolute moral certitude in what to others were situations in which ambiguity was intrinsic and irresolvable. It also led to a "physicalist" bias (in contrast to a "personalist" one) in the interpretation both of the agent and of the human good. The problems of moral theology, as a result of the way its philosophical foundations have been developed and used, are how to take into account historic changes in morality that appear to be justifiable and how to establish a view of human nature that accounts for its more personal aspects.

Thus Protestant theological ethics and Catholic moral theology currently share a serious quest, namely, for a philosophical foundation for Christian ethical thought and Christian moral activity which takes the Christian tradition seriously, which provides a common ground with nonreligious persons and communities and with other religions, and which has openness to historic changes and to personalistic values without becoming utterly relativistic.

"Historicism" and Existentialism in Protestant Ethics

Protestant ethical thought in the modern period has been no less varied than it has been since the time of the Reformation. On the whole, however, there has been consensus on the rejection of the natural law tradition and particularly on the metaphysics of that tradition.[1] The charges most commonly made against natural law have been three: its reliance upon a human natural inclination toward the good does not take sufficiently into account the seriousness of the human condition of sin, which for many Protestants not only perverts human desires and will but also distorts human reason; its reliance upon reason to formulate the norms and principles on which all humans can agree has persistently failed, for all rational persons do not come to the conclusions of the Catholic tradition; and the substantive norms and principles it has developed always seem to reflect the social and cultural conditions of the medieval period in which the theory developed. To a considerable extent these charges have been more asserted than thoroughly argued; they frequently were not made on the basis of a thorough study of what the theory in its classic Catholic theological setting did and did not maintain. For whatever reasons, no major figure in Protestant ethics in the post-Enlightenment period has thoroughly developed and defended a *theory* of natural law, though one does find theologians who have "natural" bases for ethics which function to provide a universal ground for morality comparable to what natural law theory does.

The centrality of Scripture in Protestant ethics can be accounted for only in part on the basis of the authority of accepted tradition. Even theological arguments for it are supported by reasons which are extratheological and extrabiblical in character. On some occasions the findings of Scripture are corroborated by human experience and reason. Rauschenbusch, for example, in his little study book, *The Social Principles of Jesus*, moves with considerable ease between the biblical narratives and teachings as a basis for ethics and observations from human experience. Scripture is the principal source for understanding the moral will of God, but by inobtrusively indicating that "the will of God is identical with the good of mankind,"[2] he provides a warrant for interpreting the ethics of Jesus in the light of his perceptions of "the good of mankind." Reinhold Niebuhr's view of love is grounded in Scripture, both in the teachings of Jesus and in the paradigm of his self-sacrificial love on the cross. Yet Niebuhr also claims that "love is the law of life."[3] This opens the possibility for reflection on the *law* of life through an interpretation of human experience and of the *nature* of life of which love is the law, though Niebuhr did not take this route very far. Scriptural teaching is corroborated by human experience in much of Protestant ethics, though an argument which could sustain this possibility and take into account its implications for a theory of theological ethics is seldom made.

A combination of philosophical and theological judgments led to another set of reasons for the centrality of Scripture in Protestant ethics. For many theologians in the Protestant tradition the consuming passion in the matter of theological method for well over a century has been to come to grips with the difficulties created by Hume and Kant for the enterprise of "natural" knowledge of God. Although Luther and others asserted the principle of Scripture alone, subsequent Protestant theologians from the sixteenth to the early nineteenth centuries generally found ways to indicate that "reason" could also come to firm convictions about God's existence and attributes. For some it can be said that natural theology led them to the same conclusions, or to similar ones, as those revealed in the Bible, but by a different route of inquiry. For some, natural theology took precedence and provided principles for purifying biblical theology of its archaisms and irrationalities; natural theology provided the principles for selecting what was valid in the historical texts. For some, natural theology could be put into apologetic service by a dominantly biblical theology; it could be used to expound revelation in other than historical biblical language and concepts. All assumed that to some extent one could know God as he is and of himself by processes of natural reason. To this assurance the writings of Hume and Kant dealt a shaking and in some instances a devastating blow.

If one could *not* have clear and certain knowledge of God by reason, there were only certain possibilities left for theology. It was a myth or fiction which was in basic error, and thus was an offense to be destroyed for its backward and distorting consequences; or it was an innocuous weed for less rigorous minds to tend which would wither away from lack of nourishment. Or theology was an enterprise worthy of attention but had to have a different grounding. One response was to view the Bible as a miraculous revelation undertaken by divine volition, and verbally inspired; it was in principle a different kind of knowledge exempt from philosophical critiques of its authority. Or, since man cannot move by reason to knowledge of God, God chose to reveal himself to man through the history and events of a people with whom he made an old covenant and a new covenant; thus the history recorded in the Bible is the place to look for knowledge of God, although the book is not verbally inspired. Or, if one could not be persuaded of the validity of these options, one could say that any knowledge of God that humans can have occurs through his relations with the world and particularly with humans in particular historical circumstances; thus all knowledge of God is relative to historic occasions and no final certitude is possible via either reason or revelation. The options were a rather credulous *fideism* which only avoids and does not answer the issues raised by Hume and Kant; a reliance on a particular *history* as a trustworthy source of knowledge of God, a reliance supported by a radical faith; or reliance on that history as providing a meaningful account of God's dealings with humankind that is historically and existentially confirmed in human experience. In theological ethics the options are similar to those for theology in a restricted sense.

If rational knowledge of the moral order of Being or God is judged to be impossible or dubious after the impact of Hume and Kant, ethics requires another grounding. The history of much contemporary moral philosophy is the story of how nonreligious thinkers have come to terms with this requirement—for example, by finding a formal principle of universalizability to be a test of any moral rule or principle, or by disclaiming any general tests and grounding morality in the emotions or interests of individuals and groups, or by secular existentialistic confirmation of the rightness of a choice in the moment of action. In Protestant theological ethics we have legacies comparable to those in theology proper. There is a fundamentalist option—the Bible is a revelation of morality, and by its miraculous divine authority is exempt from philosophical criticism. Thus the ethics of "the Bible says. . . ." There is what has been called "biblical realism"; God has made himself, his commands, the way of life he wills, known in his revelation in the historic events whose meanings are recorded in Scripture, and Christians will be followers of that revealed way. Or, this is combined with an existentialistic note; by being steeped in that historical biblical revelation, persons are better prepared to hear the command of God in the moment of decision. Or, with less certitude, all persons and communities are historically conditioned and there is no overcoming the relativization of knowledge both of God and of the morally right and good; Christians find the Christian story to be meaningful to them and thus live out that story in the common life without claims for its truth or universal validity.

To make a thematic interpretation of recent Protestant ethics in comparison with contemporary Catholic ethics, I focus first on "historicism." The word can be used to refer to a rather clearly defined movement and set of philosophical issues, symbolized by the work of Ernst Troeltsch, or to a more general cluster of movements and concerns. I use it in the looser sense here. When Protestants became convinced that the structure of the human mind does not correspond to the structure of reality, or more particularly to a moral order of the universe, human history took on new significance. All knowledge was seen to be historically situated and thus relative to the history within and from which anything is known. Thus the enterprise of Christian ethics had to reckon with the implications of this for any claims writers made about the validity of its basic standpoint, or the moral principles and values it proclaimed. Historical accounts of past human experience disclosed alterations in moral teachings, in the ordering of moral and human values, even within the Christian tradition. This posed a problem: either change was due to a distortion or error and history had to be overcome, or it was an unavoidable aspect of morality and had to be justified theologically and ethically. Thus under a general term, "historicism," I refer to the Protestant responses in ethics that implicitly or explicitly accepted history (in contrast to immutable nature) as the necessary starting point for ethics.

A historicist assumption can ground a variety of views of Christian ethics. One view rejects in principle the need to make the particular ethics of the Christian tradition universal in its implications; the theologian rejects the need to show that Christian ethics are applicable to all persons. Rather, the Christian community is a particular historical community with a special vocation to follow its Lord, Jesus. The conduct of the community and its members, and the community's views of politics and economics ought to be governed by radical obedience to the biblical witness to Jesus. From this view Christian ethics took a wrong turn early in the history of the church by absorbing the Stoic natural law tradition into its thought, for this was the beginning of a process by which the particular historic identity of the community was compromised. The use of natural law weakened the radical claims for distinctive moral witness by Christians; rather than Jesus being the norm, other principles, borrowed from philosophical ethics, became normative. A statement of this view does not need to take into account the impact of the critical philosophy of the eighteenth century; the view has historical precedents that antedate that philosophy. But such a view is "historicist" in the special sense that it eschews a general philosophic justification for the morality of the distinctive historic tradition. It can be grounded in a "biblical realism" of classic Protestant conception which centers on the *historical* revelation of God in Jesus.

The most eloquent and persuasive American who represents this view is the important Mennonite theologian John Howard Yoder, whose book *The Politics of Jesus* states well a case for the position that the churches have a particular social ethics with

Jesus and the biblical materials providing its norm and content. Yoder does not develop a philosophical justification for his return to the Bible, indeed to do so would be at least ironic and perhaps even paradoxical. He invokes "the radical Protestant axiom" of "biblical realism": "it is safer for the life of the church to have the whole people of God reading the whole body of canonical Scripture than to trust for her enlightenment only to certain ... filtering processes through which learned men of a given age would insist all the truth must pass."[4] Yoder cites a variety of contemporary positions he believes to be in error; for our purposes the most important is one which holds to the conviction that moral and social responsibility requires the Christian community to be something other than "a faithful witnessing minority." The acceptance of a "majority" status was historically correlated with the developments of ethics which found principles to justify Christian ascendancy to political power and to compromise the radical obedience claimed by the gospels. Yoder is an admirable heir to the Anabaptist tradition noted in Chapter 1. For him, Jesus, a historic person, is known through a text (in a nonfundamentalist way) which is the norm for guiding the church in its aggressive but nonviolent resistance to political and social oppression.[5] Fidelity to Jesus is the moral principle of the church; not rational concepts of justice or of the common good. This view does not believe that the historical developments in which the churches find themselves require a basic reconsideration of their ethics; the view is *not* historicist in that sense. It does, however, have a norm which is found in a particular historical event rather than in "nature" or in universalizable moral principles. A history is the normative source of morality, and the churches are called to be faithful in any particular historical events to that history.

A second view that has followed from historicist assumptions can be captioned "the ethics of God acting in history." Underlying this view, which for decades had strong Protestant support and can now be heard echoing from liberation theology, is the turn toward biblical theology noted above. The steps toward this pattern of Protestant ethics seem to be these. Christian theology is not "natural theology"; the philosophical criticisms of natural theology made it both possible and necessary to affirm this. If it is not natural theology, it must be "revealed" theology in some sense. God is revealed in a historic text, the Bible, but the use of critical historical and literary methods rules out revelation in a fundamentalist sense. The Bible is an account of the history of a people, one with whom Yahweh made a covenant; it is an account of God's action in their history and in the historic event of Jesus and the primitive church. Thus historical events are the medium of God's revelation; as such they disclose that he is a God who acts in history. An important move is to be emphasized here: descriptively, God acts in history—this is how he is known to the people of the Bible; this description becomes theologically normative— God acts in history. Thus theology becomes historical in several senses: there is a historical source for it; that source is itself about historical events; those events testify to God as one who acts historically; subsequent theology involves the discernment of God's action in subsequent historical events, or in "all actions upon you."[6]

Theological ethics, then, involves a process of interpreting how God acts in current events. The norm is not grounded in "nature," or in universalizable moral principles, but in a historical source used to interpret subsequent historical events. Since historical events have elements of novelty, and since there are historical developments which foreclose some possibilities and create the conditions for others, there is an openness to reform and revision in theological ethics. Actions and social structures are not to be judged by the degree of their correspondence to immutable moral principles derived from nature, but by the extent to which they conform to God's action. The notion of action in history lends itself also to more "personalistic" ways of understanding events; actions are by persons ("whole persons" as many Protestants like to say), and in large measure they are actions upon persons. The notion of history as an arena of action, God's action and human action, correlates with less emphasis on the physical characteristics of the "nature" of humankind. Terms like "dialogue" and "ability to respond" seem to be more appropriate for citing what it means to be human, and for the relation between man and God (who as actor is "personal"), than the impersonal "physicalist" concepts of God's moral *law* of nature. Since knowledge of God's actions in history is grounded in and developed from the Bible, that historic text has a highly privileged position for theological ethics. If one does not believe intellectually and affectively that the Bible is the place to learn about a God who acts in history and about the sorts of actions he does, then it is difficult if not impossible to be persuaded that moral attitudes, judgments, choices, and actions justified by this theology are ethically justifiable. Communication with the non-believer has a serious obstacle. A number of influential Protestant theologians who have written in the field of ethics are examples of this view: Karl Barth, H. Richard Niebuhr, Paul Lehmann are but three.[7]

It is a fairly short step from the theology of God's actions in history to an affirmation of "historicism" in another sense, that is, historical relativism or "relationalism." From a descriptive point of view, it is clear that some of the moral teachings of the churches and the actions and conditions that they condemned or approved through the ages have changed. The approval of slavery finally died only in the nineteenth century; usury was long condemned but later the teaching about it was modified. Either the teachings in the past were in moral error, or there is some continuity in teaching though the alterations seem more noticeable (as in some Jewish legal teachings based on historic Torah texts), or the religious community develops moral insights through historical experience, or God's actions are relative to particular historic conditions and thus require human responses relative to those conditions, or God is free to command different acts in different times and places to different persons. All but the first of these options accepts in fact, if not in principle, a measure of historical relativism.

If one argues that the Bible is the historic authority for ethics, and at the same time chooses not to apply its moral teachings literally to present circumstances, one must take recourse to some procedure which permits change at various levels of generality or specificity. Biblical moral and religious teachings can be said to provide a basic life-orientation, but actions from that orientation are not completely determined by it. Other considerations must be taken into account in that determination, including the historical circumstances of action. For example, a "respect for life" orientation can be grounded biblically, but in certain circumstances taking human life is justifiable. Or, biblical teachings can be claimed to have in them implicitly what is historically made explicit as the community ponders their meanings in changing circumstances. Changing experience enables the community to have new insight into the teachings, or to see new implications in them. A biblical theme like *agape*, love, can be taken as normative, and more specific principles can be derived by inference from it which in turn have different applications relative to particular occasions, so that to kill soldiers in a morally justifiable war is grounded in love, but to kill fetal life is almost never justifiable. Or the Bible may be taken to be a source for reliable insight and guidance in the interpretation of the significance of the historical circumstances and events in which action is called for; it might provide analogies that are applicable, or general but exceptionable rules, or a basis for presumption in favor of certain human values; more precise determinations of a course of action are made in relation to the particular historical occasion.

How a theologian describes God's actions, or God's purposes, will determine to some extent the range of historical moral relativity that is permitted. If God were free, that is, not even self-bound, to do what he wills, moral reflection with a theological reference would be impossible, for there would be no moral generalization that would be applicable to his purposes and actions. If God's action directly and strictly determined each event and human action, no moral reflection would be necessary, for what *is* would be what *ought* to be. If God's action is described by a single adjective such as humanizing or liberating, the possibility occurs that in certain historical circumstances the human response requires violent revolution and in others nonviolence. If God commands only what is consonant with his grace, he might command very different actions in different historical circumstances because each action could be what grace required then and there. If God is in the future, then one can be assured that what is now, is not what is yet to be; but what a community ought to be and do now is largely to be open to the future, and there is little theological ethical guidance for possibilities of present courses of action.[8]

How different theological ethics becomes, when generally historicist assumptions are made, from the form it takes when a moral order of nature is its ground is clear by implication. The foundations must appear shaky, the ground in which they stand sandy to the traditional Catholic moral theological mind. Questions raised from a Roman Catholic viewpoint are warranted. Historicism, with epistemological, ontological, and other aspects built into it, makes the theological bases and the practical outcomes of Protestant ethics very insecure, indeed. How can a community which accepts such philosophical principles make moral claims with the requisite certitude of their validity? How can a community which acknowledges its own history and sources to be relative make moral claims that are universally applicable? How can it avoid the looseness of moral pragmatism or of utter "situationism"? Why don't Protestants relate their historically particular history to the natural law by building in some way on Romans 1:18–32? (Some Protestants do use this text, but not to engraft a *theory* or the moral law of nature.) Why don't Protestants use the cosmic christologies of Colossians, Ephesians, and the gospel according to John for a biblical foundation for natural law? (Again, these texts are used to base universal claims, but not a theory of natural law.) That Protestantism's historicist assumptions have bequeathed a fundamental problem to its contemporary ethicians cannot be denied. That recent Roman Catholic natural law theory, as it has been used in moral theology manuals, has bequeathed problems to contemporary moral theologians is also the case. How are history, historic experience, "revelation" in history, changes in moral teachings, and so forth to be taken into account? How is what is claimed to be universally valid related to what is historically particular? Here is an area of shared problems to which Protestant ethics comes on a road we have called historicism.

The second post-Kantian philosophical movement to influence Protestant theological ethics deeply is existentialism. Among the many elements that can be found in existentialist philosophies, two are particularly important for understanding recent Protestant ethics. One is an emphasis on radical human freedom and on the need for a subjective confirmation of moral choices, in contrast with confirmation by the correspondence between the choice made and principles that are derived from an objective moral order. This we have seen as one aspect also of Roman Catholic situational ethics.[9] The other aspect, which is correlated with this one, I shall call occasionalism, that is, a view of moral action which emphasizes the uniqueness of each moment of serious moral choice in contrast to a view that emphasizes the persistent, perduring order of moral life and the continuities of human experience. Both of these aspects are grounded in a conviction that if there is a moral order of the universe (and likely there is none) it is not knowable by human reason. Thus the moral life is without the props of principles of natural law, which have provided a basis for great objective certitude and for moral absolutes universally valid across time to all who share a common human nature.

Occasionalism

The "crisis of decision," a term frequently used by Protestants deeply influenced by existentialism, resonates with the sense of radical freedom, the sense of anxiety in the absence of principles that provide objective certitude, and the sense that the rightness of a decision (the use of "decision" rather than "choice" has its own existential overtones) can only be subjectively verified and confirmed. Scripture itself has been interpreted in these terms, and the interpretations are often claimed to be not only historically valid but also theologically normative. Rudolph Bultmann's classic book, *Jesus and the Word*, is an example. The "intrinsic significance" of the demands of God in the teachings of Jesus, he wrote, "are not mediated to man through Scripture as a formal authority,"

> and they are not derived from an ideal picture of man and humanity. They cannot be deduced from a universal ethical theory. Then whence do they come? They arise quite simply from the crisis of decision in which man stands before God. . . . Its meaning is simply that this moment of decision contains all that is necessary for the decision, since in it the whole of life is at stake. . . . In this crisis of decision, the continuity with the past is accordingly abrogated and the present cannot be understood from the point of view of development.[10]

This quotation suggests the occasionalism I have noted, but here I am more interested in noting the condition of the religious moral person. In considering a response to God's demands in the moral teachings of Jesus, he or she does not have a guaranteed formal authority of the Bible, nor a generally verifiable moral ideal of humanity, nor teachings derivable from a universal ethical principle. Each of these in some way would provide some degree of objective certitude, so that actions in conformity with these teachings could be judged to be right or good by some standard held by a particular community or by reason. The past is abrogated, and the present is not to be viewed as a continuous development of the past; even the continuity of human experience is of no real significance as a confirming test. The person is in a crisis; human freedom makes that inevitable, as does the absence of general or universal principles which have some objectivity. The only confirmation, it appears, can be a subjective or existential

one; everything else is corrupted by inauthenticity. Indeed, the *Bultmann*
subjective authenticity of a decision makes it valid.

Intense subjectivity and occasionalism, as we have noted, are
correlative. In Barth's theological ethics the occasionalism is as
vivid as it is in Bultmann's, but the theology in which it is
grounded is very different. Here is Barth's strongest statement of
it.

> The command of God as it is given to us at each moment is
> always and only one possibility in every conceivable particu-
> larity of its inner and outer modality. It is always a single deci-
> sion, including all the thoughts and words and movements in
> which we execute it. We encounter it in such a way that abso-
> lutely nothing either outward or inward, either in the relative
> secret of our intention or in the unambiguously observable ful-
> fillment of our actions, is left to chance or to ourselves, or
> rather in such a way that even in every visible or invisible detail
> He wills us precisely the one thing and nothing else, and mea-
> sures and judges us precisely by whether we do or do not do
> with the same precision the one thing that He so precisely wills.
> Our responsibility is a responsibility to the command as it is
> given us in this way.[11]

This statement occurs in the context of an extensive critique of
various forms of "formal" ethics, that is, ethics which derive
content and method for understanding the nature of human
experience and for formulating moral norms which are universally applicable. The notion of law, which Barth uses, itself must
be reconceived; the law of God "is not merely a general rule but
also a specific prescription and norm for each individual case."[12] *Barth*
The occasionalism is correlated with a theological principle,
namely, that God acts and commands in a "vertical" way, that is,
with a sovereign direction in each event and to each person. It is
correlated with an anthropology of covenant partnership with
God, which makes other metaphors such as speaking-hearing,
command-obedience more appropriate than the language of a
moral law of nature. It is correlated with a view of moral life
which finds the language of response and responsibility the most
apt. All of this is significantly different from natural law theory
and its implications for ethics.

It must be noted that the most radical occasionalists qualify
their more extreme statements. Bultmann and Knud Løgstrup

have phenomenologies of orders of creation or human experience which provide some continuities that their most radical statements would appear to rule out.[13] Barth speaks of the "spheres" in which the command of God is heard and warns his readers that if what they hear God commanding in his living word in the moment is significantly different from the teachings of Jesus, the Decalogue, and other biblical materials, it might well not be God's command. But the practical import of these qualifications is a restraint upon the prior existentialism; it is a movement from radical freedom and occasionalism to limitations of context in which they are lived out. It is not a priority of moral order which must be related to moments of freedom and particularity, as is the case in the philosophical basis of Roman Catholic ethics.

Other Protestants, both contemporaries of those referred to and of a subsequent generation, have found that the legacies of historicism and existentialism provided insufficient bases for ethics, in its practical outcomes and its philosophical and theological foundations. The idea of "orders of creation," though they were more biblically than philosophically justified, provided one base which was less shifty; this idea was expounded by Lutheran theologians and by Emil Brunner.[14] Dietrich Bonhoeffer's concept of "mandates" was another device. What is needed, however, is not a confessionally biblical basis but a way to provide a perdurable content and a more critical method for ethical reflection than more radical historicist and existentialist philosophies make possible. The openness of these perspectives requires partial if not full closure, and the principles used to enable such closure must be testable by persons outside the historic Christian community. I believe we are now seeing moves that absorb insight from two current philosophical positions to overcome the more radical relativism of important thinkers in the immediate past. These are phenomenology (in a loose sense), which provides a way to determine pervasive and perdurable patterns of personal and communal existence without necessarily purchasing the totality of the assumptions of natural law theory, and a sort of Kantian moral philosophy, which provides formal criteria for testing moral norms such as the principles of universalizability or generalizability. The former, like natural law theory, opens the box of the is-ought problem; the latter seeks to avoid that.

Knud Løgstrup's exceedingly perceptive account of the sig-

nificance of trust as crucial to human life and as a source of
moral claims is one example of a phenomenological account of
the interpersonal world (though clearly it is unsatisfactory as a
basis for dealing with institutionalized power for what Americans
call social ethics). "[T]rust and the self-surrender that goes with
it are a fundamental part of human life";[15] this is Løgstrup's
basic descriptive theme which he supports by making many
observations on human experience. Trust is the ground for the
ethical demand: "our existence demands of us that we protect the
life of the person who has placed his trust in us." "[T]his trust
means that in every encounter between human beings there is an
unarticulated demand irrespective of the circumstances in which
the encounter takes place and irrespective of the nature of the
encounter."[16] In one sense, Løgstrup can be said to be developing
an account of the fundamental "nature" of human interpersonal
existence, and from this "nature" obligations or "demands"
arise. Because of the character of his account and its elaboration,
the view of the moral decision required of a person remains more
a description of the factors involved in a choice than a set of
principles or values which can be relied upon in making a choice;
his "phenomenology" leads to an "existentialist" ethics. Nonetheless, we have in Løgstrup's work a major effort to provide a
description, without developing a theory-laden view of "nature,"
of the fundamental aspects of human existence from which
obligations arise.

Other theologians have taken similar paths. H. Richard Niebuhr's account of the primacy of an ethics of response and
responsibility over teleological and deontological ethics is
grounded in part in his perception that responsiveness is a
universal characteristic of human existence; there is a phenomenology (if not an ontology) that undergirds his development of
the most proper form of ethics.[17] Paul Ramsey borrows Barth's
language of "co-humanity" and "covenant relations" and uses
them not only because they have a biblical theological authorization but also because they provide terms that reflect general
human experience as a basis for morality.[18] Gibson Winter, as he
develops his constructive alternative to social theories that he
perceptively analyzes, intends "to make explicit the norms of
sociality which are implicit in this essential structure of sociality."[19] This is in a formal sense the intention of natural law
theory, that is, to find the *essential* structures of the nature of

human life in which there are implicit norms. Winter's conversation, however, is with phenomenological philosophers and not with Aristotle.

David Little is more ready to use the term "natural law" than are others. In the development of a natural law theory two things have to be shown about "the everyday world." It must be "possible to establish a set of empirical generalizations about human nature that is constant, both spatially (cross-culturally) and temporally (historically)," and to show that these "descriptive generalizations" can be the basis for a set of moral prescriptions.[20] Important to note is the language of "empirical generalizations" and "descriptive generalizations"; these terms avoid the stronger claims of traditional natural law theory but appear to seek a similar outcome, that is, a way to describe "human *nature*" that is constant. Little follows through on this by using the works of modern cultural anthropologists such as Clyde Kluckhohn, Ralph Linton, and Margaret Mead to establish "empirical generalizations." Basing himself on this work, he can write that we are "coming close to an empirical definition of 'humanity'" (in distinction from primates); that is, we can say that "*to be human is to order life cooperatively.*"[21] The further task, then, is to specify and elaborate "*the conditions for social cooperation.*"[22] To describe how Little proceeds to show that this enterprise can be a part of a Calvinistic ethics would take us afield, but the essay as a whole must be commended as a major effort to formulate constants ("natural law"), without grounding them in an explicated ontology (such as a traditional theory of natural law), for the sake of theological ethics.

These Protestant efforts all move toward a "natural" basis for formulating persisting and perduring moral norms. The status of that basis, ontologically speaking, remains obscure. Clearly, phenomenological observations and empirical generalizations do not have the same status as natural law in the traditional sense. But these are departures from a radical historicism and extreme existentialism that can be observed in the thought of some Protestant theologians.

Other writers are turning to phenomenology and to contemporary British and American philosophies of mind and of action to develop concepts which account for the persistence and continuities of moral agents, that is, their characters. The most systematic effort is that of Stanley M. Hauerwas. Hauerwas poses as his basic problem the absence in recent Protestant theological ethics of a view of the person which can account for "character"; although his treatment of their thought comes only toward the end of his book, Barth and Bultmann are the foils for his argument for reasons similar to those which bring them under scrutiny in this chapter.[23] Both of these influential theologians shape their conceptions of the moral life around the metaphor of command, he notes; correlated with this metaphor is an "individualistic and occasionalistic understanding of the self."[24] To overcome occasionalism, Hauerwas returns to the language of character and virtue. By character he means "the qualification of man's self-agency through his beliefs, intentions, and actions, by which a man acquires a moral history befitting his nature as a self-determining being."[25] To return to the terms "character" and "virtue" is to take seriously the Aristotelian and Thomist traditions in theology, but after a sympathetic critical account of them he moves to the recent British and American philosophies of mind and action to establish the constructive proposal embodied in his definition quoted above. Like those in the Catholic tradition of virtues, Hauerwas does ethics oriented from the agent's continuities of "selfhood"; unlike those in the tradition he does not invoke an ontological theory to ground the possibilities and actualities. Rather, he uses the theories of intention and action formulated by contemporary philosophers to ground his view of how a self-determining being can be somewhat consistent in his actions. To the traditional Catholic reader, this procedure is "ontologically weak"; to some Protestants it is deficient because of its avoidance of the issues raised by more deterministic views of the behavioral sciences (which in their own way "explain" continuities of behavior). Yet, as with Løgstrup, Little, and others noted above, Hauerwas (with his attention to character) is trying to overcome Protestant occasionalism without purchasing a theory of natural law.[26]

The other philosophical tack that is taken is a more formal one that applies to choices and acts, namely, to find principles of universalizability or generalizability which can test moral principles (even those derived from the Bible and historical tradition) for their general applicability. This can occur together with the tentative approaches toward something like natural law, or it can be independent of them. The basic intention, I believe, is to overcome the particularity and relativism of much of Protestant

Agape
&
Eros

ethics without surrendering a Christian theological orientation. The practical necessity for this task is thorough and critical familiarity with and competence in the literature of contemporary moral philosophy.

The most intensive and extensive study of this sort is Gene Outka's *Agape: An Ethical Inquiry*.[27] The matter of *agape*, or Christian love, has had intensive discussion for decades as a result of Anders Nygren's classic treatment of it in *Agape and Eros*. Nygren's characterization of *agape* in sharp distinction from *eros* poses the issues for Protestant theological ethics in general and for Outka in particular, exceedingly sharply. God's love, agape, is characterized by several features: it is "sacrificial giving"; eros is "acquisitive desire and longing." It "comes down," is "God's way to man"; eros is an "upward movement," "man's way to God." Agape is "unselfish," "gives itself away"; eros is egocentric. Agape is "freedom in giving," depending on plenty, in contrast with the possessiveness of eros, which depends on want and need. It is primarily God's love, and in human form it is patterned by divine love; eros is man's love, and when attributed to God is patterned on human love. Agape is spontaneous and unmotivated; eros is determined by the beauty and worth of its object and is thus evoked or motivated. Agape "creates value in its object"; eros "recognizes value in its object— and loves it."[28] These are radical distinctions that claim for agape, both in its primary form of God's love and in its human form of Christian love, characteristics which are particularistic. Human knowledge of them comes from "revelation" and not from observations about human experience or knowledge. Thus Nygren radically poses the issue of Protestant revelational particularism concerning the nature of love.

While Outka is concerned with many facets of the discussion of agape elaborated by many authors, his basic approach is indicated by his subtitle, "An Ethical Analysis." This implies not only that he will use ethics "primarily as treated in contemporary Anglo-American analytic philosophy,"[29] as a procedure to analyze theological ethics and clarify its amplitude of confusions, but also to suggest a normative view of agape which stresses its aspects that are defensible on grounds of reason alone without abandoning "the theological center of gravity." From the richness and subtlety of Outka's discussion one theme comes to the fore, namely agape as "equal regard." This theme is introduced early in his book as the basic content of human love (in the sense of agape) in the following way.

> Agape is a regard for the neighbor which in crucial respects is independent and unalterable. To these features there is a corollary: the regard is for every person qua human existent, to be distinguished from those special traits, actions, etc., which distinguish particular personalities from each other.[30]

For the purpose of this chapter it needs only to be noted that "equal regard" is justifiable rationally as a primary feature of normative ethics. A religious or particularistic historical backing for equal regard is thus reduced in its significance. Indeed, in Outka's final comments on self-sacrifice, which for Reinhold Niebuhr marked the most distinctive characteristic of agape, with the death of Jesus on the cross disclosing this, he writes, "Self-sacrifice must always be purposive in promoting the welfare of others, and never simply expressive of something resident in the agent. It is simply one possible exemplification and by-product of devotion to others for their own sakes."[31] Agape is "disinterested" with reference to the agent of an act and seeks the welfare of the other as a human existent; this is the case even in self-sacrifice, which for many Christians has been an ideal, if not an obligation, based upon fidelity to Jesus Christ and not upon benefits to others.

Outka's purpose, I believe, is not only to provide rational analysis of texts dealing with love but also to suggest rational justification for agape in his normative sense. This overcomes the radical occasionalism and emotivism of some Protestant uses of love and provides instead a universally applicable principle. Thus it accomplishes a practical outcome similar to what principles derived from the natural law accomplished in Catholic moral theology. The foundation, however, is different; Outka is not a natural law theorist but rather is oriented from more formal considerations which are the stock-in-trade of a significant group of analytical moral philosophers. His work is an effort, however, to overcome historicism and existentialism in Protestant theological ethics.

If contemporary Protestants have been seeking a philosophical basis to overcome some of the openness that is the legacy of their immediate predecessors, Catholics have been seeking a philosophical basis to loosen the rigidities of the natural law tradition as they have received it from writers in the recent past.

Revised Natural Law Theory, Existential Phenomenology, and Pragmatism in Catholic Ethics

On the Roman Catholic side, as we have noted, there has been a growing criticism of the "nonhistorical" character of traditional natural law theory, of the impersonal character of the theory as it was formulated in the manuals of moral theology (the view of individuals was "physicalist" rather than "personalist"), and of the absence of a decisive role of a biblically based theology in moral thought. The third, the biblical concern, is a matter deferred; to respond to the first two criticisms there have been reinterpretations of natural law theory which stress the internal dynamism of natural law itself and the historical process as a way to grasp its significance. This is a relatively conservative attempt to ground some greater "openness." There have also been more radical attempts to replace the basically Aristotelian concept of nature as a ground for ethics with the patterns developed by the general movement of existential phenomenology. And efforts have been made to incorporate elements of both of these into a new amalgam.

The evidence which *prima facie* requires a reconsideration of the relation of natural law to history is the changes that have occurred in moral teachings in the Catholic tradition. There has been historical development not only of basic theological doctrine but also of moral teachings. An unsophisticated question requires a sophisticated answer: if Catholic moral teachings on particular questions have changed, and if the moral teachings are based on an immutable eternal moral law of nature, then how does one explain the changes? Does an explanation of the changes require an adjustment or a thoroughgoing alteration of the philosophical theory of the natural law?

John T. Noonan's work on the history of moral teachings provides evidence of changes. He has written on usury, abortion, and contraception.[32] On all of these issues Noonan, a historian of law, shows how the teachings at any particular time can be adequately understood only in the context of social, economic, doctrinal, and other factors. For example, in his book *Contra-*

ception, Noonan demonstrates the diversity of the teachings of theologians and canon lawyers on the ordering of the ends of marriage and thus makes clear that the natural law theory has not issued in a single or unambiguous answer to the question of the moral permissibility of contraception. His conclusions to a chapter on "Counter Approaches" during the medieval period indicate the significance of such historical scholarship.

> All the theories, values, practices, reviewed in this chapter ran counter to the theory and valuation which required that the purpose of lawful intercourse be procreative; which treated the act of coitus as intended by nature to be procreative; which implied that the generative process was an absolute, immune from human interference.
>   If the counter elements had been assembled into a system of values, a different synthesis from the dominant Augustinian one would have been made. . . . The doctrine on sexuality, as it stood, was a balance—not the logical projection of a single value, but a balance of a whole set of competing values. The balance was weighted at a particular point which excluded contraception. [33]

The general point to be inferred from Noonan's study is that historical factors determined the weighting of competing "values" in a particular period; the teaching did not historically come into being as a result of a single norm grounded in a simple theory. Once this is demonstrated, a question is posited, namely, how does natural law theory account for the historical alterations in moral teachings? Contemporary Catholic moral philosophers and theologians perceive the need for a rethinking of the philosophical bases of their work in order to account theoretically for historical development of moral teachings; indeed, the tradition is a historical one, and a theory is needed to interpret, understand, and justify the importance of history for a theory developed from "nature."

One way in which development and change can be justified is by returning to Thomas Aquinas' texts, for they can be fairly and honestly interpreted as providing for more dynamism, more extension and development, and for less certitude than the manualists in moral theology claimed. An important text frequently cited is one of which Thomas distinguishes between speculative or theoretical reason and practical reason. Speculative reason is concerned with necessary things; "the practical reason ... is concerned with contingent matters, which is the domain of human actions." While there is necessity in common principles, "the more we descend towards the particular, the more frequently we encounter defects." In speculative matters the truth is the same for all men, but "in matters of action, truth or practical rectitude is not the same for all as to what is particular, but only as to the common principles; and where there is the same rectitude in relation to particulars, it is not equally known to all."[34] A fault with some of the moral theology traditions is that they consigned to the practical reason the certitude of the speculative reason and did not sufficiently take into account the contingencies in action which are subject to change and to error. Columba Ryan, O.P., argues that the function of describing general directives for conduct as belonging to natural law is "not so much to call attention to their content as to the moral character of their obligatory force."[35] These directives serve as principles in the reaching of individual decisions, but in this process "the natural law is indefinitely extendable." The extension and development take place with "constant reference to a wider and more sensitive assessment of experience," and this requires "exacting enquiry" which is subject to errors.[36]

When one steps back from this use of Thomas' text, the procedure seems to be as follows. There are levels of principles of natural law ethics, with accompanying degrees of generality and specificity and of certitude and risk of error. As persons think about the rules that ought to govern conduct in contingent and specific circumstances, they must take recourse to human experience in its complexity as a source of information and insight. "To *discover* what it is to be human and to achieve properly human fulfillment" requires not only attention to man as a biological species; what is "natural" to man is constituted by relations to the world the species has created (including culture) and to other persons as subjects.[37] Thus natural law extends and develops, though its first principles do not alter, in the course of changing historical and social experience. "To be forever progressing is a characteristic of man"; thus the unalterable first principles of natural law require new applications in detail, and some previous applications are no longer valid in new circumstances.

A distinctively different approach is that of Bruno Schüller,

S.J., who for many years has persistently dealt with the problems of this chapter and the next. In a 1965 article, "To What Extent Can Moral Theology Dispose of Natural Law?" Schüller addresses his colleagues who have become skeptical of the tradition out of their awareness of historical development. His interests are several: to show that there is a biblical basis for natural law (as do Josef Fuchs, S.J., and others), to show that the New Testament does not provide a different content than does the natural law (his concern in several articles, which he also shares with others), and (for my purposes, the primary interest) to reiterate the fundamental conviction of natural law, namely, that the moral imperative is grounded in being. Even with his reaffirmation of the tradition, Schüller has to account for historical changes in moral teachings. To do this he distinguishes between the element of continuity in man's being and the element of change. The problem of more static views of moral theology is that they restricted the formulation of moral norms to the unchangeable characteristics of man; this was done out of fear of relativism. Natural law norms must also be developed from the changing aspects of man's being, he argues; this does not make them any less *natural* law norms. Thus to the extent which man's *being* is altered in the course of historical experience the ethical norms governing his behavior must also be altered. The argument is still from being to "ought," but since being changes, the "ought" changes.

One of his examples will show how he makes the case in practical matters. It is clear that in much of the Western world the pattern of relationships between husband and wife has changed from one of clear subjection of the wife to the husband to one of greater equality of partners in marriage. Approval of this change does not invalidate a doctrine of natural law even though arguments for the subjection of wives have been made from it. Nor is it a change that is explainable by the theses of historical relativism. Rather, the relationship between husbands and wives has "objectively" changed, and thus the moral precepts appropriate to the relationship must change. It is not unfair to say that for Schüller the *being* of the relationship has changed, and this can be correlated with changing aspects of man's nature. Thus, specific precepts must change.[38]

In one of his few essays devoted to fundamental rather than practical moral theology, Richard McCormick, S.J., addresses all the issues introduced in this section. Like Columba Ryan and others, McCormick intends to overcome the caricatures of natural law that have developed rather than abandon it. He quotes with approval Louis Monden, S.J., whose *Sin, Liberty, and Law* was exceedingly popular among Catholic seminarians in the last half of the sixties. Natural law is not an abstract blueprint but a *"dynamically inviting possibility*, a concrete project to be carried out in the midst of a concrete situation in which man's 'self' presents its demands to an 'ego' conscientiously realizing itself." McCormick adds, "In other words, it is man's being charting his becoming."[39] Subsequently he elaborates, "Man's being is the basis for the norms of his becoming," his "being is the basis of the significance of his action." That "man changes, matures, develops, transforms himself" is an accepted fact. Not only is this true of individual humans but also of the species, as Chardin has made clear.[40] This developmental process requires that moral theology be open to various sciences to understand this growth and its significance, that due attention be given to the consequences of actions and to the subjective communal aspects of the perception of human development. But by taking the traditional stand that norms (in McCormick's case, of "becoming") are grounded in being he fends off more radical Catholic grasping of pragmatic, utilitarian, historicist, and existentialist modes of thought.

A more personalistic interpretation of natural law is given by the influential Redemptorist, Bernard Häring, who understands natural law to refer to "the nature or meaning of man insofar as man has the capacity of understanding his nature, meaning, and vocation"; it refers to the realization of "what preserves to the greatest extent the full meaning of his person."[41] Because of the development of the species from the Stone Age to our time, and because of the changing capacities for human self-understanding, human ways of experiencing and thinking are altered. "Thus we are faced with a changing man gifted with a somewhat changing faculty of self-understanding."[42] "Historicity" belongs to the "constitutive structure of man," "human life means growth," and thus moral teachings are subject to alteration.[43] Häring turns toward love as the central motif of his personalism and by combining love with his "dynamic" view of natural law becomes more open to change than some of his contemporaries;

but his views, as can be seen in his massive text *The Law of Christ*, do not abandon the tradition.[44]

Evidence could be mounted to a point of diminishing utility to indicate how Roman Catholic moral theologians attempt to open the concept of natural law. Charles E. Curran, always a fair interpreter of trends, and a writer who always seeks to account for the complexities of theological ethics, sums up the discussion by moving dialectically between the "classicist" and the "historical" methodologies. Against the rigidities of the older tradition he asserts that modern moral existence does not primarily call for conformity to a "detailed and unchanging plan"; the "meaning of human life is not already given in some pre-existing pattern or plan." Rather it is to be found creatively in life and experience. Yet, a historically conscious methodology must avoid "the pitfall of total relativism"; we need "to understand the ontological foundations of historical development."[45] It is an effort to find a *theory* which will account for continuities, if not universals, while also accounting for historical change and development, that occupies the minds of the Roman Catholic reformers of a more conservative inclination. The contemporary Protestant comes to the same problem from the opposite direction.

None of the persons noted above has adopted the existential phenomenological writings as a basis for his thought. Roman Catholics who do that provide a more radically different philosophical option and one that is attractive to some Protestants. To indicate this possibility, I shall attend to the writings of two persons, William H. Van Der Marck and William A. Luijpen. Neither is radically historicist in the senses I described for Protestants; neither is individualistic or occasionalistic in his existentialist proclivities. Both, I believe, wish to ground moral norms in human "nature"; what distinguishes them from Schüller et al. is that they perceive and conceptualize the human in very different terms.

Luijpen writes not as a moral theologian but as a philosopher of law. Since natural law theory is at the heart of both Catholic jurisprudential thought and moral theology, his *Phenomenology of Natural Law* would be applicable to moral theologians.[46] Whether his interpretation of Thomism, written from the philosophical viewpoint, is adequate is not our concern; that some of

his objections are similar to those we have already noted is
sufficient for our purposes. He accuses Thomists of manipulating
"an uncontrollable concept of 'nature'" so that contradictory
moral and legal prescriptions can be justified by the same
concept.[47] He argues that "the Thomist does not, or at least not
sufficiently, take into account that a man simply is not what he is
without his fellowmen," which results in an ahistorical individualism.[48] "Never . . . does the Thomistic theory of natural law
emphasize that man's 'seeing' is a historical 'seeing.'"[49] The
consequence is a rigidity grounded in the "objectivism or essen-
tialism" of the Thomistic concept. While Luijpen insists on
objectivity, the error of Thomism is that it makes "objectivity
entirely independent of the subject."[50] The knowing subject is
not, for him, a "pure *cogito*."

Luijpen's project is to replace the objectivistic and essential-
istic view of human nature with what he judges to be a more
adequate view. For his principal sources he draws upon the
writings of Marcel, Merleau-Ponty, and Heidegger. The most
basic term for his reconstruction is "co-existence." "[M]an as
existence *is* co-existence." "Being through others, then, is an
essential characteristic of man."[51] Man not only knows as a
"co-existent" in an interpersonal and cultural life-world; his
affective life and his life of action occur in and through the
meanings of a shared world of culture and language. Man is a
personal subject, capable of creativity and spontaneity in reci-
procity with other subjects. The social structures are made by
man and embody human intentions in the world. Though the
following quotation is cryptic, it illustrates both the vocabulary
and the way of reasoning that characterize this mode of thought
on a major issue, namely, that of human right.

> The *minimum* of the demand of love, the demand which hu-
> man existence as co-existence itself *is*, can thus be formulated
> as the most fundamental right of the other. The other's right
> is the minimum of my "yes" to his subjectivity, a "yes" called
> for by my existence as a "having to be for the other," as an
> "ought" on the level of co-existence. . . . Thus the other's right
> is a "natural right," better still, an "essential right," for it is
> implied in the "nature," the "essence" of co-existence. For the
> execution of his "having to be for the other" belongs to that
> through which man is authentically man, hence to his "na-

ture" or "essence." In a certain sense he is not a man if he
does not execute it, namely, in the sense that he is not a man
on the level of his authenticity.[52]

Luijpen's strained and strange theory of the "ethical genius" in
whose existence the truth of human co-existence is "uncon-
cealed," indeed in whose life the truth "happens," can reasonably follow from this, but is not a matter of primary interest to
our purpose. What is of interest is that the historicity of
knowledge of the essence of the human means that "the natural
law is never 'finished,' but takes part in endless history," and that
"many societies at many times and in many places live in many
different historical phases of the natural law," that is, "they live
on different levels of humanity." Yet Luijpen feels called upon to
return to classic terms of the eternity and immutability of natural
law; there is an initial demand of justice in the essence of man's
"being-man-together-with-his-fellow-man" which is the "already" present in each historical "now" and which once "uncon-
cealed" will "compel" persons to affirm it in every subsequent
phase of history.[53]

New wine is poured into old wine skins, and the taste of it is
very different to one who imbibes. We have the terms "nature,"
"law," "eternity," "immutability," "rights," "justice," and
"man" as a species term. But either the referents of these terms
are radically altered or the content which they are given is
radically different. The objectivist Aristotelian view of nature and
of a *telos* is gone; the paradigm shift is drastic. Humanity is
known in terms of co-existence of subjects, or intersubjectivity
and historicity; humanity is known through a process of uncon-
cealing. The process of historicizing both human being and
human knowing is far more radical than Schüller, McCormick, et
al., will accept. Existential phenomenology provides the understanding of the human, and the implications for moral theology
are vast.

It is William H. Van Der Marck who has made available to the
English reader a sketch of what moral theology would look like by
drawing upon the same general movement that Luijpen finds
compelling. His 1967 book, *Toward a Christian Ethic: A Renewal
in Moral Theology*, has a comprehensive purpose: it formulates a
coherent fundamental theological ethical position and thus inte-

grates doctrinal theology with a philosophical anthropology.[54] I shall limit the discussion of his theology here and note only how his philosophy of man alters the traditional structure and function of moral theology. The language is basically the same as Luijpen's: corporeity, intersubjectivity, authenticity, and so forth. The formal move of all natural law thinkers is made, that is, from the essence and nature of man to the end of the good, man's fulfillment. It is the understanding of the essence that is radically different. "The very essence and nature of man is intersubjectivity." "Person is community."[55] "If there is one thing that may be called fundamental and central in anthropology, it is intersubjectivity, communication, love, human solidarity, justice, or whatever name one chooses to call it."[56] All these terms express the same reality in Van Der Marck's judgment. From this essence is derived the *telos*: "The ultimate aim of man is none other than intersubjectivity, communication, community, a share in common humanity, love, justice—or whatever more or less historically conditioned or even loaded term one wishes to use."[57] Happiness or joy comes by sharing in and contributing to intersubjectivity. "Good and evil," then, "refer to the success or failure of intersubjectivity."[58] This way of viewing human life and the context of human action does not of itself solve moral problems but points toward a basis of judging the worth of actions; where the effects of actions form community they are good; where they destroy it they are evil. Similarly the moral worth of persons can be judged; a person is virtuous insofar as he or she fulfills this essence—virtue is authentic humanity (sharing in community), and vice is deficient humanity, "a qualitative deficiency in the state of being directed toward others and toward community."[59] This leads to an ethic of virtues in distinction from an ethics that primarily focuses on the moral principles that determine specific acts.

That Van Der Marck's proposal keeps a formal structure similar to that of natural law theory is clear; one delineates the essence of the human and derives values and ends from it. The perception of the essence and the conceptualization of it, however, are radically different from the traditional view. The concepts used are clearly less "physicalist" and concentrate more on what distinguishes the human than on what makes it continuous with the rest of nature. The end to be fulfilled is interpersonal in a sense qualified by existential phenomenological overtones. A procedure of practical moral reasoning from this view of the human must be different from one that relies even on the newer interpretations of natural law; so also must the relations between doctrinal theological principles and ethics be different. Clearly the meaning of existence cannot be derived from what Curran calls "some pre-existing patterns or plan"; actions are judged qualitatively by a different principle from conformity to an immutable order.

Some of the same themes developed by Luijpen and Van Der Marck can be found in the writings of a Catholic philosopher who considers himself to be an "ontological pragmatist," namely, Robert Johann. Johann, whose writings were very influential in the sixties, charted a course which, without being eclectic, incorporated elements of American pragmatism and other philosophies and theologies influenced by that movement. The Scottish philosopher John MacMurray, whose Gifford lectures are aptly titled *The Self as Agent* and *Persons in Relation*, the Protestant theologian H. Richard Niebuhr, and others, including John Dewey, contributed to the shaping of Johann's *Building the Human*.[60] This book, a collection of finely wrought essays with varying degrees of technical discourse, establishes a vision of the human which replaces the traditional Thomist one and which, if taken seriously by moral theologians, would have profound implications for their work. Johann's criticisms of conventional natural law theory are not distinctive; it is his recourse to experience and to a philosophy of the person which is important. His ideal is "creative responsibility" which has its final test in experience; this ideal entails a way of knowing, a view of action, and an understanding of the world. Human nature is not "complete and self-enclosed" but rather "a task, a project of promotion, a work of love." The role of reason is "not simply to record but, in the light of Being, to innovate"; reason is to judge and transform experience.[61] Morally right action, then, is not what conforms to determinate nature but what conforms to reason in the service of love in human experience. Knowledge, including moral "knowledge," comes from "the perceived consequences of our active dealings with our surroundings."[62] Man seeks through inquiry to integrate his experience as a responsible agent, his participation in the interactive process, with a whole range of others. The meaning of a person's life, then, "is the difference his presence makes in the overall process." "Being human means coming to grips creatively with the concrete situation in which a person finds himself."⁶³ This does not imply a radical "situationalism" of an existentialist individualist sort, for the situation includes a wide range of experience and Being itself. The person is Being's agent, "reshaping the face of the earth in the light, not of his whims, but of those wider possibilities that his very presence to Being continually opens to him."⁶⁴ "Mankind is thus a reality summoned to share in its own making," the goal of which "is a genuine community to which each member gives himself and, in the very giving, finds himself."⁶⁵

Johann's vision, then, is of persons being in relation to each other, though he has no penchant for hyphenated terms and novel words. His view of individuals stresses their capacities to be agents, to be actors, more than it stresses the determinate features they share with other creatures. While he has, and develops at some length, an ontology, it is one that recognizes development, openness, and change as inherent aspects.⁶⁶ His ethics is clearly consequentialist; humans develop moral insight and knowledge through experiences, through the consequences of their intentional acts. There is a goal, a movement toward wholeness in individuals, in communities, in all of life, toward harmony of a common good. The method is not "phenomenological" in the sense of the Husserlian movement; it is not the method of the traditional natural law theorists; it is not a personalistic individualism. Rather it is rigorous inquiry into experience which yields an awareness of structures and processes, of ends and means, without foreclosing them on the basis of a determinate order. Although Johann has not published a comprehensive, systematic work, the outlines of a distinctive philosophy can be discerned which, if absorbed by moral theologians, would be different from the natural law revisionists and from Van Der Marck.

Running through the criticisms of traditional natural law theory there has been a persistent query, namely, is it necessary to distinguish between nature and person when one is concerned about human individuals? What is the most fitting interpretation of the relation between nature (the determinate aspects of human life shared by all humans and with other species) and freedom (the capacities of human agency which transcend determination)? The issue was addressed both in theory and in practical application by the tradition. It can be argued that St. Thomas was not purely "physicalist" in his understanding of human nature, and in practical moral theology the distinction between the use of ordinary and of extraordinary means for the preservation of humans seems to imply that in the absence of more "personal" qualities of human life it is not necessary to use heroic procedures to sustain physical life. The celebrated "turn to the subject" in Catholic philosophy has provided bases for a reconsideration of the nature/person relationship, and the impact of this is occurring in moral theology. The thought of Bernard Lonergan, S.J., has not yet been thoroughly applied to moral theology by others nor has Lonergan himself developed the implications of his thought for ethics and moral theology in a systematic way. Karl Rahner, S.J., has given more explicit attention to the philosophical foundations of moral theology and has in a few essays made his own applications to practical moral problems.[67]

The basic issue of the relation of the determinate to the indeterminate in human life and action has evoked speculation since the dawn of reflective human consciousness, and its dimensions and ramifications are manifold. Indeed, the notion of "nature" itself has been interpreted in various ways: for some it excludes all particularity and individuality and refers only to what is universal in humans; for others, since "freedom," which is the condition for individuality of action, is characteristic of all persons, it must be included in human "nature." A summary statement by Rahner indicates his way of holding the determinate and the indeterminate together. Moral action, he argues, "is more than just a realization of a universal idea happening here and now in the form of a case." It "has a positive and substantial property which is basically and absolutely unique." Man is not "merely the appearance of the universal," "his spiritual individuality cannot be (at least not in his acts) merely the circumscription of an, in itself, universal nature through the negativity of the *materia prima*." Yet a person is not unrelated to his material being which he or she shares with others.

[I]n so far as man belongs to the material world by his concrete activity, his activity is an instance and fulfillment of something universal which determines his actions as something different from the individual and opposed to it, i.e. as a *law* expressed in universal propositions. In so far as the same man subsists in

his own spirituality, his actions are also always more than mere
applications of the universal law to the *casus* in space and
time; they have a substantial positive property and uniqueness
which can no longer be translated into a universal idea and
norm expressible in propositions constructed of universal
notions.[68]

While there is an "essence" in man which is the ground of law in
the sense of universal propositions, it is also part of man's
"nature" to be spirit, to be free, and thus to be creative.

There are implications in this both for interpreting the moral
acts of individuals and for understanding how morality itself
develops in the course of history. Discrete acts of individuals with
their particularities occur not merely through the virtue of
prudence in the application of principles to concrete cases but
through the exercise of human freedom, which is distinctive to
the nature of the human. While, as I noted, Rahner was a critic
of "situational ethics" in its extreme form, his alternative is not
the moral theology of the manualists. Man's freedom is an object
"of a binding will of God," but the "creative will" of God is not
perceived by abstraction from essences. The contrast term to
"existentialist" ethics is "essentialist" ethics, and as the Catholic
tradition has developed essentialist ethics there is a violation of
the substantial being of man, that is, the transcendental freedom
and individuality of humans. From Rahner's point of view, there
is "a binding ethical uniqueness."

This does not imply a normlessness in moral decisions, or in
moral theology as an activity. Since personal freedom is the
nature of humans, it also becomes a norm of action. Man
proceeds to discover and to develop what is distinctive to the
human species, and as such is its end; indeed there are as yet
undiscovered potentialities even in the "essence" of the human
species. Rahner's two essays on human genetics are of particular
importance because in complementing each other they indicate
both the openness and the limits that his philosophical anthropology permits. From "The Experiment with Man," it is possible
to view Rahner as supporting a normless creativity; this interpretation has been made in scathing terms by Paul Ramsey.[69] The
human capacity for "self-manipulation" is, descriptively speaking, changing man. This capacity is grounded in the radical
"transcendental" human freedom, thus it is part of the "nature"
of the human. In the light of this, Rahner warns against

responding to proposals for self-manipulation and "self-crea-
tion" too hastily in a negative fashion. Clearly, he has moral
rigorists in mind, and, clearly, what is at stake in *theory* is the
status of human "nature" and the significance of freedom as its
distinctive aspect. The possibilities for destructiveness as well as
for some benefits are admitted by Rahner. There must be norms
derived from "nature" which guide man's "categorial self-
manipulation."[70]
In "The Problem of Genetic Manipulation" these norms
become more definite. While continuing to insist that human
freedom implies that man is "handed over" to himself and is thus
self-manipulating, he is clear that this does *not* imply that
everything that can be done ought to be done. Again "nature"
provides the norm, and the argument between Rahner and the
manualists is over what that nature is. "Man is essentially the
subject; he is a person, aware of himself as a free being, and
related, in this freedom, to the absolute mystery which we call
'God.'" "Man's nature is constructed with a built-in transcendental necessity; man must inevitably affirm his own nature even
in an action which seeks freely to deny it." The immoral, then,
occurs when this *transcendental* nature (man's radical freedom as
subject) is violated by his self-determining action.[71] This transcendental nature is intimately connected to the human biological
constitution. The practical moral question with reference to
genetic manipulation then becomes: "Just *when* would a biological alteration seriously damage a man's 'nature' as a person?"
How Rahner resolves particular questions of genetic manipulation is not our concern here. What is important to see is that
descriptively and normatively freedom is the nature and the end
of the human. But there are conditions in which this freedom is
grounded; there are predeterminations and "essential" aspects of
the human. What alters these conditions (in the case of genetics,
the biological) in such a way that man's nature (freedom) is
diminished or destroyed is evil; what respects that nature in the
determination of the rightness of an act, and what sustains it and
enables it to flourish, is good. And, humans *discover* through
exercise of their natures (freedom) potentialities for fulfillment.
Thus human life is, in a sense, a project.
I hope I have been sufficiently clear about Rahner's thought,
even though manifestly unfair to its nuances and highly technical
distinctions, to indicate that it provides a philosophical option

useful to moral theologians who desire to "open" the tradition.[72] It provides a way of dealing with the person (human nature is subject, it is transcendentally free); it provides a way for "natural law" to develop (it is through the acts of freedom that humans come better to understand what their natural potentialities are). For more conservative reformers the safeguards against irreversible moral errors are not sufficiently stringent, but that norms (though somewhat elusive) are present can be demonstrated.

Though the strokes have been broad, I hope they have been plain enough to indicate a general convergence of direction in which contemporary Roman Catholics and Protestants are moving. There continue to be Protestants who resist forming theories of ontology, for whom the possibility of "knowledge" of being is a matter of dispute and for whom the task of finding generalizations about man that are philosophically defensible is not engaging. There continue to be Roman Catholics whose anxiety about moral relativism makes them mightily resistant to any change which would historicize natural morality or make moral decisions more "existential." But a common problem is shared, and it is fair to propose that both traditions in their recently received forms are insufficient. If this minimal claim is correct, then the prospects for ecumenical Christian ethics are more encouraging than at any time since the Reformation. It now remains to deal analytically with theological developments in which there are convergences and divergences. The issues I believe are crucial are the uses of Scripture, the relation of grace to nature (or gospel to law), and ecclesiology.

Theological Bases

As we proceed from one chapter to the next the difficulties in fulfilling the purpose of this book grow. We have noted the plurality of procedures of practical moral reasoning and of philosophical foundations in both traditions, though these are more notable in Protestantism. Attempts to generalize are necessary to fulfill this project, but the accuracy of generalizations is difficult to insure even when they are made cautiously. As we turn to convergences and divergences in the theological bases for ethics in the two traditions the problematic character of the necessary generalizations becomes more intense. The historic reasons for this must be noted.

The Reformation controversies with the Catholic church were basically religious and theological rather than ethical. Thus the introduction of theology as a topic poses the roots of the historic differences between the traditions. Protestant theology had by the latter part of the sixteenth century already developed discernible traditions, in significant measure defined by controversies of Protestants with each other: Lutheran, Calvinist, Anabaptist, and Anglican. Each of these traditions in various ways had its own historical development, its own responses to subsequent cultural movements like the Enlightenment. To some extent each of them and offsprings of some of them continue to inform our contemporaries; thus it is apparently desirable to have commissions of Lutherans and Roman Catholics, Reformed and Roman Catholics, and Anglicans and Roman Catholics to deal with the distinctive theological issues each Protestant group has with Catholic theology. And each Protestant tradition has varieties of theology within it. In addition the movement of "liberal theology" had impact on all of them in the nineteenth and twentieth centuries, as did the eighteenth-century form of liberal theology, Deism; even modern fundamentalism has found homes in these traditions or been a historically decisive point of contention.[1] In recent decades we have seen such a proliferation of theological movements, indeed theological fads, that it is really impossible to make significant generalizations about Protestant theology.[2]

Catholic theology since the Council of Trent has had a more stable history, though the seeds of diversity were planted at the turn of the century. But the flowers and weeds in the Catholic theological garden have also proliferated in the past two decades (some live only for a season, some are killed by the frost of ecclesiastical authority) so that it is increasingly difficult to make accurate generalizations about Catholic theology.

There is, however, another sort of difficulty involved in the project of this chapter. Ethical writings have had different relations to theology, more strictly conceived, in Roman Catholic and in Protestant thought. In Catholicism moral theology took on a great deal of autonomy relative to fundamental theology, ascetical theology, and scriptural studies. Its next of kin was canon law rather than theology. No doubt it was properly assumed that basic theological tenets were established by the Council of Trent or by standard theological treatises. The moral theologian could assume a secure basis in Christian doctrine and proceed to become a specialist. The role of Scripture was frequently one of citation of texts that supported natural law arguments. The Protestant penchant for doing both theology and ethics in close relation to biblical texts was absent, with few exceptions, in Roman Catholicism. Thus moral theology became a discipline in its own right, rather autonomous, and not in continuous relation to fundamental and dogmatic theology and biblical studies.

In Protestantism a special field called "Christian ethics" is a rather modern innovation. From the Reformation forward until very recent times the great thinkers were theologians, more or less systematic theologians, and what they wrote about ethics was integrated with the basic Christian doctrines or flowed from them. There are ethical treatises in Luther's works but no systematic Christian ethics text; Calvin has important sections on ethics in *The Institutes* and in commentaries but no systematic ethics per se. Ethics could not be separated from theology. Schleiermacher wrote about ethics in a philosophical way, and he wrote a systematic theology. In that book he indicates what Christian ethics would be in the framework of his theology. Christian ethics "will answer much better to its true relation to Dogmatics, and so to its own immediate purpose, if it drops the imperative mood altogether, and simply gives an all-round description of how men live within the Kingdom of God."[3] His lectures on ethics took the form of a description of "Christian morals" that is, of the forms of activity in which Christians are engaged. In the nineteenth century one begins to get books of systematic Christian ethics, such as those by Dorner and Martensen,[4] but to get at the ethics of the influential theologian Albrecht Ritschl one must read his texts in theology. In the decades of this century one finds theologians who incorporate sections on ethics into their theological treatises, and one finds those who write separate books in the field of Christian ethics. The main point is that theology and ethics have been more closely intertwined in Protestant than in Roman Catholic history. And theology has always drawn upon the Bible (and in turn has had to take into account biblical scholarship). Thus the ethos in which ethical writing has been done has been different in the two traditions.

In contemporary Catholic thought one finds a renewed relation between moral theology and fundamental dogmatic and biblical theology in a number of leading figures. Of great importance historically in this century is the remarkable work of Bernard Häring, *The Law of Christ*.[5] In spite of its somewhat eclectic character this work has had a broad and deep impact upon the Catholic world, in part because Häring (following a German Catholic tradition in which Scripture was more central) grounds his moral theology in themes of Pauline and Johannine Christologies, and develops fundamental concepts which he finds more congenial to Scripture than the traditional concepts of natural law theory. Karl Rahner has throughout his career written essays of central importance for fundamental moral theology, such as the famous article, "On the Question of a Formal Existential

Ethics," which build bridges between his philosophical and "revelational" theological principles and practical moral theology.[6] While Rahner has addressed moral issues, as we have seen, it may be the task of others to order his ethical thought more systematically; that his theology and philosophy can be the basis for a "developmental" view of natural law has already been demonstrated.[7] J.B. Metz, Edward Schillebeeckx, and Bernard Lonergan are other theologians whose thought is being directed toward ethical questions by themselves and by others.[8] The fact that fundamental and doctrinal theology are now in a renewed conversation with moral theology in Roman Catholic thought is itself important for some rapprochement with Protestant writers. Persons who are primarily moral theologians, such as Josef Fuchs, Charles Curran, and others, show concern to develop the theological and biblical implications of their ethical thought.

The remainder of this chapter examines three general areas in which important developments in Roman Catholic thought converge somewhat with Protestant thought—areas where some Protestants can converse seriously with Catholic authors. These are a turn to Scripture as a more explicit and developed resource for theology and for ethics, the interest in articulating a theology in which grace is prior to nature, and the discussion of the nature and authority of the church. The indices of convergence and divergence are not as clear, in my judgment, when theological bases of moral thought are considered as they were in the two previous chapters. This is not only because of deeply rooted historic differences but also because the diversity within Protestantism is even more pronounced.

Scripture as a Source for Theological Ethics

In Chapter 1 some of the consequences of the legacy of the Reformation principle of *sola scriptura* were developed. In Chapter 2 it was necessary when analyzing practical moral reasoning in recent Protestant writings to indicate how Scripture functions for various theologians in that regard. Even in the discussion of the philosophical bases of Christian ethics in the previous chapter, it was necessary to indicate how biblical thought was integrated with historicist and existentialist judgments, assumptions, and principles in Protestant theology. Thus at this juncture attention is given primarily to Roman Catholic authors. A brief sketch of the uses of the Bible in Protestant ethics will suffice to recall and order what has been suggested previously and also developed in others of my publications.

First, the Bible has been used in one way or another as a source for a revealed moral law, the precepts of which are applicable to the governance of human action. As one has Torah in the Old Testament, so one has a "new law" in the New Testament. Second, the Bible has been used in one way or another as a revealed source of knowledge of God and of God's relations to the world and especially to humans. I shall indicate briefly only some examples of this use. With reference to what is known about God and how he is present in and to the world, Protestant theologians used Scripture to develop doctrines of God the creator, the governor or ruler, and the redeemer; they have dwelt on the creative, the governing and judging, and the redeeming activity of God in history. Ethical thought has been elucidated in relation to these doctrines. They have interpreted the status of humans in terms derived from Scripture: man is creature; he has turned from God and thus is sinner; man is loved by God or has been in principle redeemed by God and thus is justified before him; man is given by God a newness of life. All of these and other doctrines which relate to the status of persons as moral agents have affected the ways in which ethical thought is developed. Biblical symbols and concepts have been used to interpret the broad circumstances of man and history: biblical theology has been grounded in "resurrection faith," and thus ethics can be grounded in hope; eschatology has been constructed from scriptural texts, and ethics can be developed in relation to that doctrine. The moral teachings or patterns found in the Bible are interpreted in the light of basic theological themes: in Christ God's work is both known and done, and Christ becomes the norm and pattern for a moral life of discipleship; God as known in the Bible is "for man" and thus the elements of "law" are interpreted as permissions as well as commands, as indication of how life is to be lived under God's grace. These examples are by no means exhaustive and are used only to recall how much of Protestant theology turns to the Bible for its basic doctrines, symbols, and concepts, and how these in turn have consequences for Protestant ethics.

As was earlier indicated, Roman Catholic theological ethics

did not ignore Scripture; there have been basic theological premises drawn from it which have framed and grounded the more philosophically derived expositions of the moral order of nature, the purposes of creation, the end (*telos*) of the human. The only claim being made here is that in recent years, for varied reasons, some Roman Catholic moral theologians have been distinctively more interested in demonstrating the theological and moral significance of the Bible.[9] That the impact of this renewed interest in biblical concepts and symbols is visible in documents of the Second Vatican Council has been noted by many persons. The concept of God as acting in history, developed by Protestant biblical scholars and theologians, is used in a central way in Roman Catholic theologies of revolution.[10] These theologians come closest to the Protestant tendency to move from Scripture through a principle of interpretation to theological ethics (or politics) and thus to recommendations for action. The authors to whom I shall principally refer, however, maintain more of the philosophical posture of the tradition and thus continue to keep an intellectual distance from the Protestant biblical confessional approaches while accenting the biblical materials more than their immediate predecessors.

I shall develop two related, but distinct, themes in recent Roman Catholic moral theology which take into account biblical theological themes in a way that moves conversations with Protestant ethicians to a different plane. First, the biblical basis for an authorization of natural law has been explored to argue that natural law thinking is not "unbiblical." Second, in some writings new attention is given to the participation of the Christian community in Christ; this leads to a development of Pauline and other New Testament themes and within this framework to a distinctively Christocentric ethics. It must be reiterated that these themes are not novel in the Roman Catholic tradition; the present interest in them, however, is in part generated by a new openness to traditional Protestant concerns for biblical theology. At least they make discourse between Protestant theological ethicians and Catholic moral theologians possible on some common bases in a way that has not occurred since shortly after the Reformation.

To represent how Catholic moral theology has recently given greater attention to the biblical basis for natural law I have selected a book by Josef Fuchs, S.J., professor of Moral Theology at the Gregorian University in Rome. His *Natural Law: A Theological Investigation* goes to the heart of the issue and contains its own critical analysis of recent Protestant theology. Although a relatively short book, it is a comprehensive interpretation of natural law theory and addresses issues raised in previous chapters of this book. Attention is given here only to passages relevant to the biblical basis for natural law. Three aspects are of particular significance: the use of Romans 1 and 2, the biblical view of man being in the image of God, and the biblical sources for a logos Christology. Fuchs' development of the natural law itself remains close to the tradition, emphasizing distinctions between nature and supernature and the like. These matters are peripheral for present purposes.

The first two chapters of Paul's letter to the Roman Christians have been debated for centuries. To what extent do they authorize a "natural theology" and a "natural law"? Particularly important are 1:20 and 2:14.

> Ever since God created the world his everlasting power and deity—however invisible—have been there for the mind to see in the things he has made. That is why such people are without excuse. . . . [P]agans who never heard of the Law but are led by reason to do what the Law commands, may not actually "possess" the Law, but they can be said to "be" the Law. They can point to the substance of the Law engraved on their hearts. [Translation from the Jerusalem Bible]

For Roman Catholics these texts have provided a biblical warrant for natural law, though Paul does not develop the substance and form of a theory of natural law. Fuchs endorses this view. He acknowledges that Paul is primarily concerned with other matters, but for him " 'the natural law' is a self-evident domain which raises no problems as such. For us, it is legitimate to discover the notions of natural law implicit in his treatment of law, sin and grace."[11] Thus the church's use of the language of natural law and natural right "can be grounded" in Paul's writings even though Paul does not offer an explanation of the natural character of this knowledge or of its ontological foundations. When the apostle proceeds in various epistles to indicate the guilt of the pagans, he has a moral order in mind that is "equivalent to that called natural law by the church now."[12] The difference between good and evil is not *established* by the Torah;

what is historically revealed *teaches* humans about what is already good and evil. Even the "Law of Christ" is an appearance of the natural law given a "positive and new *authority*."[13] To claim a warrant for natural law in Romans, however, is not a sufficient argument to establish its theological basis, and thus Fuchs turns to other arguments as well.

One of them, also a classic argument, is based on the biblical doctrine of man in the image (likeness) of God. "Being a creature always includes being God's image." "By creating an image of himself God, through this image, gave a binding and necessary *in-formation* to the behaviour of the creature composed of body and soul."[14] By this emphasis and interpretation Fuchs is able to answer two Protestant criticisms of natural law, namely, that "nature" rather than God becomes the authority for morality, and that in practice the norms of morality become heteronomous. Contrary to what is supposed in such criticisms, Fuchs can argue strongly that the moral order stemming from the *imago Dei* is based on God's being and at the same time on man's being. "Man's own being within the being of the world surrounding him, is indeed God's *demand*."[15] Even social institutions such as the family and state are "pre-figured" in man's being. An argument with the "actualism," personalism, and dynamism of Protestant theological ethics becomes explicit; a Protestant penchant for using the concepts of man being called by God and responding to him reflects this way of using biblical theology. Fuchs' view, in contrast to a Barthian view which finds the likeness to God in a relation, enables him to authorize the analogy of being on biblical theological grounds. Indeed, he attends to another favorite Protestant term, theonomous ethics, and can legitimately conclude from his argument that "the natural law is the foundation of true *theonomous* ethics."[16] The argument also leads to the conclusion that a "rationalistic conception" of the natural law is no less in error than a Protestant reliance on revelation alone or on divine actualism, for such a conception gives absolute value to man and to abstract ideas. Human autonomy, which is restricted, is a gift of God, and participates in the autonomy of God. Not only *can* natural law ethics be grounded in theology derived from Scripture; a Christian doctrine of natural law *must* be so grounded.

The basic thrust of the argument is not novel; distinctive, I believe, are the author's reasons for making it (to answer

Protestant criticisms that natural law is unbiblical and to show that rationalistic views of natural law are theologically unsound) and some of the points of reference used (natural law can properly speak of God's command or demand; it can be *theonomous*).

If a Protestant theologian should choose to rebut Fuchs' theological interpretation of biblical bases for natural law, it is clear what would be crucial to the argument thus far. He or she would have to argue by exegesis that the passages from Romans 1 and 2 cannot bear the weight that Fuchs puts on them; that, while they indicate that humans are without excuse before God and thus in need of repentance, they do not *imply* a natural law *doctrine*. And, he or she would have to argue that the likeness of man to God is not one of being but one of relation, or historicity, or something else, and show the consequences for ethics.[17] The arguments would have to be theological, not practical or philosophical; they would have to be about the proper interpretation of biblical theology. To note that Fuchs gives a very Catholic interpretation of these passages would not be sufficient; another biblical theological argument would be required to indicate the error or implausibility of his argument. Such arguments about these texts abound in Protestant literature; my intention is to note that a Roman Catholic moral theologian is explicitly arguing a case on biblical texts and themes, territory historically claimed by Protestant theology.

A second theological theme in Scripture that Fuchs uses to provide a biblical theological foundation for natural law is Christology. Natural law, grounded in the act of God the creator, is no less grounded in Christ; not exclusively in the historical Christ but "the Logos as the eternal son of God."[18] The cited biblical texts are those one would anticipate: the prologue to John's gospel, Colossians 1:15–17, Ephesians 1:9–23, 1 Corinthians 8:6. All things, including man, were created in, through, and for Christ; thus the human likeness to God is "the mirror of the divine image" portrayed by the eternal logos of God. The historical and "pneumatic" Christ no less than Christ as Logos is with the Father, the creator as "first principle." Thus Christ is the prototype and the norm of the human; he is not an historical norm distinguished from the norm of the natural law.

The texts cited above have had an important role in some Protestant theological ethics as well. One cannot understand the

Christological basis of Barth's theology and of the ethics of divine permission, the ethics of "thou mayest," without taking them into account. Interpretations of the universal significance (for all persons, nonbelievers as well as believers) of the person and work of Christ have always relied on these passages to provide both an authorization and explanation of such significance. Indeed, in Barth's case, it can be argued that these texts grounded the principle of universality in his ethics so that all persons can hear the command of a gracious God.[19] But what Barth has refused to do, for theological reasons, is to develop the universal implications of the logos Christology in terms of the natural law. It is again clear that Fuchs has taken up his argument for the authorization of natural law in biblical theological terms, and thus a discussion with him must be in part on exegetical and biblical theological grounds.

For Roman Catholics or Protestants who favor the Johannine, Ephesians, and Colossians texts an issue that has been present in the church since its beginnings has to be faced, namely, whether the teachings and life of Jesus present a different moral norm from that of the natural law. Although we have already faced this issue in previous chapters, we must address it again in the context of the theological bases for ethics. The issue has exercised Fuchs considerably.[20] The lines of his basic argument are clear from what has been indicated above. God the creator has made man in his likeness; this grounds the natural law. The creative work of God is in and through Christ, the Logos, the Son, the God-man. Thus what is known in and through Christ in the sphere of the moral cannot be inconsistent with what is known through the natural law. What principally distinguishes the morality of Christians from that of others will not be the specific rules of conduct or moral values they adhere to, or their specific acts or deeds. It will be, as Fuchs puts it in two later articles, their transcendental, supernatural, and Christian intentionality which is nourished in various ways by the "treasure of Christian reality."[21] The stakes that theological interpretations of natural law have in this argument are sufficiently great to warrant some elaboration.

For Fuchs, Christian morality is "a human morality, in the best sense of the word"; "the moral conduct of the Christian must essentially be human conduct."[22] Texts from St. Paul and from Thomas Aquinas are cited in support of this. He proceeds to raise the issue that both Roman Catholics and Protestants have raised, namely, whether the love commandment, particularly the command to love one's enemies, does not require a "new law," or a virtue of love which is specifically Christian and goes beyond the justice of "human morality." His response is not explicitly theological but could be defended on his theological ethical grounds, namely, if these were specifically Christian commands, "then those who do not know or acknowledge Christ would be permitted to leave unregarded their neighbour, the sick, the needy, the underdeveloped countries, indeed they would be permitted to hate their enemies and, consequently, to practice the methods of hatred, violence, and so on. . . . [I]ndeed, love of neighbour is *the* absolute value of every human morality."[23]

The same concern has been taken up by other contemporary Catholic moral theologians, though often for practical motives (to show how Christians can agree with others on moral issues) rather than for articulated theological reasons. Fuchs' general theological argument is, however, assumed if not suggested by all. A more general way of addressing the issue than by the application of the law of love is to look at actions described in the Bible which are difficult to justify on the basis of reasoning from natural law. John Giles Milhaven, in an important study, "Moral Absolutes and Thomas Aquinas," examines the biblical texts which posed this problem to the medieval synthesizer.[24] I shall cite only one such example, the suicide of Samson. Thomas makes three basic arguments to show that suicide is unlawful: it is a sin against oneself, for by nature one loves oneself and thus wills to keep oneself in being; it is a sin against the community, for one is a part of the whole and thus the community is injured by a suicide; and it is a sin against God, for life is a gift of God. On the basis of these three principles, two derived clearly from the natural law and the third more directly from Scripture, it appears that Samson's act is not justifiable. For Thomas, Augustine's comment seemed to be a sufficient way out. "Not even Samson is to be excused that he crushed himself together with his enemies under the ruins of the house, except the Holy Ghost, who had wrought many wonders through him, had secretly commanded him to do this."[25] There are some contemporary moral theologians who would argue that recourse was taken too quickly to excusing Samson's deed by a secret command of the Holy Spirit. Bruno Schüller, S.J., discusses Thomas' article on suicide and

some recent treatments of it in moral theology. He desires to go
beyond the principles normally adduced and sets the issue of
suicide in a larger context. "To what purpose or end could God
have given such a law [against suicide]? This purpose can finally
be only the realization of the good."[26] Thus the law against
suicide can never be its own end. An evil is permissible only
insofar as this evil is proportionate to the realization of a good.
While Schüller does not at this point take up the example of
Samson, one can infer from the questions he details that it would
be possible to give a rational justification for Samson's deed. For
example, is the death of a man chiefly a means, and the only
means by which the good can be realized? The reader can infer
that in the Samson narrative the answer would be affirmative.
Similarly in the application of the love command, Schüller argues
that one can make a rational argument from teleological ethics of
natural law for each specific action. What some would argue is a
"secret command" of God, or is a specifically Christian morality,
Schüller argues can be rationally justified.[27]

Thus, while on the theological grounds for natural law there
are no differences in actions and the reasons for them given by
Christians and others, there is a difference in the transcendental,
supernatural Christian intentionality of the Christian. In *Natural
Law*, Fuchs uses the Thomistic distinctions between the natural
and the supernatural to explain how the morality of Christians is
affected by faith.

> It is true therefore that, objectively, Christ is the moral stan-
> dard and measure for all men, both in the supernatural and
> natural order. For if all created things, natural and supernat-
> ural, are rooted in him the same is true of the corresponding
> natural and supernatural moral orders.
> But as in Christ human nature was intended as a vessel of
> the Word, so our nature seems to be meant to be a receptacle
> of the supernatural life; the consequence on the moral level
> being that the natural order, moral in itself, is directed to-
> wards the supernatural; more, it is a part of it, since grace is
> the final perfection of man as created in Christ.[28]

Thus while the natural law and the moral law of Christ are one,
by participating in the supernatural life, the moral life of
Christians has a supernatural end; "just as nature is essentially
open to the supernatural so is the natural law open to supernatural supplementation."[29]

In later writings by Fuchs the concepts of "transcendental
Thomism" become more pronounced as he gives an account of
the same thing. He writes that two elements of Christian morality
are to be distinguished, though they are always found together;
the particular *categorial* conduct in which specific categorial
values, virtues, and norms are realized, and the *transcendental*
bearings (*Haltungen*) and norms, which as transcendental pene-
trate (*durchdringen*) and exceed (*überstiegen*) the particular
moral categories.[30] It is the transcendental bearing that truly
distinguishes Christian morality and can properly be called the
Christian intentionality. This bearing or intentionality is directed
in and toward God incarnate in Christ. "The Christian has
become a son of God in the spirit of Christ, which is given to him,
and thus relates himself with Christ as son to the Father of the
salvation he has attained in Christ."[31] In awareness of "this
Christian reality," the Christian lives out the specific (categorial)
moral actions in faith, hope, and love, and relates them "to the
Father of our salvation in Jesus Christ." "[T]here is nothing in
the moral life and conduct of the Christian that is not filled with
this Christian intentionality and consequently also the expression
and manifestation of this Christian intentionality—that is, of the
personal, conscious and freely-willed relation to the Father of
Jesus Christ."[32]

Clearly we have here an effort to formulate a classic Catholic
position in a contemporary context. In a brief way, Fuchs has
sought to formulate what, I believe, St. Thomas indicates in his
discussions of the new law as the grace of the Holy Spirit written
on the heart and in his discussions of the relations of life in Christ
and the theological virtues to the natural virtues and to moral
actions. Thus the effort is not novel. What is significant,
however, is that in the contemporary ecumenical context the issue
of "specific Christian ethics," something explicitly claimed by
some Protestant authors and implicitly by others, becomes a
matter of special attention. Fuchs, in effect, says that what is
distinctive about Christianity is the new relation it creates with
the triune God; what is distinctive about the Christian life is that
it is fully personal life with and in God made present in Christ. Its
morality is not unique; to live in faith, however, is to have a
different transcendental intentionality, a Christian orientation
toward God, which "fills" the conduct of the person of faith.
Fuchs clearly intends to show that Catholic moral theology is

grounded in the biblical themes of incarnation, justification, faith, and life in Christ. Protestants do not have an exclusive claim to these "Christian realities." Yet moral theology, while articulating this personal reality, also is grounded in natural law which is grounded in biblical theological principles and thus can make universal claims.

Again, one sees that the basis for discussion between Catholics and Protestants has shifted significantly when one compares Fuchs (and others) with the manualist moral theologians. The common ground is a very biblical and Christocentric view of the Christian life; the continuing difference will be how to explicate this theology in moral terms, and what *philosophical* principles are appropriate to "annex" to theology (to use a term Barth likes).

This discussion has already carried us into the second theme to be developed in examination of how recent Roman Catholic moral theology has become more centered on biblical thought, namely, the participation of the Christian community in Christ as explicated in Pauline and other New Testament texts, and the Christocentric ethics that can be developed from this. Here I wish to attend especially to the work of Bernard Häring. Häring is the most prolific writer in Catholic moral theology in our time and is a person of worldwide influence. Although Charles E. Curran's judgment that Häring's major work, *The Law of Christ*, "betrays its age and reveals its transitional character"[33] is correct, the great Redemptionist churchman is worthy of attention particularly at this juncture. To move into his writings from an interest in biblical theological themes is only one possible way. His personalism and historical consciousness have already been noted in Chapter 3; other significant elements are his interpretation of law as the form of love and his use of the natural law tradition, of objective value theory derived from Max Scheler, of sociological materials, and of the concept of virtue. Here our concern is to indicate how his use of biblical materials makes possible a different conversation with Protestantism than was the case with the previous manual writers.

Antecedent to Häring's work and the milieu out of which it comes, is the Tübingen school of moral theology. Particularly relevant to some Protestant interests is the very biblically based moral theology of Fritz Tillmann, *The Idea of the Imitation of Christ* and *The Realization of the Imitation of Christ*.[34] Häring's

work stems from the Tübingen tradition. The ground text of his
The Law of Christ is Romans 8:2: "For the law of the Spirit of life
in Christ Jesus has delivered me from the law of sin and death."
The law of Christ is the law of the Spirit of life in him; this
grounds central themes in Häring's work—Christian "maturity"
in the life of faith, life *in* Christ and the Spirit, love as a
dynamism, imitation of Christ, and the concepts of the person, of
response and responsibility, and of historicity.

Some quotations from the Foreword of *The Law of Christ* give
the flavor of the theme that will be developed here.

> The principle, the norm, the center, and the goal of Chris-
> tian moral theology is Christ. The law of the Christian is Christ
> Himself in Person. He alone is our Lord, our Savior. Christian
> life may not be viewed solely from the point of formal enact-
> ment of law and not even primarily from the standpoint of the
> imperative of the divine will. We must always view it from the
> point of the divine bounty: God wills to give himself to us. . . .
> In the love of Christ and through the love of Christ for us He
> invites our love in return, which is a life truly formed in Christ.
> The Christian life is following Christ, but not through mere
> external copying, even though it be in love and obedience. Our
> life must above all be a life in Christ.[35]

To use language from Protestant discussions, one notes here the
priority of the indicative over the imperative. One also notes the
centrality of the life of faith and piety; of a personal relationship
between the Christian and Christ. Moral life is grounded in the
Christian life of faith; moral theology is grounded in a Pauline
and Johannine conception of life in Christ. My judgment is that
Häring finds in the New Testament a basis for morality that is
open, dynamic, positive, and personal; he finds in the New
Testament the *theological* basis for overcoming the closed, static,
negativistic, and impersonal moral theology of the manuals. The
practical correlate of this is the nourishment of the life of faith
and piety out of which moral action flows.

Thus Häring can say, "the basic demand of Christian morality
says: *Live from the grace you have received.*"[36] This grace is a
stimulant to growth in Christian maturity; it is a call to a life of
response to God which is not really expressible in terms of law.
Involved are a constant deepening of conversion, a participation
in the sacramental life of the church (which had erroneously
become a religious duty), the life of prayer, a striving toward the

fulfillment of the goal of perfection to which Christ calls, a
turning toward the concerns of his kingdom. The doctrine of
Christian life in Pauline writings is appealed to for theological
foundations of this view. Häring seems to imply that the situation
of Catholic morality in the received tradition was comparable to
that which Paul saw in the scrupulous Judaism and Jewish
Christianity of his time: legal modes of thought were dominant
and defined morality in terms of minimal boundaries; defensive
attitudes were fashioned which were more concerned with avoidance of deeds proscribed as wrong than with growth in outgoing
love. The antidote that Häring prescribes is basically a Pauline
one: the individual Christian and the Christian community are
called to "being-in-Christ," to participation in him through the
church, and thus to a freedom, a love, an openness which serves
the world in its social and individual needs.

In some passages Häring adopts a language that Martin Buber
and many Protestants have judged to be the basic biblical
metaphor. It is the language of response, responsibility, and
dialogue. "The pure type of religious ethic is of the nature of
response, in which moral conduct is understood as response to the
summons of a person who is holy, who is absolute."[37] God speaks
to man and man responds to God's call; man then lives in
fellowship and communion with God and with others. This does
not, for Häring, lead to an ethics of intuitive response to what is
occurring in particular situations, though it imbibes of that more
than most of his Catholic colleagues find comfortable. The
language of law and commands, of casuistry and right order,
these terms and the explication of their significance for particular
actions are used in the context of love, of vitality and life in
Christ. "Ethic of right disposition and inner spirit must be
wedded to the ethic of commandment."[38] The ethic of the created
moral order is to be lived in response to the call of God and in a
personal responsibility to God on the part of moral agents.
Within the context of what Häring sees as a Christocentric view of
the Christian life, then, he can engraft the basic patterns of
natural law ethics.

As I have not entered into internal criticisms of other authors
used in this book, so I shall not analyze the internal strains in
Häring's work. They are there, palpably. What is important is
that, insofar as many Protestants have desired to establish
Christian ethics on the basis of a New Testament view of the

relations of Christians to God through the work of Christ
(granting always that such theological ethics are shaped by
principles of interpretation around which they cohere), the work
of Häring and of the German tradition in which he is nourished
offer a basis for some common reflection. Some old theological
questions are being answered in a way similar to that used by
many Protestants. What are the consequences of the person and
work of Christ, as these are indicated in the New Testament, for
Christian morality? How does one move from Christian doctrines
authorized by the New Testament texts to ethics, that is, to an
interpretation both of the fundamental characteristics of moral
life and of the prescriptive principles and values that are to guide
human action? If Protestants for theological or philosophical
reasons eschew the annexation of natural law to a biblical
theology (or find unconvincing arguments that natural law is
aleady implicit in biblical theology), what alternative theories,
principles, and procedures of moral reasoning do they propose to
fulfill the function that natural law does for Catholic biblical
moral theologians? And, how are these to be theologically (and
particularly biblically) grounded?

With the work of Fuchs, Häring, Charles Curran, and others
available, certain stereotypes of Catholic moral theology as
unbiblical are even less warranted now than previously. Indeed,
though it has not been cited in this discussion, Protestants must
reckon with the work of Catholic biblical scholars on the "moral
theology" of the New Testament itself.[39] The discussion between
Protestants and Catholics must now include dimensions of biblical theology. This does not resolve any issues; indeed, it may
complicate matters, given the disputes of various sorts that occur
about the proper interpretation of Scripture. What is significantly different is that important Catholic moral theologians are
interpreting Scripture more centrally in their work and that
Protestants can appreciate that intention and frequently the ways
in which it is executed.

Grace and Nature

The language of "nature and grace" has been historically more
appropriate to Catholic theology than to (at least) recent Protestant theology, especially theology that has become very biblical
and confessional in perspective. A distinction that is functionally

similar and that has a history in Protestant theology is one we noted in the first chapter, law and gospel. Law and nature function as terms to indicate, in part, the persistent continuities of requirements for individual and common welfare, for the right ordering of human life universally. Gospel and grace function to indicate, in part, the redemptive newness of life and power that the church has known through the person and work of Jesus Christ. But the term "nature" in Catholic thought has had particular connotations, philosophically derived from Aristotle, that Protestants have eschewed in the modern period. And "gospel" in Protestant thought has tended to refer to the forgiving mercy and justifying and sanctifying grace that Christians personally experience more than it has to the goodness or grace that is present in the creative work of God. This does not imply that grace in creation, and prevenient grace, are unknown in Protestant theology; on the whole this grace has not been included in the term "gospel."

American Protestants since 1951 have been accustomed to using another set of terms that have a functional similarity to nature and grace, law and gospel, namely, Christ and culture. H. Richard Niebuhr's extremely skillful development of a typology of the relationship between these concepts and that to which they refer has become a standard device for many persons when thinking about these issues.[40] Niebuhr's typology can be interpreted to be a refinement of Ernst Troeltsch's equally famous types which correlate Christological principles with general ethical positions and with ecclesiological views. Troeltsch's general pattern is as follows: Christ as Lord (basically Jesus of the synoptic gospels) is correlated with a rigorous ethics of conscientious obedience to his teachings and deeds, and with the "sect" which draws a sharp line of exclusion of its members from the world; Christ as universal redeemer (the Christ of the high Christologies) is correlated with an ethics of cultural responsibility and of compromise in all aspects of life (for Christ is redeemer of all), and with the church, as inclusive in its membership, and with the sacraments as redeeming powers; Christ the indwelling Spirit is correlated with an ethics of spiritual perfection or of mysticism, and with a loose form of Christian community.[41] Niebuhr's extreme types are Christ of culture and Christ against culture; his intermediate types are Christ

above culture, Christ and culture in paradox, and Christ transforming culture. It is not farfetched, I am suggesting, to
substitute grace or gospel for Christ, and nature or law for
culture, and thus to provide a set of ideal constructs for the area
to which we are here attending.[42]

In a sense one is only indicating the logical possibilities for
relating terms. One possibility is identity: Christ of culture—
grace and nature are one and the same. A second possibility is
mutual exclusivity: Christ against culture—grace and nature are
mutually exclusive and in a relationship of opposition. Niebuhr's
three intermediate types represent clear distinctions between
Christ and culture, and each indicates a possible relationship
between them; Christ above culture, a "dialectical" relation
between them, and Christ transforming culture.[43] Grace is
"above" nature and is its fulfillment; grace and nature are in a
dialectical relationship; grace transforms nature. As ideal constructs, types are not really conformed to actual historical patterns,
they are not historical generalizations. Rather they accent or even
exaggerate distinctive features of historical materials for the sake
of contrast. Seldom will one find a text that is an example of a type in
its pure form.

It is not necessary here to recapitulate the examples from
Catholic and Protestant theology that Niebuhr used in his book.
We can note, however, that much of Protestant ethics has been
built on a "unitarianism" of the second person of the Trinity.[44]
This has taken a number of forms: Jesus and his teachings were
the basis for much of Christian ethics, including the ethics
applicable to politics, international relations, and economics, in
much of liberal and even some "postliberal" Protestant thought;
the gospel accounts and person of Jesus have been the source and
norm of ethics in the Anabaptist tradition (Christ against culture); the revelation of the second person of the Trinity is the
source of theology and theological ethics in Barth; ethics as
"eschatological ethics" is grounded in the resurrection of the
crucified God in Moltmann; and so forth. The ways in which
Christ, or grace, have been related or not related to "nature"
differ in various forms of Protestant Christocentric ethics, but on
the whole "nature," or even the common experience of humanity,
has been ignored or been difficult to encompass in a coherent way.

All of this is described to indicate that *how* a theologian interprets the relation of Christ to culture, gospel to law, grace to nature has forceful implications for his or her ethics. Indeed how one interprets the relations of the creative activity of God to the redeeming activity of God in one's doctrine of God itself has forceful implications for theological ethics.[45] Because this is the case, the recent Roman Catholic literature on nature and grace is of the greatest significance, in my judgment, for an examination of the possibilities for rapprochement between Catholic and Protestant ethics on the theological level of discourse. Protestant theologians who write about the priority of gospel over law, of grace over nature, though they may work this out philosophically and theologically in quite different ways, have made a crucial move which can be exploited in relating Protestant theological ethics to Roman Catholic thought (especially that of Karl Rahner and those influenced by him) in potentially fruitful ways. The principal issues involved are theological, though they involve crucial philosophical judgments and have practical implications; that this is the case by no means enhances the prospects for a rapprochement, but one can indicate a possible course along which certain theological judgments that are similar could lead to greater convergence in theological ethics.[46]

The writings of Karl Rahner, S.J., are clearly the most significant to explore in this regard. I have already noted in Chapter 3 certain philosophical moves he makes pertaining to the relations of human nature and human freedom. This suggests that philosophical judgments cannot be divorced from basic theological ones when nature and grace are the subjects of attention. That the arguments made to support Rahner's ontology and theology are highly complex and involve concepts and terms that are not easily mastered is widely acknowledged; my noting of crucial points here is necessarily superficial, though I believe not inaccurate. That Rahner intends to be in basic continuity with Roman Catholic theological tradition is also widely known. This is important; as was indicated in the previous section, so also here—the contemporary developments, while innovative, draw upon themes present in the tradition and are not in discontinuity with it.

One of Rahner's less technical passages helps to locate his discussion within the possibilities outlined above.

> [I]nstead of placing the orders of redemption and creation alongside each other, we speak of the order of redemption

within the order of creation; this states the thesis that divine grace, the fruit of redemption, actually penetrates the created order itself, healing and sanctifying it; that it incorporates the world, in all its abiding naturality, into the *mysterium Christi;* and that this process of taking the world by grace into the life of God is also meant, according to God's will, to be carried out by the activity of men.[47]

When Rahner is writing about the order of redemption within the order of creation, he is concerned *not* with the *ontological* status of grace and nature, to which I shall return, but with the *historical concrete existence* of the members of the human community. We shall remain at this level of discourse briefly, for it is here that his thought may be elucidated in relation to Niebuhr's typology.

If the "order of redemption" can be provisionally equated with "Christ" in the sense of the benefits of Christ experienced in the human community, then Rahner is ruling out several of Niebuhr's types. The order of redemption is not a counterculture; it does not create an alternative community to life in the created order; it is not *against* creation. Nor is it *above* creation; it does not raise life out of creation with a separate intentionality directed toward a redemption from created existence. Nor is the relation one of paradox or dialectic; it is not "alongside," as Rahner specifically says, so that participants in both have two orientations dialectically related to each other. Nor is the relation one of identity. The order of redemption, as the "actualization" of grace in concrete experience, "includes the order of creation as an essential factor within it."

> The two orders are still, indeed, not identical, but neither are they adequately distinguishable from each other; they are related as the whole to the part.[48]

The relation is one of unity without identity; the order of creation is part of a whole, which includes the order of redemption. (This points to the ontological theological conviction to be elucidated, namely, the priority of grace over nature, the orientation of all persons toward their true end, the love of God, by their very "natures.")

In the end then, Rahner is best understood in the light of Niebuhr's type of Christ transforming culture, the order of redemption transforming ("penetrating" and "sanctifying") the order of creation. But the type can only be used heuristically (as ideal types should be used); we have in Rahner's thought, as I understand it, not an order of creation into which redemption subsequently comes to transform its fallenness (Rahner, of course, has a doctrine of the fall and of sin). Rather, we have an order of creation grounded in grace in which the order of redemption is also grounded, and the whole is in process of transformation through the actions of humans. To be noted is Rahner's assertion that the order of redemption, not to mention grace, is not coterminous with the church. The redemptive processes in creation are accruing through the actions of persons who do not belong to the church as well as through actions of those who do; this is a matter that also requires theological explanation.

Rahner's theory of grace and nature provides a more general set of theological principles which ground and explain his ethics of transformation.[49] My understanding of this, pared down for my purpose here, is as follows. Rahner perceived a fault in the received Thomistic manuals of theology. The fault was that God's grace "elevated" human nature and oriented it toward its supernatural end, but it did not make any fundamental "ontological" difference in human nature. Thus grace made no significant difference to human moral activity; "[s]ince conscious moral activity would be the same, as far as awareness went, in the natural and supernatural order, the values and goals for which men strive would be the same whether a supernatural order existed or not."[50] This suggests that Niebuhr's use of his Christ-above-culture type to elucidate the traditional Catholic position was not wholly inaccurate. The efficacy of grace was based on God's positive will to redeem humankind through the death of Christ; it was soteriologically essential but not morally significant; it directed life toward salvation, but this made little difference to human moral activity. The "order of redemption" was above "the order of creation" rather than within it. The basic theological error was that grace was not intrinsically related to Christ as the Logos, the one in and for whom all things were created.

One objective of Rahner's work is to correct this error. I believe that, in order to do this, in each of three realms of theological discourse two aspects have to be related to each other in a different way. In the concrete historical realm the order of redemption has to be "within" rather than alongside of or above the order of creation. In the realm of the *telos* of human life, the two ends, natural and the supernatural, must be conceived in such a way that the natural end is "within" the supernatural end; the two must not remain relatively discrete. Put differently, the moral end is within the redemptive, penetrated by it. In the realm of theology/ontology, the correlative relation is established by conceiving of God as grace, freely communicating himself as grace in "nature," in all persons, and creating the capacity in all persons to be responsive to this grace in their actions, whether they are atheists, faithful to other religious traditions, or communicant believers in Christ. The being of humans depends utterly on God, on grace, and thus there is an orientation of all human beings (and not just of those who know grace as grace) toward their redemptive "supernatural" end.

Another statement of this position, with "coordinates" that are more familiar to Protestant readers, might be useful. If I am correct in judging Rahner's ethics to be best elucidated by the transformationist type, then I can indicate his theological reasons for this preference, and also indicate some distinctive features of his ethics. The transforming efficacy of Christ (for purposes of this exposition, read "grace") in moral life and in culture is not limited to the consequences for human action of explicit faith in Christ, to the vital experience of justifying and sanctifying grace in Christ, or to participation in the historical Christian community. It is not limited to those who know grace as grace. The "benefits" of Christ are not merely the "positive" experiential and historical benefits of a historical death and resurrection of Christ. Christ (grace) is in culture *qua* culture (part of the "order of creation"); grace is in the world *qua* world; it is in humans *qua* human. The Johannine language ("through him all things came to be; not one thing had its being but through him"), which Rahner develops in a philosohical theology, means not merely that God in a gracious act created all things but that all created things are graced and that this grace is the grace of Christ. It is not merely that all created things are good because God the Father created them; Christ is ontologically present in all humans, in the being of the world. Thus the grounds for transformation are Christ (grace) but they are present in man and the world (in a loose sense, in nature). All persons are in Christ (grace), and are "Christian" though many are anonymously so and do not know grace as grace.[51] All persons have a capacity to respond to grace (the "supernatural existential"), and the proper moral actions of all persons are graced. Thus there is a unity of love of God and of neighbors.[52] All persons, not merely faithful believers, are disposed or oriented toward a "supernatural" end, toward redemption. The transformation is ontological and universal and is not confined to the explicitly Christian experiential and historical arenas. All ethics are Christian ethics, all morality is Christian morality.

What distinguishes Rahner's theological ethics from the received tradition of the manuals of moral theology is that the "natural law," which is knowable and acted upon by all persons, is, theologically speaking, Christian; it is graced. It is Christian and graced because it is created in, by, through, and for Christ, the Incarnate Logos of God. It is graced not merely because a gracious disposition in the Creator was expressed in bringing "nature" into being; it is really graced—ontologically, grace penetrates nature. Persons know grace who do not know grace *as* grace; those who are acting in conformity with their true natures are acting in grace. Those who act morally are Christian; they are not to be thought of only as autonomous rational beings governing their conduct in accord with principles derived from the moral order of "nature" (in the sense of something distinguishable from grace). Though anonymously so, they are Christian. Those who act morally are not only preserving the created moral order in the face of threats to it; they are participating in the "order of redemption." The redemptive work of Christ is taking place in culture, society, and individual life through all persons who are morally praiseworthy. Those who properly love their neighbors are at the same time loving God; whether they are atheists, Hindus, Catholics, or Protestants is not a decisive factor. To be sure, the mission of the church is in part to increase the number of persons who know grace as grace; to be sure, there are additional "benefits" of grace to those who participate in the life of the church. Morally speaking, however, to be Catholic or, more inclusively, to be Christian in the explicit sense, is not necessary in order to live a life that is Christian in a moral sense.[53]

Rahner's philosophical theology, which develops the concepts that explicate and justify these views, can for my purpose be bracketed here, though clearly a major argument looms on the intellectual horizon when one seeks to find the principles that traditional Protestants could share with him. Rahner's concept of "the supernatural existential," his concept of transcendental freedom in relation to concepts of nature in the human sphere, his concept of the anonymous Christian, and others are likely to be objectionable to one or another Protestant who might be sympathetic to the theological intention to rethink the relations of grace and nature, redemption and creation, church and world, Christ and culture. When I now suggest that there are theological motifs in Protestantism that have a family resemblance to this aspect of Rahner's theological project, I do not mean to indicate that a consensus can be easily established.

As Niebuhr's *Christ and Culture* makes clear, various Protestant theologies have related the terms of the above polarities in different ways. Theological, and not only ethical and practical, choices are involved; indeed for the theologian (in the most restrictive usage) these choices are decisive. If, for example, God's work is not only distinguished but divided between that which is creative and that which is redemptive, two ethics are likely to follow—the ethics of the orders of creation and the ethics of the redeemed person. If, however, the gospel is a revelation of God as gracious and redemptive, and if the "law" is interpreted as the "form of the gospel" and the world is in principle but not in fact redeemed, there will be different consequences for a basic position in ethics, consequences closer to those of Karl Rahner's theology. Ethics within the range of the transformationist type are likely to be developed.

Several Protestant theologians have moved in the direction of a theology that leads to ethics that have some similarity to Rahner's. Among the Reformation theologians, Calvin would be more similar to Rahner by a large measure than Luther or the Anabaptists.[54] The Victorian Anglican F. D. Maurice was discussed by Niebuhr under the transformation type for good theological reasons.[55] The affinities of Karl Barth's theology with Roman Catholic theology, as well as the differences between the two, have been extensively discussed by two major European Catholic theologians, Hans Küng and Hans Urs von Balthasar; though I know of no major study of Barth's and Rahner's ethics, I believe such similarities as can be drawn are possible because of a basically similar judgment on the relations of grace and nature, gospel and law.[56] H. Richard Niebuhr himself, while distinguishing response to God the Creator from responses to him as

Governor and Redeemer, insisted that the creative activity of God was redeeming and governing, the governing activity creative and redeeming, and the redeeming activity creative and governing; thus Christian activity ought to be basically transforming of culture.[57] Joseph Sittler's most recent book, *Essays on Nature and Grace*, clearly reflects Rahner's influence.[58] I shall confine my discussion to Sittler and Barth as authors who take steps in the direction Rahner has gone, though neither is sympathetic to the philosophical theology which grounds and explicates Rahner's work.

Sittler, who was on the way toward formulating a theology of grace before Rahner was widely read in America, saw the "cosmic dimensions" of Christology before Allan Galloway had articulated them for his theological generation.[59] As Rahner objected to the order of redemption being placed "alongside" of the order of creation, Sittler perceived that, in Protestantism particularly, "the doctrine of grace has been almost exclusively administered in relation to man as sinner."[60] This confinement left "entire ranges" of grace unadministered. Thus a question locates Sittler's project.

> Might it be possible ... to recover and release such an understanding and celebration of grace as shall locate its presence and power and hope within man's life in the world-as-creation as well as within man's hearing and receiving of grace through the Word and sacrament of forgiveness?[61]

The answer is affirmative. The resources for sustaining the affirmative are found in part in the Bible (Colossians and Ephesians receive special attention, as is to be expected), in part in the Patristic tradition (Irenaeus receives special attention) and Eastern theology, in part in Western theology, particularly Augustine's. What these and other resources are marshalled to support is that grace is the "fundamental ascription" in the Christian faith's understanding of the God relationship. To speak of God as gracious is to say that "God is a creative and redeeming reality, presence, energy, and allure."[62] This presence is located "within history and nature, and amidst the most common and formative episodes of experience." The theological point (in a restricted sense) that grounds this view is that grace is postulated of God the Creator, God the Redeemer, and God the Sanctifier; thus "the presence and power and availability of grace must be postulated with equivalent scope."[63] Anything natural or historical can be the occasion for grace. Grace is "the sheer *givenness-character* of life, the world, and the self—the plain *presentedness* of all that is." Thus man does not move from nature to grace, nor is grace only the therapy for human sin; rather the whole of creation is "a theatre of grace."[64] As a consequence of this, Sittler writes, "*Theological* ethics . . . must address man in his strength as well as his weakness, in his joy as well as his sorrow, and in his accomplishments—to direct them and hold them in proportion to larger goods—as well as in his failure—to forgive and console them."[65] Christian ethics is an ethics of grace, relating the presence and availability of God's goodness to all occasions of life and action.

While Sittler does not work out either his theology or his ethics in a rigorous, systematic way, and while his biblical orientation and other factors deter him from developing the technical philosophical theology and anthropology that one finds in Rahner, his basic theological view is sufficiently similar to Rahner's to merit inclusion in this discussion of grace and nature. Sittler's anticipation of the current interest in the issues of ecology was in considerable measure grounded in this theology of the universal presence of grace in all of creation; this area has marked his most distinctive contribution to practical matters of human action and values. On other issues that occupy moral theologians he has written little or nothing, but it is clear that at least the moral attitude toward the world which coheres with this theology is, like Rahner's, one of the affirmation of possibilities for responsible human participation in the moral and redeeming work of God in the world. Though a Lutheran by ecclesiastical and theological tradition, Sittler has moved from a dialectic between the poles of law and gospel, creation and redemption, to a view in which, similar to Rahner's, nature is within grace, and the order of redemption is penetrating all of creation and not only forgiving penitent sinners.

Another Protestant theologian of the "triumph of grace," Karl Barth, has developed his theology, his ethical theory, and his practical moral theology in an amplitude equal to Rahner's.[66] Rahner's philosophical theology and anthropology, articulated in sophisticated technical detail, is a matter on which Barth would have basic debate, though the imaginative interpreter of both might find points of affinity worthy of attention. The morphology of the relation of the universality of grace to individual actions that one finds in Rahner is different from what Barth uses. Barth's dominant language is drawn from personal and social relations—commands and permission, command and hearing, command and obedience, decision and action, response and responsibility—and leads to what I have described as occasionalism. But the priority of grace in both leads to a plausible suggestion that further exploitation of the significance of their theologies of grace for ethics is worthy of consideration.

Barth opens his major discussion of ethical theory with the assertion of this priority. "In the true Christian concept of the covenant of God with man the doctrine of the divine election of grace is the first element, and the doctrine of the divine command is the second."[67]This, in one swoop, rules out the language of "alongside." Grace cannot be conceived as only a remedy for sin; gospel cannot be cast in a dialectical relation to law. Rather, "[r]uling grace is commanding grace"; "[t]he Gospel itself has the form and fashion of the law"; "[t]he one Word of God is both Gospel *and* Law." It is first Gospel and then Law"; its content is Gospel and its form is Law.[68] Command becomes permission and permission takes the form of command; the grace of God is expressed in the moral commands.

Human action, then, is to correspond and conform to God's gracious action. Thus in a section on "The Content of the Divine Claim," the first answer to the question, "What are we to do?" is, "We are to do what corresponds to this grace. We are to respond to the existence of Jesus Christ and His people."[69] The most general moral norm of action is the grace of God made known in Christ; the Christian is to accept the action of the gracious God as right. Thus ethics is basically the imitation of God; it is human action that is in conformity to and bears witness to God's action. To see how this works out in a biblical confessional way is not too difficult, for the form and content of God's gracious action is disclosed in Jesus. Thus the command of God's grace is itself bound to be coherent with the one in whom that grace is revealed, and therefore with biblical teaching. An ethics of conformity to grace is clearly possible for Christians who know grace as grace. In what Rahner would cite as the positive historical order of those who have an explicit faith, there is clearly an ethics of grace. But does this leave Barth without an ethics of grace for all persons? Does this make Christian ethics exclusively relevant to Christians? Barth rejects an "esoteric" implication to his theology and thus also to his ethics. God's revelation is of "the truth" and not merely of certain ideas and obligations alongside of different ones; it has a universal validity. Part of that truth is that all persons are de jure, though not de facto, in Christ, that is, in a relationship of grace to God.[70]

> There is no humanity outside the humanity of Jesus Christ or the voluntary or involuntary glorifying of the grace of God which manifested itself in this humanity. There is no realization of the good which is not identical with the grace of Jesus Christ in its voluntary and involuntary confirmation. For there is no good which is not obedience to God's command.[71]

The "distinctive essence of all who live in the world" is "that the decision that has been taken in Jesus Christ does actually affect them too and their being." Jesus Christ is the "Lord and Head" of each and all humans; and unbelievers, "whether they have known him or not, are only provisionally and subjectively outside Him and without Him in their ignorance and unbelief." They are really Christ's, objectively; "they belong to Him, and they can be claimed as His *de jure.*"[72] Thus there is an "ontological connection" between Jesus as the one in whom all are elect of God and all humans.

   In light of this claim, it is possible to state that there is a functional equivalent in Barth's ethics to Rahner's concept of the anonymous Christian. Barth clearly eschews the concept of natural law for theological reasons;[73] nonetheless, on his grounds it can be claimed that all ethics are theological or even Christian because all persons are elected to a relationship of grace through Christ, and this is their "essence." This is warranted by biblical theology that accents the Christologies to which I have previously referred, as well as by aspects of the tradition. All realization of the good is identical with the grace of Jesus Christ (not with "the moral law of nature"), and all moral commands are commands of the gospel, of grace. Thus those who are morally praiseworthy, it seems reasonable to conclude, are implicitly Christian in the sense that they hear the command of grace even if they do not know it as grace. As Rahner has a further development of the meaning of the Christian life for those who are in the church, so Barth discusses in his passages on sanctification just what knowing grace as grace effectuates in believers.[74] Basically it

brings into existence de facto what is already de jure. At the level
of de jure existence, however, there is an "ontological connection" between Jesus and all persons which is the basis for the
functional equivalent of Rahner's concept of anonymous Christians.

As we saw in the previous chapter, Rahner's ethics provide a
warrant for a positive, open relation to the world; thus there is not
a totally negativistic attitude toward new developments, though
there are principles to be derived from the essentially human
which guide and limit action. In a generally similar manner
Barth's theology sustains a positive and affirmative attitude
toward the world; the import for ethics is that prohibitions
become basically affirmations. The meaning of prohibitions
against killing, for example, become "Thou mayest live!"[75] This
does not rule out a divine "No," but the "No" is for the positive
intention of the Divine "Yes" to human life and the world.

To indicate similarities is not to be blind to vast differences
between Barth and Rahner. Barth's knowledge of the universality
of grace is known through Scripture alone, and his explication of
it is intentionally confined as much as possible to biblical
language. Rahner's concept of the "supernatural existential" in
each person would violate Barth's principle that he used against
all Protestant views invoking a point in human life that naturally
responds to God. While for both human freedom is at the heart
of the essentially human, clearly Barth would avoid the philosophical anthropology that Rahner develops to state his case. Similar as their openness to newness is, for Rahner the openness
involves a discovery of new aspects of the character of human
freedom (human "nature"), whereas for Barth it is based on the
freedom of God, in his grace, to command something different in
new circumstances (though he is not likely to command anything
that countervenes his revelation in Jesus Christ). While grace is
triumphant for both, for Rahner it is grace in and through nature
that has consequences for morality; for Barth it is grace in and
through a more immediate command of God, a command that is
permission.

The general point I desire to make should be clear. At the
theological "level" of discourse, judgments about the relations of
grace and nature, gospel and law, redemption and creation,
Christ and culture, are decisive for theological ethics. When Karl
Rahner, much in the tradition of certain biblical themes, and

themes from patristic and classic Catholic theology, develops a theology of grace and nature in which the first word is grace, certain Protestant theologians (my examples being a revisionist Lutheran, Sittler, and a revisionist Calvinist, Barth) are within speaking distance of him on a crucial issue. In looser language, we can say that Christian theological ethics in both traditions becomes universal rather than particularistic; morality becomes more open as against closed; accent is on the affirmative and positive principles rather than on prohibitive and negative principles; moral life becomes dynamic as against static. I have not developed, as a fuller account requires, the coordinate views of sin and evil within these theologies of grace; surely a comprehensive assessment of them and their implications for ethics requires such a development. Sin as the "ontological impossibility" for Barth has raised comment about the sufficiency of his view, and similar matters would have to be addressed to other theologies.[76] The basic thrust, however, is clear: ethics begins from the basic supposition of grace rather than sin.

For some of us in the Protestant tradition the Roman Catholic development of a theology of grace has to be taken seriously as a theological proposal; the ethical principles and procedures that are coherent with the theology must also be taken seriously. They force one to take seriously what the ethical "shape" of grace is and ought to be, not merely in terms of general moral principles and human values, but also in terms of practical moral decision-making. There can be a practical casuistry within a theology of grace, as Barth himself makes clear in *Church Dogmatics* III/4, though for Barth its intention is to help one to hear the command of God. *If* one is persuaded that grace and nature are the proper terms (rather than gospel and law as command of God), then moral principles can be established on the basis of "nature," or its functional equivalents in a different moral theory; this "nature," then, is a "form" of the gracious presence and purpose of God. "Grace" is not reduced to spontaneous or occasional goodness but is the fundamental designation of the divine and its relation to the human. Grace provides a different context within which principles are established and applied and within which experience is interpreted. One possible effect is that individuals and the community, while being morally serious and seeking clarity and precision in determining action, can live without the absolute moral certainty that some manuals of moral theology offered and required. Action without absolute certitude can be taken not only in the confidence of the mercy of God, the forgiveness of sin, but also in the acceptance that finite humans are engaged in an ongoing task of discovering what the right ordering of the human community is and in what its well-being consists in changing historical and natural circumstances.

Many Protestant theologians have made rather crude charges against Roman Catholics for being "legalistic." This charge has meant several things: legalism leads to works-righteousness and thus is soteriologically in error for not relying upon God's grace; it leads to what Catholic moral theologians themselves call "scrupulosity" so that absolute certitude is expected before an action is undertaken, and so that one lives out life in the fear of committing a sin; and it leads to excessive rationalism. A theology in which the priority is on grace can avoid a legalistic moral theology. Indeed, Roman Catholic theology of grace can have a valid attraction to the Protestant theologian, especially if he or she objects to the obscurities permitted in most Protestant accounts of the relations between God's grace and human action. It is "nature" that is graced, and thus within a theology of grace there is not only "permission" (a "Thou mayest") but also an obligation to think through carefully, using resources of moral philosophy, of human experience, and of scientific information, what the moral ordering of the community and moral actions of individuals ought to be. Rationality within a theology of grace can avoid legalism, but requires rigorous moral reflection; a theology of grace that does not conceive of grace working through nature and rationality can lead to careless intuitionism and occasionalism.

Ecclesiology

I indicated in Chapter 1 that one of the historic differences between Roman Catholicism and Protestantism has pertained to the authority of the church in matters of morals. This authority continues to be problematic in both traditions; because the institutional powers of the Catholic church are at the center of current discussions, it remains an extremely thorny issue.

Differences of judgment and tradition on the questions of the nature and purpose of the church have far wider ramifications for Christian ethics, however, than the matter of authority of

moral teachings. I have noted Troeltsch's correlation of views of
the church, Christological emphases, and characteristics of Christian ethics. This could be one approach to elaborating other
aspects—the view of the sacraments, the roles of the ordained
ministry, and so forth. The language used to point to the nature
and purpose of the church could be correlated with views of the
purpose of moral teaching and theory in communities. The shift
of weight from the metaphor of "body" of Christ to the term "the
people of God," for example, has carried with it a new emphasis
on the notion of "pilgrims" living and acting in historic circumstances. The Vatican II document "Gaudium et Spes" reflects
this shift and with it clearly came less confidence in natural law as
the foundation for Christian moral thought.[77] I shall not explore
the whole range of ecclesiological issues which have some implications for ethics; this area has been deeply neglected, and there is
only a minor correction of that neglect here.[78]

Within Protestantism the discussion of the authority of the
church in moral matters is far more chaotic, and the points of
reference are more numerous and less clearly defined, than in
Roman Catholicism. Paul Ramsey in *Who Speaks for the
Church?*, his passionate polemical response to the 1966 Geneva
Conference on social issues sponsored by the World Council of
Churches, raises a number of relevant matters that cohere around
his provocative title.[79] The title is one good question; it suggests
others. Who listens to the church? Why do they listen or refuse to
listen? Put in other terms, what and who authorizes the church to
be a moral teacher? (I mean to include in moral teaching
prophetic criticism, pronouncements on social policies, specific
designations of wrong conduct, and so forth). What authorizes
what is taught? (Institutional authority, persuasiveness of argument, and biblical warrants are some possible answers.) To whom
does the church address its teaching? (All persons of good will, a
denomination's own members, the Christian community as a
whole?) Why are the teachings taken seriously or why are they
ignored? (The answers would be in the reasons of the hearers that
correspond to reasons which authorize teachings: institutional
authority is accepted or rejected, the arguments are found to be
persuasive or not, and so forth.) Of particular significance in a
study of theological ethics is the matter of the authority of
theologians as a class or of individual theologians. Roman
Catholics can more precisely locate the disputed issues in answers

to these questions than Protestants can, largely because there is a clearer tradition of authority to accept, reject, or modify.

The one point of consensus within Protestantism is that there are no bases for a claim to infallibility for any Christian moral teaching just because it is endorsed by an ecclesiastical institution. Beyond this, diversity of opinion is so great as to make generalizations difficult. The absence of clear institutional authority makes it difficult to apply any sanctions against moral behavior that does not conform to even such consensus as does exist on a particular moral issue. While church discipline in some Protestant groups exists in principle, it is seldom exercised on persons who violate moral teachings and is declining in efficacy in all mainline Protestant groups and also many evangelical ones. Protestant churches do not claim a biblical or historical authorization for a continuity of institutionalized authority from the Apostles forward, as the Roman Catholic tradition does. They do not claim that the church has a special gift that enables it rightly to understand what the natural law requires, as certain papal documents claim. Nor, as I noted in Chapter 1, has the sacrament of penance been maintained as a quasi-judicial device to exert specific sanctions against conduct that is judged to be morally errant.

Protestant church bodies do, however, function as moral teachers. The authorizations for this function are varied and complex, and the variables relate in part to the polities of different groups. The Bible contains moral teachings, and thus churches explicate and apply those teachings. Fundamental theological principles grounded in Scripture authorized moral teachings in biblical times and continue to do so. The moral sensitivities evoked, sustained, and cultivated by religious faith and life require explication of the good ordering of society and of the right conduct of persons. Gatherings of church members provide occasions, frequently authorized constitutionally, for the collective religious moral opinions to be expressed; these opinions carry such authority as constitutions allow or consensus evokes.

Further specification of the reasons why what is taught ought to be attended to by those who read and hear would require a rehearsal of all the forms of theological ethics and moral theories that exist in Protestantism today, many of which have been discussed in previous portions of this book. Because specific moral teachings are usually provoked by current events or movements in society and culture, they have a time-bound character. The teachings frequently have no consistent pattern of argumentation but are *ad hoc* appeals to different principles and arguments. Sometimes they support whatever seems to be the prevailing moral opinion on an issue, and sometimes they dissent from prevailing opinion. For example, many Protestant church statements on abortion have paid little attention to the Bible and to dominant traditional church teaching on this issue. Rather than be explicit about how a strongly pro-abortion position might be grounded biblically and theologically, or about why traditional anti-abortion arguments have in principle been wrong or must in present circumstances be altered, the justifications by church bodies have in an *ad hoc* way borrowed various arguments from a strong pro-abortion movement in the culture.[80] (This illustration has special significance for ecumenical discussions of morality. Protestant groups which differ from the official Roman Catholic anti-abortion position *must* show the errors in the theological and moral arguments that authorize that position rather than simply declare an alternative opinion or make political arguments.) In contrast to the abortion issue, Protestant arguments against the war in Southeast Asia with some frequency appealed both to biblical norms and to a church tradition of just-war theory to support dissent from government policy. The diversity and inconsistency in Protestant church moral teachings could be proved conclusively through a document-by-document analysis. There is little or no consensus on theological principles and on moral theory in Protestantism; this clearly weakens the authority of church teaching.

To whom are Protestant moral teachings addressed? Generally the intention is to address both the members of the Christian community (or a denominated segment of it) and the wider human community, especially those who have power to influence the course of events. The character of the arguments made and the evidences adduced in their support clearly ought to appeal to the intended audiences, especially since the churches have neither legal nor socially designated power to function as moral teachers in most modern societies. Previous sections of this book pertain also to this subject. Protestant church teachings carry the weight of their arguments and little in addition to that. Thus the arguments have to be developed in an honest and coherent way to be at least considered by, and at best persuasive to, the Christian

and secular communities. This requires clarification and defense
of the principles that sustain the teachings to both intended
audiences.

Who listens to the moral teachings of Protestant churches?
This is an empirical question that has been answered to some
extent by sociologists of religious behavior.[81] When the teachings,
even though theologically and biblically grounded and "pronounced" by official church bodies or leaders, diverge too far
from the prevailing moral opinions of church members, the
members either do not listen or become hostile. Class identification, ethnic identification, and other factors seem to determine
the moral opinions of Protestant people more than church
identification does. Beyond church membership, no doubt persons sympathetic with the teaching (for their own moral reasons
or interests) welcome additional support. Pious Protestants can
be virulent racists or civil right activists. They can be militarists or
pacifists, socialists or defenders of the free-market system,
regardless of what church agencies teach about these matters.

This brief and general account indicates that the situation of
Protestant churches with regard to moral teachings is only a little
short of chaos. It remains to make a few observations about the
role or authority of theologians in Protestantism. Few professional theologians are church officials; few denominations continue to exercise the authority of appointment to theological faculties. (In one dramatic instance where authority has been exercised,
the Lutheran Church, Missouri Synod, the ecclesiastical pressure
to conformity has been resisted, and finally an independent
theological faculty has been created.) Protestant theologians,
particularly in noncreedal and non-"evangelical" denominations, are not answerable to church authorities or bodies in
a formal way. They are free agents, exercising the same pre-
rogatives of the academic profession that scholars in other
fields do. In addition, many of them avoid participation in
ecclesiastical bodies even when their participation is welcomed.
Thus the influence of theologians in the determination of the
moral teachings of the churches is usually indirect and informal.
Clergy and laity feel little or no compulsion to consult theologians
in forming moral pronouncements or shaping moral opinions,
and many theologians are unwilling to make the effort to have a
more direct influence. (There are exceptions to these generaliza-

tions; theologians in denominational seminaries tend to take ecclesiastical responsibilities more seriously than those in nondenominational schools. There are examples, however, of theologians in nondenominational schools who participate conscientiously in denominational and ecumenical bodies.)[82] Suasive influence, rather than institutionalized official authority, is the means by which theologians affect the church moral teachings in most of Protestantism.

The circumstances that mitigate the authority of Protestant churches in the area of moral teachings are not themselves without theological and traditional authorization. Since the time of the Reformation, with its stress on the work of the Spirit in and through laity as well as clergy, clericalism, institutional claims to certitude, and any presumptuous claims by theologians have been questioned on the basis of theological principle. (In practice, of course, clericalism and other authoritarian practices have occurred.) One impact of a characteristically Protestant view of the church has been to make it difficult, if not impossible, for Protestants to deflect moral accountability from themselves to official church teachings or to ecclesiastical authorities. Accountability had to rest, finally, on moral agents themselves. Thus the churches could be moral teachers and communities in which the moral outlooks and consciences of their members were formed, but they could not be authoritative teachers in the sense that official pronouncements stated what was to be conformed to by their members. (Again, exceptions should be noted; violations of certain of the Ten Commandments and, in certain groups, of rigoristic behavioral rules, have sometimes been the basis for institutional sanctions.) The Protestant "church" has always been a *Magister*, a teacher, in matters of morality, but if churches claimed an absolute certitude for teachings beyond the confines of the most traditional rules ("Thou shalt not commit adultery," "Thou shalt not murder"), and if they claimed obedience to teachings on the basis of institutional authority, something essential to Protestantism would be violated. Teaching had to win the consent of the minds and hearts of chronologically mature Christians. If it did not, it became (to use a modern term) heteronomous; obedience to it was "inauthentic" compliance to a norm that was extrinsic and alien to the conscience. Moral teachings had to have "subjective" authority, not in the sense that their authority was determined by individual interests and desires, but in the sense that agents were persuaded intellectually and spiritually of their validity.

This has left Protestantism with a legacy, namely, the final authority of the individual informed conscience, that is not foreign to an aspect of the Roman Catholic tradition and is attractive to both theorists in moral theology and to persons responsible for Christian nurture in the Catholic church. The legacy creates a very difficult practical problem. What activities are required and possible for Protestant churches in secular and pluralistic cultures in order for them to be moral teachers, to influence the formation of moral outlooks and of consciences? Not only the procedures to achieve this end are in question but also the content of the teaching. What is the proper curriculum (not so much in terms of its pedagogical attractiveness as its substance)?[83] Culturally and socially there are obstacles to effec-. tive answers to these questions.

Descriptively as well as normatively there are similarities between the Protestant tradition and recent Roman Catholic life and thought that render certain stereotypes dubious. First, Protestants must remember that since the First Vatican Council, which authorized papal infallibility, no specific moral teaching of the church has been declared under the specified conditions which make it infallible. The authority of moral teachings has to be discussed within a margin short of that claim. Second, the authority of moral teachings has been grounded mainly in two basic ways: the natural law and faithfulness to tradition and Scripture. The teachings have not been promulgated on the basis of arbitrary (reasonless, willful) authority and power, but on bases which are open to rational scrutiny within both the Christian community and the larger human community. The pertinent point at issue here for Protestants is the claim that has been made for a special competence to interpret natural law, tradition, and Scripture, that is, an ecclesiological claim. Third, the Roman Catholic Church has always *taught* morality through its various institutions and pedagogical procedures; it has in principle provided reasons for the rules to those who were to conform to them. The issues for Protestants are the adequacy of the reasons and the motives appealed to for obedience. (Clearly, Protestants, like Roman Catholics, have appealed to fear of punishment and promise of rewards, so a simpleminded judg-

ment is ruled out.) Fourth, *in principle* Catholic moral theology
has always honored the right of the individual informed conscience to be the final arbiter of moral choice. Discussions by
moral theologians about dissent from the magisterial authority of
the episcopacy assume the propriety of these four points. In
question form these points are: What is the authority of a
noninfallible moral teaching? Are the arguments made from
reason and from Scripture and tradition valid? Can alternative
arguments be made from the same bases? How ought the
teaching function of the church in matters of morals be carried
out? What is the scope of permissible conscientious dissent from
moral teaching by individuals, and what are legitimate reasons
for it?

These matters have come to the fore in what Charles E. Curran
has called the "creeping infallibility" that progressed in the
nineteenth and first half of the twentieth centuries. Not only
encyclicals by the popes, but their speeches or allocutions, the
words of bishops in dioceses throughout the world, the judgments
of local pastors, and the words of nuns in the classroom were
accepted with more authority than in principle they have. But the
acceptance of authority has been selective. Pope Pius XI is
remembered for two encyclicals, *Quadrigesimo Anno*, which had
radical enough social implications to lead John A. Ryan to argue
that it supported the New Deal in the United States, and *Casti
Connubii*, which rules out birth control by any means other than
periodic continence.[84] Surely the latter has carried greater authority at least for American Catholics than the former. My
impression is that currently Pope Paul's *Progressio Populorum*,
which gives encouragement to significant social reform, is turned
to by socially liberal Catholics for support while *Humanae Vitae*,
on birth control, is conscientiously neglected.[85]

Particularly as a result of the latter encyclical, the discussion of
the authority of the church in moral teachings has become more
intense and widespread.[86] To indicate a representative response
which seeks to make important distinctions, I have chosen an
essay by Bruno Schüller, S.J.[87] While Schüller's disposition is
more conservative than some other authors', the terms he uses
have wide currency. He argues that Christ commissioned his
church to preach and teach both his gospel and his law. This
preaching and teaching must be "authentic," but to be authentic
it need not be or claim to be infallible, without error. Indeed,

there is no certainty that the will of Christ can be known without a margin of error. Thus we see the major distinction: teaching can be authentic without being infallible. Such teachings bear authority, for they issue from reflections of the church, which is overall better protected from error by the fact that its insights into both the gospel and the law of Christ are deeper than those of any single individual. Consequently, there is always a presumption in favor of the authenticity and truth of church teachings on moral matters. Yet when the church speaks *merely* authentically it cannot offer the certitude of absolute accuracy to the laity, who are themselves rational moral agents searching for moral truth. If it becomes clear that a presumed authentic teaching is actually in error, the church must admit that Schüller's views on natural law, indicated in previous chapters, require the principle that individuals, as well as the magisterium, have access to knowledge about what is proper in the sphere of morality. By implication then, when the laity and individual theologians come to certainty that a decision by the magisterium is wrong, they are obligated to withdraw their consent to authorized teaching.

The distinctions drawn are not mechanically applicable to matters of dispute. Only the criteria for infallibility are clear and precise, and, as we noted, no moral teaching has been given that status. To many Catholics the distinction between an infallible and a noninfallible but authentic teaching has not been made clear. Once it is, and both laity and theologians accept a class of teachings to be "merely" authentic, to be accorded the presumption of truth but also the possibility of error, difficult choices abound around the legitimacy of dissent, the criteria used to judge its legitimacy, and subjective certitude about its rightness. Theologians have undertaken extensive discussion to clarify the theological, ecclesiological, ethical, and other principles required to distinguish between reasonable and unreasonable doubt about noninfallible moral teachings.

The role of professional theologians has been a matter of particular delicacy in the past decade. Richard A. McCormick, S.J., states a position on this issue in a carefully formulated response to Thomas Dubay's criticisms of Charles E. Curran and others.[88] He sets both the official magisterium and theologians in a wider framework, namely, "the teaching-learning process of the Church." The bishops and the theologians are both subordinate to the purpose of finding "the behavioral implications of our

being-in-Christ" and "moral truth." Thus it is proper "to speak
of a duty and right to exercise a truly personal reflection" within
that process; that is "a duty and right that belong to all who
possess proportionate competence." Neither theologians nor bishops are "exempt from this arduous task."[89] Indeed, as long as
the magisterium does its job well there are few occasions for
dissent. Theologians are fallible but surely have an obligation, as
participants in the teaching-learning process, to indicate errors
they detect in official teachings. In a sense there are two
teaching-learning offices in the church, the bishops and the
theologians, which serve the same purpose while having distinguishable functions.[90] It is a mistake, then, to charge, as
Dubay did, that theologians "are not sent" and therefore must,
as a matter of office, subordinate their teaching to official
authority.

A return to the questions developed above provides a way to
summarize this discussion of moral theology in the context of
ecclesiastical authority. Authentic noninfallible moral teachings
are to be given the presumption of truth. But since their
authenticity is based on the quality of their arguments, and not
just on the official authority of their promulgators, the arguments can be judged for their validity by others, particularly by
theologians. The competent arguments and teachings of theologians have authenticity in their own right. If McCormick is
correct, the teaching function of the church is a continuing
process of learning and teaching. I infer from this that also, in
relation to the laity, persuasion by the validity of arguments and
teachings, rather than recourse to institutional authority, is the
preferable way (perhaps the only proper way) to gain consent.
While the conditions of "proportionate competence" are not
delineated by McCormick, I take it that in principle those
conditions can be met by conscientious laity within the "teaching-learning process" and that conscientious informed dissent to
particular teachings is thereby legitimate. Also, it is apparent
that increased attention is being given to the special competence
of the laity in the development of moral teachings.

A generalization is warranted similar to those made in Chapters 2 and 3. Ecclesiologically, the Roman Catholic church is
moving from a position of clericalist authority to determine
moral truth that is binding (or received as such) on the laity to one
which permits, if it does not encourage, a greater measure of

tolerance of diversity in coming to moral "truth," in the forms of its dissemination, and in the conduct of church members. While moving in this direction, the presumption of authenticity to be accorded the official teachings provides a relatively solid baseline from which alternative teachings are to be distinguished only for good reasons. Surely social and historic factors play roles in this movement, but these are not my concern. The rhetoric of "people of God" and of the "pilgrim church" symbolizes an altered perception of the church which has implications for the authority of moral teachings as well as for the processes out of which they are formed.

Protestant leaders, in denominational and in ecumenical meetings, seem to desire more authority for their various teachings than many persons in that tradition find desirable. The presumption of instant authenticity (if not infallibility) that seems to accompany pronouncements on particular topics has little in the way of a theory of the church and its competencies to sustain it. The weight of authority primarily must be borne by the quality of the argument and the rhetoric; only secondarily do the degrees of competence and breadth of representation of those who write the pronouncements and who vote approval bear upon their reception. In my judgment there is an unspoken longing in Protestant church bodies, and Protestant-dominated ecumenical bodies, for greater authority for moral teachings. Plurality of theologies, ecclesiologies, moral opinions, and methods of ethical analysis all militate against the fulfillment of the longing.

Both traditions share a common practical problem, namely, how to form and inform the moral action of their members individually and collectively, or how to render McCormick's "learning-teaching process" more effective. Catholics are clearly attending to this, if one can judge from the interest in studies of moral development and from the number of publications addressed to the laity and to persons directly responsible for their education. Protestant efforts are not as noticeable, in part because there has been no dramatic change in church trends in the past two decades; many such efforts, however, do exist. The rapprochement can increase at least on a practical level. On the matter of doctrine of the church there also is manifestly more common ground now than earlier, in the recognition of the importance of the laity in Catholicism and in the use of more historical symbols for the church.[91]

The remaining task of this book is not so much to summarize these chapters as it is to point to some of the basic principles and structures that underlie both possibilities of rapprochement and continuing differences. To these even more formal considerations attention must now be given.

Basic Issues and Prospects
for the Future

In the three previous chapters an analysis has been made of the lines of convergence between Roman Catholic and Protestant ethics or, if that is too strong, of the bases on which some rapprochement between the traditions can develop. Also noted have been the points of continuing significant divergence, the issues that for various reasons remain intransigent. Although many generalizations were made, I remained quite close to the evidence drawn from the writings discussed, quoted, and cited. With reference to both Roman Catholics and Protestants, I indicated that some authors can be cited to support the generalizations developed. My purpose was not to develop irenic or optimistic views of developments for the sake of ecumenical sentiment or polemically to attack the Roman Catholic tradition. My Protestant heritage is no doubt evident, but those chapters were written in the conviction that there are deficiencies in both traditions and that both traditions must face some common questions in new ways. While representatives of traditions cannot be expected to shed their historically conditioned wraps or to deny that there are good reasons for past answers, nonetheless I believe that theological ethics (or moral theology) as a field can be developed in some fresh ways in common.

In this chapter, I move to another level of formality or

generalization before turning to more particular summary generalizations. On the basis of the previous chapters I can point to
certain even more underlying patterns which I shall develop in the
form of two theses. Then I shall develop six general theses which
point toward basic requirements for greater rapprochement
between the traditions. Finally I shall make some references to
the present state of affairs, recalling materials from the previous
three chapters, in order to indicate what the prospects for the
future are.

outline

Systematic Theological Ethics in General

In this and in other publications, I have attempted to show that
writings in theological ethics have certain base points, or certain
points of reference that are developed with some coherence or
that by virtue of incoherence are subject to criticism. Not many
writers of theological ethics have attempted to develop a comprehensive, coherent view that explicitly relates these principles or
base points to each other. Not many authors have articulated a
basic perspective, a unifying perception, intuition, concept,
symbol, or principle around which other considerations are
developed coherently, such as H. Richard Niebuhr's concept of
responsibility. My own attitude toward the development of
inclusive systems has itself been ambivalent. While I have been
concerned to inquire whether what a theologian says about *a*
coheres with what he or she says about *b, c, d,* and so forth, I
have had, and continue to have, doubts about the merits of a
theology which so rigorously systematizes its concepts that the
richness of Christian faith and of human experience become
oversimplified. The failure to press for comprehensiveness and
coherence, however, is a greater deficiency in contemporary
theological ethical writing than is the lack of richness. How
tightly systematic, how rigorously consistent, one expects a
theologian to be, is not a matter to be settled now. Here in a very
formal way, two basic theses about systematic theological ethics
are developed to suggest some of the criteria by which Catholic
and Protestant ethics can be tested, as well as future developments of ecumenical ethics!

The first thesis pertains to coherence. *The organizing perspec-*
tive, metaphor, analogy, or principle of any comprehensive theo-

logical ethics must be developed so that four distinguishable base
points, or points of reference, are coherently related to each other.[2]
These are: (a) the theological base in a restricted sense, that is, the
understanding and interpretation of God, the ultimate power and
value, his relations to the world and particularly to humans, and
his purposes, both "moral" and "nonmoral"; (b) the interpretation of the meaning or significance of human experience, of
historical life of the human community, of events and circumstances in which humans act, and of nature itself (in short, the
interpretation of the significance of the world, and of human life
in the world; (c) the interpretation of persons as moral agents and
their acts (for example their freedom and its limits); (d) the
interpretation of how persons *ought* to make moral choices and
judge their own actions, those of others, and the state of affairs
in the world (this includes the prescribed or recommended
procedures for choosing or judging as well as the normative principles and values used in choices and judgments).

A brief illustration can put sufficient flesh on these bones to
make the point of this thesis more intelligible. The writings of
Thomas Aquinas, in my judgment, present the most comprehensive and coherent (that is, systematic) account of theological
ethics in the history of Christianity. In an analysis of his thought
one can begin with any one of the four base points and find that
what he wrote about the other three is reasonably coherent with
it. The test is an elementary one; if he says x about d, can one
predict with some accuracy what he has to say about c, d, and a?
A brief sketch of the work of Thomas will be sufficient. With
reference to d, moral choices and judgments ought to be made
rationally in the light of moral principles and values which
protect and enhance the common good and the realization of the
potentialities of individuals. For example, recall his discussion of
suicide cited in Chapter 1. Suicide is morally wrong and is a sin.
Three reasons for this are that it violates the common good of the
community by depriving it of a member, it violates the natural
and proper love of the self which seeks its fulfillment, and it
denies that life is a gift given by God and under his sovereignty.[3]
Not only are the principles clear, but the reasons for them adduce
in a coherent way aspects of c, b, and a. With reference to c,
persons are directed by a basic desire to keep themselves in being;
thus there is a natural inclination toward their good which suicide
violates; they also have a freedom of will to act in accord with, or

to violate, this inclination toward the good. They can know what the real good is, formulate principles derived from it, and exercise their wills to protect it by not taking their lives. With reference to *b,* persons are a part of the whole creation (including society) which is oriented toward its well-being. With reference to *a,* God is the power who has graciously created all things so that they exit from him and return to him, their final good; thus the theological base is coherent with the principal aspects of the other three. The basic perception around which all four cohere is that of a teleological order. His epistemological views also cohere with what he says substantively. While this is too simple and sketchy, I believe it illustrates my thesis.

Within Protestant theology, Karl Barth has offered a comprehensive and roughly coherent account of ethics. His "actualist" view of God acting and speaking (*a*) coheres with his normative claim that moral acts ought to be done in obedience to God's commands (*d*); these roughly cohere with his notions of agents as covenant-partners with God, responsive and responsible to him (*c*), and with use of historical and relational analogies rather than analogies drawn from nature for interpreting life in the world (*b*). One of Barth's basic perceptions is that life is open and active; whether Barth would acknowledge this to be the formative intuitive perception or not, it brings the base points into coherence.[4]

At least a *prima facie* incoherence between these four bases, detected by inference or explicitly found in the writings of a single author, gives pause and requires a special explanation.

The data, information, ideas, and other "content" used in a comprehensive and coherent account of theological ethics are drawn from various sources. Two important judgments are made by the theologian in this regard. One is the choice he or she makes of the basic perspective: the unifying perception, intuition, concept, metaphor, analogy, symbol, or principle that organizes other "content." From the works of some authors this must be inferred; in others it is articulated; in still others it becomes apparent that a clear judgment has not been made. The second judgment is made by a theologian when he or she determines which sources are to be included as relevant and valid and which sources are to be excluded. For example, a judgment that only a vigorous application of the principle *sola scriptura* is proper sets strict limits to what can be appealed to in an argument. I indicated in previous chapters how various theologians use Scripture, and at what points (as in the four base points above) it is used; how various theologians use philosophical principles; and how they use data from various sciences or appeal to confirmation in human experience. These different sources are applicable in principle to each of the four base points, though for various reasons theologians have used certain sources for some points and others for other points. Thus we come to the second thesis about comprehensive and coherent theological ethics; in some respects this is a normative proposal and thus will not be as widely acceptable as the first. It is drawn from the materials analyzed, however, and thus is also a descriptive and analytical proposal. It is comparable to David Tracy's use of the term "relative adequacy."

The second thesis is one about judgments of adequacy, or about the relevance and validity of data, information, ideas, perceptions, and other aspects of the "content" used in the four base points. *A comprehensive and coherent Christian theological ethics must be adequate with reference to the following sources:* (a) the historically identifiable sources of Christian thought, that is, the Bible and the Christian tradition; (b) philosophical methods, insights, and principles; (c) scientific information and methods that are relevant and about which there is little dispute; and (d) human experience broadly conceived, including the consequences of the theological ethics when applied to human action. I repeat: *judgments* are made about these sources. These are judgments about (a) which sources are valid and relevant; (b) which sources are to be decisive when they conflict, and why; (c) what specific "content" is to be taken and what to be ignored from these sources, and why; and (d) how this "content" is to be interpreted and why it is interpreted as it is.

It is apparent that judgments about the validity and relevance of sources are extemely difficult to make, particularly if a theologian has chosen to use a wide variety of materials. (Almost all theologians writing in ethics do use all the above sources, implicitly if not explicitly; thus the thesis is a descriptive and analytical one, and not a purely normative proposal.) Since these judgments by different theologians are based on different factors —for example, a fundamental intuition, strict creedal principles, or commitments to a philosophical tradition—disputes about them are extremely difficult to adjudicate. This is truer about

Protestantism than about the Roman Catholic tradition. In instances of more systematic theological ethics the author has decided which of the above four sources is most authoritative or decisive and has provided reasons for this choice. This decision is extremely important, for other sources are tested for their relevance and validity by this source, and the theologian's system then coheres around this source.

For example, Karl Barth's ethics (and his theology) are formed by a judgment that Scripture determines the relevance, validity, and interpretation of other sources. (To be sure, there are theological and perhaps philosophical principles which determine his interpretation of Scripture.) The Bible is the primary and normative source; other sources can be used (or "annexed") insofar as they cohere with his biblical theology. When one compares Barth with Schleiermacher, it is apparent that Scripture and Christian tradition do not have the same normative function in the latter. I would argue that Schleiermacher uses a basically organic metaphor to interpret human experience which in turn determines the relevance, the validity, and the interpretation of other sources, including the interpretation of Scripture. Christian ethics describes the activity of those who are within the Kingdom of God; like a seed planted and nourished, so faith grows and spreads and is expressed in the moral activity of Christians. From these sketchy examples, I believe one can see that judgments about which sources, and about which interpretive principles, are normative determine the relevance, validity, and interpretation of other sources.

The two theses are clearly interrelated, and the interrelation takes different forms in different theologians. It follows from a determination of which *source* is finally decisive what much of the content of the base points will be in a coherent theological ethics (note Barth's use of Scripture as primary in all the base points). It often follows from which of the base points is judged to be central, for example, a doctrine of God, what sources are judged relevant and valid and how they are coherently related. In looser accounts the interrelationship between the two theses is more complex and is often confused.

In my judgment, many of the reformist or revisionist materials discussed in the previous chapters are only loosely systematic; Karl Rahner's work is the clearest exception. This is not to claim they are drastically at fault, for in a transitional period when

moral theologians (Protestant and Catholic) are correcting perceived errors in their traditions there has not been time for the
maturation of more comprehensive and coherent accounts. Yet,
while intellectual modesty is a virtue, and one particularly
appropriate to us with modest talents and limited learning, it is
fair to press for greater comprehensiveness and greater coherence. We must ask ourselves: if I say x about base point d, and
primarily use b sources, what are the implications for what I will
say about base points, a, b, and c, and how I will say it; and how
will I then use sources a, c, and d? These two theses do provide a
way to assess what the state of affairs is in a Christian ethics
today and a way to make some more precise observations about
what issues remain within each tradition and between them.

Prospective Rapprochement between Catholic
and Protestant Ethics

Theses will again be used to make critical observations about the
materials previously introduced in order to indicate the prospects
for rapprochement between the traditions. Some of these are
observations of a generally empirical sort; others involve more
critical analysis; and in some my personal judgment is crucial.
The sequence of the theses is from the more general to the more
specific, and from the more descriptive to the prescriptive.

The first thesis is a retrospective observation about certain
fundamental characteristics of the recently published materials
discussed in this book. *Reconstructive or revisionist proposals
made by Roman Catholic and Protestant moral theorists address
explicitly or implicitly the following traditional and persistent
polarities*: being and becoming, structure and process, order and
dynamics, continuity and change, determination and freedom,
nature and history, nature and grace, law and gospel.

To claim that all of the first terms have the same reference, or
that all of the second terms do, would be patently false. Gospel
and change do not necessarily have a common reference any more
than do law and being. Yet this thesis is warranted by vague but
significant similarities in the functions of the polarities in the
literature. The vague similarity of function is that these polarities
are used to account for two distinguishable but related concerns,
neither of which authors are willing to give up. These terms have
a similar reference to more persistent and generalized, or univer-

sal, characteristics of "things" (and different sort of things—the
nature of all that is, individual human persons, principles of
moral conduct) on the one hand, and to more changeable and
particularistic aspects of "things" on the other hand.

Some examples will illustrate this. (I do not attempt to adduce
sufficient evidence to demonstrate the validity of the observation
here since its importance for subsequent theses is suggestive
rather than decisive.)[5] Richard A. McCormick is concerned to
account for persistent and unchanging moral principles as well as
extensions if not alterations of some principles; thus he uses the
language of being and becoming in his crucial statement that
man's being "charts" (perhaps an intentionally ambiguous word)
his becoming. David Little is implicitly, but I believe clearly,
impressed with the historical and other evidences for diversity
and change in moral behavior, but is not satisfied that radical
moral relativism is fitting either as an empirical generalization or
as a basis for normative ethics. Thus he uses materials and ideas
developed by cultural anthropologists and others to establish his
own "empirical generalization" about what constitutes humanity;
this, he believes, points to constants both across space (cross-
culturally) and through time. In turn, "to be human is to order
life cooperatively" becomes the basis for specifying "the conditions for social cooperation," which I presume can differ across
space and time.

Karl Rahner faced a received tradition that justified a defensive posture toward innovation, and an ethics of extrinsic authority requiring conformity to its rules; these were defended on the
basis of an interpretation of nature that implied severe limits to
human freedom. In his reconstructive response, he argues that
human nature, in one sense, is characterized by a radical
transcendental freedom; he does not forget, however, that in
another sense human nature is subject to biological necessities.
And, even from the aspect of transcendental freedom, he can
determine universal principles which judge and direct human
conduct.

Paul Ramsey faced a received tradition that was pragmatically
responding to changing courses of events, and thus often was not
only unclear about what made a course of action morally proper
but also was haphazard and inconsistent in its justifications of
judgments. His response is not to deny historical particularity and
change but to develop a method and substance of Christian ethics

that can be used in all similar circumstances, and to ground these rules in more basic, comprehensive theological norms.

Since the purpose of this thesis is to indicate the implicit or explicit use of traditional polarities and to claim only a vague, but nonetheless significant, similarity in function of the first terms and of the second terms, further illustration would be redundant.

The second thesis is an observation about general tendencies which distinguish the Catholic from the Protestant authors in most of the contemporary materials used in this book. *Reconstructive Catholic writers are generally and characteristically attempting to take greater cognizance of the second terms in the polarities*; they are moving toward becoming, process, dynamics, change, freedom, history, grace, and gospel. (Certainly in popular liberal or reformist Catholic literature and speeches these are commonly heard words.) *Reconstructive Protestant writers are generally and characteristically attempting to include the significance of the first terms in the polarities*: being, structure, order, continuity, determination, nature, and law. (One can hardly, however, point to a popular use of these terms among Protestant church leaders or a recognizable party of laity.) As with all generalizations about Protestantism, this is difficult to substantiate, and even within its range of validity Protestant authors take the first terms into account in very different ways.

Since this thesis is rather explicit in Chapters 2 and 3, and can be supported by the discussion in Chapter 4, my illustrations of it can be brief. Bernard Häring writes about an "open" as distinguished from a "closed" morality, and about a dynamic and personalistic view of natural law. Charles E. Curran rejects the "physicalist" interpretation of nature for one that is more personal and historical. Robert Johann proposes an ethics of "creative responsibility." John Giles Milhaven contrasts the "classical" view of the world with the "modern," the latter being focussed on the experiential and the historical, and chooses it as a basis for his normative proposals. William Van Der Marck uses the more personalistic terms of existential phenomenology: intersubjectivity, authenticity, historicity, and so forth. From the Protestant side, the comments on Little and Ramsey made to illustrate the first thesis pertain here. Gibson Winter works to disclose the "essential structure of sociality"; Stanley Hauerwas develops a theory of character, and Gene Outka uses the principle of universalizability to make the term *agape* function more rigorously and consistently.

Apparently the penchant for stating polarities and relating the terms dialectically, which characterized so much of Protestant theology in the middle of the century, is disappearing. In the works used in this book no author says that humans are both destined and free, and then relates freedom and destiny dialectically; that humans live under law and under gospel, and then relates the terms dialectically; and so forth. I know of no authors who have consciously discarded this way of thinking and thus of no material that argues for its being in error, or even deficient. One can only infer from its decline that it is presumed to be deficient and that efforts are required to give some clearer resolution of the tensions that the poles of the dialectic provocatively indicate. Hauerwas' use of action theory from contemporary philosophy is an example; he implicitly, if not explicitly, judges that a statement that humans are both part of a determinate order of nature and free would be insufficiently precise; he finds in action theory sources for a more refined argument with a nondialectical structure.

Writers in each tradition work in patterns of basic continuity between the terms of the traditional polarities as much as they can. Analysis suggests that many authors have a reasoned primary allegiance to one pole and qualify its implications as they move toward the other. McCormick does not give up being for becoming. Milhaven chooses the second pole (history, experience) as a starting point for at least rhetorical purposes but qualifies it with elements of the first. Even Ramsey, at least in his *War and the Christian Conscience* (1961), while arguing for rigorous use of deontological ethics and "in-principled *agape*" continued to allow for moments of spontaneity in his theory of Christian love. The decline of a dialectical pattern forces a specification of issues in a more refined way. It is not hard to find many persons who would agree that humans are both "free and determined"; it requires more precise argument to make a case for how the more determinate aspects do and do not qualify "free action" to resolve the apparent paradox. Since Catholic theology traditionally has not been dialectical in the sense in which the term is used here, the change is more significant for Protestants; indeed, it can be suggested that certain presupposed ground rules for continuing discussions have been accepted which are more historically characteristic of Roman Catholic than of recent Protestant, especially neo-orthodox, theology.

In moving from one set of terms to the other, both Catholics and Protestants are locating the discussion along lines that draw *continuities* between the terms of the polarities. This, in my judgment, makes the requisite reconstructive work more difficult and demanding but also more worthwhile. (It also means that many persons in the churches of both traditions will disparage the requisite work as "academic," "knit-picking," "tedious," and unrelated to the burning issues of the day.)[6]

The third thesis in this section is an assessment of the general reason for the characteristic directions in which Catholics and Protestants are moving. (By now I hope I need not constantly qualify "Catholics" and "Protestants" with reminders that the terms refer only to the materials discussed in previous chapters.) *The directions of the movements are primarily defended on the basis of the inadequacy* (questioning the validity and the relevance) *of the substance of the arguments* (data, theories, principles, procedures and judgments) *made by authors who are part of the recent past in each tradition.* They are *not* defended on the basis of a judgment that the received traditions are *incoherent.* Put differently, revisions of received tradition are given warrants derived from judgments about the deficiencies in the substance of previous writings more than from judgments about their forms. The way Scripture was used is not valid or not relevant, therefore, it is inadequate. The way that essentially philosophical arguments were used, to show how moral choices and judgments were made, was deficient; the theories of the person were not adequate to contemporary conceptions derived from the human sciences; positions were inadequate to "experience," and so forth. The question of whether there is a basically coherent and comprehensive development of the four base points around a fundamental outlook, perception, intuition, or principle has seldom been directly raised. The question of whether a particular fundamental outlook (perception, intuition, symbol, analogy, or principle) is itself valid has more frequently been raised by Roman Catholics (classical "being" versus modern "historical" or personalistic outlooks), but apart from Rahner's work a systematic statement of both a revised central principle or perception and its coherent development has not occurred. (Intellectual giants, geniuses with

wide learning, are, after all, as rare in theology as in philosophy
and other fields.) In this exceptional case, it is fitting to observe,
Rahner developed first a fundamental, coherent theory which he
has spent much of his efforts applying and testing ever since. Put
in summary form, the criticisms of received traditions have been
primarily made on the basis of the second thesis (the "adequacy"
thesis) of the previous section of this chapter rather than on the
basis of the first (the "coherence" thesis).

To make this third thesis more intelligible I have already
illustrated it. Further illustrations might be useful. The criticisms
of Pope Paul's *Humanae Vitae* are one source. I know of no
arguments that charge that it did not coherently relate elements I
have indicated as the four base points. There are criticisms which
point to the inadequacy of the basic principle which provides the
coherence, a "biologistic" view of natural law. The principal
error is that it does not have an adequate account of the nature of
humans as "persons." Other criticisms pertain to additional
inadequacies in the encyclical: while it notes such factors as
population growth, the changing status of women, and new
medical technology, it does not take these factors into account
sufficiently. From the papal point of view, they are not valid
considerations for the moral argument and therefore not relevant
to it; from the viewpoints of some critics, they are.

Other illustrations can be drawn from the previous chapters.
Joseph Fuchs is concerned to show that many of the natural law
moralists did not adequately develop the theological foundation of
their argument and its biblical warrants, and that Protestant
charges that natural law is unbiblical can be rebutted on biblical
grounds. Häring is concerned to show that moral theologians have
tended to neglect the reality of conversion as this is developed in the
Johannine and Pauline literature; and thus their arguments have
been inadequate. Curran and Milhaven have been concerned to
show that insights and information about homosexuality and
masturbation drawn from contemporary sciences have some
validity and therefore are relevant to moral judgments on these
activities. Ramsey's most basic polemic has been against the moral
philosophical inadequacies of much of Protestant ethical literature. Both Catholics and Protestants have made adequacy to
"experience" a test.

Most of the criticisms of adequacy have been directed to
materials used in developing one or another of the four base points;

fewer have been directed to the basic perception, principle, or outlook around which the base points can cohere. Thus, on the whole, the criticisms have been piecemeal and have not pursued these questions: if the sources used to develop base point *d* are inadequate philosophically, what are the implications of my revision (1) for what I say with reference to base points *a, b,* and *c* (thesis one in the previous section); (2) for how I use sources *a, c,* and *d* (thesis two in the previous section); and (3) for the basic principle, perception, or outlook around which all my work coheres?

The fourth thesis in this section provides some explanation of why the third thesis is warranted and also suggests some further implications of it. *Rapprochement between traditions is easier to achieve with reference to more limited and special areas that can be tested for adequacy* (as in the use of psychological information about homosexuality) *than it is to achieve between the basic organizing principles or perceptions around which the base points cohere.* Consensus can occur on particular moral judgments without rapprochement on a basic organizing principle and perception or on how a comprehensive account could be organized around such a principle. An illustration will make the thesis clearer. Some Roman Catholics and Protestants might agree on certain rights of children because they can agree on certain relevant data and certain moral principles or human values; the same writers will have greater difficulty in coming to an agreement about whether H. Richard Niebuhr's concept of responsibility is a better organizing principle for a more systematic ethics than is the classic teleological principle. The former is easier to accomplish; also the particular practical matters are often more urgent and thus receive more attention.

My intention is not to denigrate the positive significance in the order of immediate practicality of consensus on more limited matters. Nor do I believe that agreement on limited matters entails, or requires a search for, agreement on a more comprehensive moral theory. The concern of this book, however, is with theological ethics, with moral theory, and thus it is appropriate to state this thesis.

In the actual discussions involving Catholics and Protestants in the United States there is an outstanding illustration of this thesis.[7] Paul Ramsey's particular judgments about moral matters in medicine, for example, on abortion, on research which uses fetal

life, and on euthanasia, are well-received by many Catholic moral
theologians, physicians, and laity. They find his policy recommendations to be congenial and agree with the more immediately
applicable rules and principles. These are not in dispute from their
perspective. Ramsey's own more general principle that provides
both authorization for his judgments and coherence to his ethical
thought can be stated, for purposes of brevity, as agape, Christian
love in the form of "covenant fidelity" between persons—physician
and patient, parents and child, and so forth. Here one finds terms,
patterns of thought, and concepts that are foreign to traditional
Roman Catholic moral theology. Yet except for Charles E.
Curran's writings on Ramsey there has been little published
discussion by Catholics of this divergence. In terms of the present
thesis, many Catholics and Ramsey agree on the immorality of
certain medical practices; they agree that arguments in favor of the
opposing judgments are "inadequate" or, more strongly, wrong.
Catholics find Ramsey's moral judgments on these matters, the
data he uses to understand the circumstances of action, the
evaluative interpretation of them, the principles and rules immediately applicable, all to be at least relatively adequate. If,
however, one presses for a more comprehensive theological and
moral theory, if one examines the moral general principles used to
validate or vindicate the matters on which there is a common
judgment of adequacy, clear and sharp divergences become
apparent. Ramsey's model for Christian ethics, as we have seen, is
basically deontological; while consequences are important, what
makes a medical act morally right or wrong is judged by the
"canons of loyalty" between the covenant-partners involved. His
model is not the basically teleological one that is used to support
traditional Catholic arguments. The authorization of Ramsey's
view of love "in-principled" in covenant-partnership is primarily
"revelational," though he also appeals to common human experience. It is not natural law in the classic Roman Catholic sense.
Although Ramsey has adopted, developed, and even refined
certain moral principles and procedures that have their historic
home in the natural law tradition, in my judgment he does not have
a theory of natural law but engrafts his principles into his own
biblical theological model.

The rapprochement is very limited. Any really significant
convergence between the theological ethical traditions requires
examination of the more general issues on which there is clear

disagreeement. An agenda can easily be established. It would follow three lines. First, one can extend the questions of *adequacy* to Ramsey's sources. Are his moral principles validly grounded from a Catholic perspective? Is his reliance on the Bible adequate? Is it sufficiently supported by argument? Is the use he makes of Scripture valid? (Compare Josef Fuchs' use of the Bible to authorize natural law theory.) Second, are the central organizing concepts around which the rest of Ramsey's ethics are developed adequate? Is love as covenant fidelity valid and relevant as the basic substantive principle? Is his deontology the right way to organize ethics coherently? Third, does Ramsey provide a comprehensive and coherent account of the four base points? Are there strains in the coherence of those points that he does develop?

This is not meant to discount Ramsey's significance or the cogency of his writings? His work and the reception of it by many Roman Catholics nicely illustrates this fourth thesis, namely, that it is easier to come to agreement between the traditions on the adequacy of more limited areas than it is to settle questions of the basic perspective which ought to provide the substance and form of a coherent and comprehensive account of theological ethics.[8] Not every Catholic and Protestant moral theologian must become a comprehensive systematizer, but more attention needs to be given to the more intransigent issues for the sake of possible greater rapprochement.

The fifth thesis of this section pertains to the central perspectives. *There is apparent consensus among the revisionist Protestants and Catholics that two extreme perspectives which provided coherence to major works in the past are in error:* an occasionalist view of ethics correlated with an "actualist" view of God's presence in the world commanding persons in "the moment"; a view of an immutable, "static" moral order fully knowable by human reason from which principles can be derived which are applicable by strict deduction to all relevant circumstances. Each of these perspectives can provide a coherent and comprehensive development of theological ethics; they are rejected because they are not valid or have limited relevance to various areas that must be taken into account.

As stated these extremes are caricatures of positions. Regarding the first, Barth has his practical casuistry, his "spheres" within which the command of God is heard and God's command is bound by his grace. Paul Lehmann has God acting to make and keep life human, and thus "humanization" functions as a persistent norm. Regarding the second extreme, only the most theoretically unsophisticated manualist in moral theology would really fit the type. Even these qualifications bear on the thesis: the writings that represent the extremes are themselves qualified to take into account more moderate positions.

Elimination of opposite extreme positions leaves more than ample space for disagreement. The reasons for the elimination, however, help to set the agenda of issues on which discussion can take place. There is no need to rehearse these again here; they are extensively discussed in previous chapters. My judgment is that, with reference to all four of the base points, the reasons pertain to finding the best way to account for the elements of the polarities listed in the first thesis of this section. If God, for example, can no longer be said to have created an immutable, static moral order, and if there are reasons to raise questions about the "classical" view of God as immutable, so also there are reasons to question whether it is sensible to speak of God as sheer dyamic potency in the world without a persisting "structure" or characteristic purposes. Or, with reference to base point *b*, while it is still meaningful to write about persistent patterns of order in the world, account must be taken of not only historical changes but also of natural evolution. At each base point the problem is how to conceptualize the point so that the two poles are satisfactorily accounted for, and then how to relate the base points coherently.

These issues are not novel, as we noted in the first thesis of this section. What is notable is a willingness, adduced in previous chapters, on the part of authors in both traditions either to attempt some fresh approaches to the issues or freely to alter received traditions when they tended too much toward the two extremes.

The final thesis involves both a prediction and an imperative that arises from it. *Any more fundamental convergence will occur only when there is more consensus on the basic outlook, principle, or metaphor that is appropriate to Christian theological ethics* that will provide the center for a comprehensive, coherent view. The imperative inferred from this follows. *Moral theologians must attend more to the analytically descriptive task that will indicate whether such consensus is emerging, and they must have the courage to develop proposals for the articulation and development of those indications.*

To propose this imperative is not to be optimistic about the possibilities of its fulfillment. Theology, like other intellectual work, is bound to cultures and historical trends. Also, in the service of the Christian community it becomes a practical virtue to fashion theological ethics that aid in making judgments about current states of affairs and give guidance to action in specific cirucumstances. Different theological themes are elevated to positions of primacy by different theologians, and reasons from Scripture and other sources are given in support of such choices. Agreement is notoriously difficult to achieve on whether Christian ethics is primarily to be governed by an eschatalogical principle or by one of a logos Christology, for example.

The imperative remains, however, in spite of these and many other observations that make its fulfillment impossible. While *uniformity* in theological ethics is no more desirable (and possible) than it is in other areas of Christian thought, a failure to seek consensus on important matters leaves the criteria for good ethics excessively subjective and pluralistic. I do *not* intend even to suggest, not to mention argue, that there is one *objectively true* system of theological ethics in the sense that its concepts would correspond to the "realities" to which the concepts of theological ethics are related. I do insist that, apart from a lure and an imperative to become more coherent and comprehensive, Roman Catholics and Protestants may be arguing over false issues, or agreeing on immediate practical issues and ignoring important intellectual issues. Also, apart from this imperative the temptation to find seemingly plausible reasons to support what are insufficiently examined moral sensitivities becomes exceedingly strong. Contemporary Protestants and Catholics are demonstrably eager to find immediately relevant reasons to justify their moral impulses without testing these reasons in a more comprehensive and coherent framework.

The imperative also arises from the common faith that finally is the human unity of the Christian community. That faith has never issued in uniformity of theological ethics. The arguments between the Apostle Paul and the Jerusalem Christians, while fundamentally theological and religious, were also arguments over the authority of Torah in Christian conduct. Similar issues have been persistent in the church ever since. Nonetheless, to be easily satisfied with diversities of theological ethics without confronting some common normative beliefs which express and nurture the common faith is an embarrassment within the life of the Christian community. At least Christian theologians ought to be clear about what they agree on, and why; where their disagreements are, and why; and to seek the criteria by which their disagreements can be overcome. This pertains to theological ethics as well as other areas; my judgment is that more work is needed on these matters for the sake of the unity of the ethically fragmented Christian church.[9]

If developments take place in ecumenical rapprochement they can likely take different forms. From much of the material analyzed one sees that the move toward a unifying principle, concept, or metaphor is likely to be made incrementally; that is, after establishing a more satisfactory view of a particular point, the author begins to see an implicit, ordering principle which then is applied to other points. Usually, the judgment about what central principle, metaphor, or concept is to order the account is not made first and then worked out with reference to the base points. Rather, it is more likely that a person will establish, for example, a view of natural law that is more dynamic and developmental, and then proceed to elucidate the implications of this for how choices ought to be made, for a theory of the moral agent, and for a doctrine of God. In some comprehensive treatments of theological ethics, or moral theology, the incremental developments never quite yield a clear organizing principle, concept, or metaphor; the various aspects of the account are not quite coherent and the whole appears eclectic. This is the case in Bernard Häring's *Law of Christ*.

Other authors are likely to make proposals for a principle, a concept, or a metaphor which in turn will be applied to the materials of a comprehensive account. We have noted how Rahner developed a philosophical theology and anthropology which in turn is tested and applied. H. Richard Niebuhr's concept and symbol of responsibility is clearly proposed in *The Responsible Self* to be the most adequate one for organizing a view of moral experience; it coheres with his view of God's action, his view of agency, and his view of decision-making. There is a sense in which "political theology" is making a proposal for a new organizing principle. For example, Dorothee Soelle states, "Political theology is ... a theological hermeneutic which ... holds open an horizon of interpretation in which politics is understood as the comprehensive and decisive sphere in which Christian truth should become praxis."[10] The consequence of this is that politics is not only the sphere to be theologically interpreted but it also provides clues to interpreting theological language, the social world, and making of choices.

Already it is clear that tentative consensus is being established by moral theologians on certain points which cross the traditional confessional lines. Some Roman Catholics have more in common in theological ethics with some Protestants than they do with other Catholics; some Protestants have more in common with some Roman Catholics than they do with other Protestants. Whether these interesting beginnings develop significantly depends on many factors, not least of which is the effort to do so. If they develop with cogency, it will not be because ecumenical sentiment is embodied but because criteria of "adequacy" and "coherence" are better met.

Prospective Rapprochement in Relation to Recent Literature

To state the boundaries within which rapprochement can be substantiated in recent literature is to court two faults: repetition of what has already been developed and generalizations so broad as to be dull. In risking these faults, I intend to suggest some elements for the future agenda.

1. Practical moral reasoning. Two extremes have been rejected as inadequate by most of the revisionist authors: an occasionalistic intuitionism and a rationalism that resolves choices by simple deductive logic. Within these margins it can be said that the exercise of practical moral reasoning is highly commended for making discriminating moral analyses and for directing moral choices and making moral judgments. At the same time there seems to be some consensus that the basic orientations of persons, affecting their dispositions and sensibilities, also have a proper function in practical moral life. The criteria by which the rejected extremes are judged inadequate and the broad consensus more adequate relate to much of the previous discussion, which I will not repeat here.

There is great divergence within the broad consensus. For some the moral principles used in practical reasoning are to be tested primarily by the formal principles of universalizability or generalizability, for others they are to be tested primarily by their adequacy to the "isness" of moral values grounded in human nature. For some the principles and rules are to be established as unexceptionable; others defend general rules with exceptions or even less binding "summary rules" that give insight to a new moment of choice. For some the "positive" biblical norms (general ones like love or more specific action guides) have greater authority than they have for others. For some a greater degree of rational moral certitude is expected from moral reasoning than it is for others. There are differences of opinion on the reliability of character, dispositions, virtues in the moment of moral discernment or choice.

Further discussion of these matters will involve clearer elucidation of the criteria of adequacy used in various proposals. Are the proposals valid and relevant with reference to human experience, behavioral science data, the canons of good logic, the Christian tradition, and so forth?

2. *Philosophical bases of theological ethics.* There is a broad consensus that some aspects of what I have called historicism and existentialism have to be taken into account; at the same time theological ethics must establish a way of developing general moral principles and values from common human experience.

Discussion continues on what are the adequate grounds for these principles and values. Some want "ontologically strong" grounding in a view of Being, some find empirical generalizations or phenomenological perceptions of the "structures of experience" to be sufficient. Some are persuaded that a hierarchy of values can be established philosophically, others are less certain. Whether the principles and values established can be confidently stated to be "absolute," "almost absolute," or something weaker is not settled. Just how historical and individual experience is to be handled is subject to dispute: are particularities to be "overcome" because they are divisive, partial, and distorting? Or do they contribute something of value to moral life? Do the general principles and values determine with great specificity what actions or states of affairs are proper, or do they provide "moral requisites" which are actualized in diverse ways in different social conditions and personal relations? Are moral agents to be understood as basically determined by an order of human "nature" (in a strong sense of determination), or are they to be understood to be radically "free." What is the relation between

"nature" and "freedom," and how do various answers affect
ethics? What are the criteria that determine which sources one
draws from to answer these questions?

   3. Theological bases of ethics. With some hesitation I suggest
that there is growing consensus on a view of God as a gracious
ordering dynamic presence and power in nature and in history
whose being and purpose are not fully known or disclosed. The
"classical" view of God as immutable and impassible, as not
involved in time and history, seems to be on the wane. For ethics
one consequence of this is that discovery of God's purpose
continues through human experience in time. I also suggest, with
equal hesitation, that there is some consensus on the priority of
grace over "nature" and that this leads to an ethical outlook that
is affirmative of nature and history without denying the necessity
for order, the reality of evil, and the distortions of human sin.

   At issue is the doctrine of God, an area in which moral
theologians have with proper modesty not made many judgments.
Unfortunately (though it may also reflect proper modesty) few
systematic theologians have spelled out the implications of their
doctrines of God for ethics. Comprehensive theological ethics,
however, cannot avoid asking the question: what is the most
adequate doctrine of God?   This includes questions about
Scripture, experience, and many other "sources."

   It is safer to suggest that Scripture has been incorporated into
Catholic ethics both theologically and morally in a way that
provides a new basis of discussion with Protestants. Many issues
remain outstanding. Does Scripture "ground" a natural law
theory? What are the proper hermeneutical principles for using
the Bible in theological ethics?

   In ecclesiology, it seems to me that the basis of commonality is
in viewing the church to be a moral teacher and a community of
moral formation, to be a pedagogue and counselor more than a
judge. As we have seen, the matter of the "authority" of the
church is under debate in both traditions.

   My aspiration is that the earlier, even more formal proposals
made in this chapter will help to sort out the criteria by which
judgments can be made, and thus foster the prospects for
ecumenical Christian ethics, particularly among the authors
whose writings contributed most of what is discussed in the
previous three chapters. The intent, I reiterate, is not to embody
ecumenical sentiment or to find a lowest common denominator.

It is to move toward a more comprehensive and coherent account of Christian ethics which has been tested in its parts and as a whole for its validity with reference to relevant sources. To say the least, Roman Catholics and Protestants share common questions that provide the agenda for Christian ethics; they also share a perplexity about how to answer them, and they increasingly share a common set of considerations to be taken into account in answering them. As long as theologians continue to write about ethics and morals (social as well as individual), and as long as moralists claim to represent the Christian tradition, the more systematic questions must be pressed. This is surely the case in contemporary ecumenical discussions.

Notes

1   Historic Divergences

1. Three recent books focus on the relations of Roman Catholic and Protestant ethics directly. Franz Böckle, *Law and Conscience* (New York: Sheed and Ward, 1966); Böckle is an important German Roman Catholic moral theologian. Roger Mehl, *Catholic Ethics and Protestant Ethics* (Philadelphia: Westminster Press, 1971); Mehl is a French Protestant. Both of these deal with basic theological issues in some depth. William A. Spurrier, *Natural Law and the Ethics of Love* (Philadelphia: Westminster, 1974), attempts a synthesis; it is so brief in its theological sections as to be only an outline and goes on to apply the synthesis to some practical moral problems. Josef Fuchs, S.J., of Rome, in his *Natural Law: A Theological Investigation* (New York: Sheed and Ward, 1965), develops his constructive argument in part in relation to the work of Karl Barth, Emil Brunner, and Helmut Thielicke, and has directed a number of dissertations by Catholics on figures and topics in Protestant ethics. One with which I am acquainted is Philipp Schmitz, S.J., *Die Wirklichkeit Fassen* (Frankfurt: Josef Knecht, 1972), a study of recent American and British Protestant ethics. See also, Charles E. Curran, "Moral Theology: The Present State of the Discipline," *Theological Studies* 34 (1973):446-47.

2. Examples of twentieth-century Anglican work are K. E. Kirk, *Conscience and Its Problems* (London: Longmans, Green, 1927), and *Some Principles of Moral Theology and Their Application* (London: Longmans, Green, 1920). See also Her-

bert Waddams, *A New Introduction to Moral Theology* (New York: Seabury, 1964).

3. See Thomas Aquinas, *Summa Theologica,* II-II, Q. 154, art. 11, and art. 12. Masturbation is in the class of "unnatural" vices (art. 11) which are the gravest sins "with regard to the use of venereal actions"; "simple fornication, which is committed without injustice to another person, is the least grave among the species of lust" (art. 12).

4. Ibid., Q. 26, art. 9. Question 26, "Of The Order of Charity," can be set to make a striking contrast with historic and contemporary Protestant discussions of love.

5. One of the most remarkable recent exceptions is Karl Barth. See his *Church Dogmatics* III/4 (Edinburgh: T & T Clark, 1961), pp. 397–470.

6. See, for example, the following words of a modern pope: "the Church, the pillar and ground of truth, and the unerring teacher of morals" (Leo XIII, "On Human Liberty," 35 [1888], in Etienne Gilson, ed., *The Church Speaks to the Modern World: The Social Teachings of Leo XIII* [Garden City: Doubleday Image Books, 1954], p. 78).

7. The differences between Protestant and Jewish views of authority have been vast and of great importance. Warrants for moral/legal arguments in the halakhic tradition are indeed complex. Biblical texts have primary authority, but any well constructed article cites the Talmud, the legal codes, and the interpretations of revered rabbis through the centuries. For two discussions, see Boaz Cohen, *Law and Tradition in Judaism* (New York: Jewish Theological Seminary, 1959), especially pp. 1–61, and Jacob Neusner, "What is Normative in Jewish Ethics?" *Judaism* 16 (1967):3–20.

8. Denominational statements on abortion in recent years provide excellent examples of the plurality of appeals to support a particular position; seldom are any historical theologians cited.

9. See, for examples, Question 26 on the order of charity, and Question 64, "Of Murder." Question 64, article 5, on suicide is a striking example. Suicide is a sin, that is, it is morally wrong, principally for three reasons, two from natural law and one from Christian theology. It violates the principle of nature that "everything naturally keeps itself in being" and the social principle that "every part, as such, belongs to the whole" (thus a suicide deprives the community of a member); it also is against the biblical theme that life is a gift of God, and under his reign only he can determine when it should end.

10. Both religious and moral rules and duties were developed in detail. The manuals of moral theology are replete with examples that can be used as evidence for the most negative interpretation. See, for example, the discussion of what a Catholic nurse

can and cannot do for a Protestant patient. "It is not, as a general rule, permitted to Catholic nurses in hospitals to send for non-Catholic ministers to attend non-Catholic patients for religious purposes; they must be passive in such cases.... This was further explained ... to mean that nurses might tell some non-Catholic attendant that a patient wanted the non-Catholic minister, and this was declared not to be active cooperation" (Henry Davis, S.J., *Moral and Pastoral Theology,* 4 vols. [New York: Sheed and Ward, 1935], 1:284). Another example is "a theological conversation piece" assembled by John J. Lynch, S.J., "pertaining to extraordinary means of administering the Holy Eucharist to those who are sick and unable to receive Communion in customary fashion" (Lynch, "Notes on Moral Theology," *Theological Studies* 26 [1955]:278-79). It is no wonder that "excessive scrupulosity" sometimes was a problem!

11. Philip Melanchthon, "Apology of the Augsburg Confession," Article II (Original Sin), in Theodore G. Tappert, ed., *The Book of Concord* (Philadelphia: Muhlenberg Press, 1959), pp. 101, 102.

12. John Calvin, *Institutes of the Christian Religion,* bk. II, chap. 1, sec. 8; in John T. McNeill, ed., *Institutes,* 2 vols. (Philadelphia: Westminster Press, 1960), 1:251.

13. Paul Althaus, *The Ethics of Martin Luther* (Philadelphia: Fortress, 1972), p. 1. "Luther's ethics is determined in its entirety, in its starting point and all its main features, by the heart and center of his theology, namely, by justification of the sinner through the grace that is shown in Jesus Christ and received through faith alone. Justification by faith determines Christian ethics because, for the Christian, justification is both the presupposition and the source of the ethical life."

14. The cursory fashion in which this is done is excusable, I hope, in view of the intention of this chapter, namely, to note historic differences between Catholic and Protestant ethics only to set a context for the contemporary situation.

15. Richard Hooker (1554-1600), *Of The Laws of Ecclesiastical Polity,* 2 vols. (London: Dent, 1954), "The First Book," 1:147-232.

16. Thomas Aquinas, *Summa Theologica,* II-II, Q. 106, art. 1.

17. Ibid., Q. 107, art. 2. The well-known discussion of law is contained, *in toto,* in qqs. 90-108.

18. Luther, *Lectures on Galatians* (1535), on Gal. 3:19, in Jaroslav Pelikan, ed., *Luther's Works,* vol. 26 (St. Louis: Concordia Publishing House, 1963), p. 310.

19. Ibid., pp. 308, 309.

20. For an impressive and useful historical theological account which moves to generalizations, see Clarence Bauman, *Gewaltlosigkeit im Taufertum: Eine Untersuchung zur Theologischen*

Ethik des Oberdeutschen Taüfertums der Reformationszeit
(Leiden: Brill, 1968). See also Robert Friedmann, *The Theology
of Anabaptism* (Scottdale, Pa.: Herald Press, 1973). Two very
different general histories are George H. Williams, *The Radical
Reformation* (Philadelphia: Westminster, 1962), and Claus-
Peter Clasen, *Anabaptism: A Social History* (Ithaca: Cornell
University Press, 1972). For an informative account of the
debates among historians (like the biblical scholars, they com-
plicate the theologian's task), see James M. Stayer, Werner O.
Packull, and Klaus Deppermann, "From Monogenesis to Poly-
genesis: The Historical Discussion of Anabaptist Origins,"
Mennonite Quarterly Review 49 (1975): 83-121.

21. John H. Yoder, trans. and ed., *The Legacy of Michael Sattler*
(Scottdale, Pa.: Herald Press, 1973), pp. 22, 23.

22. Ibid., pp. 39-40.

23. Ibid., pp. 39, 40, 41. Luther uses the distinctions between
person and office, and between the spiritual and earthly king-
doms, to avoid the hardness of the texts Sattler takes literally.
See "The Sermon on the Mount," in Pelikan, *Luther's Works,*
vol. 21 (1956), for example, pp. 98-115, on Matthew 5:33-42.
Calvin's critical response to the Anabaptists on oaths illustrates
his differences with them; see *The Institutes*, bk. II, chap. 8,
secs. 26-27, in J. T. McNeill, ed., *The Institutes*, 2 vols.,
1:391-93. For Calvin on the magistracy, again in distinction
from the Anabaptists, see *The Institutes*, bk. IV, chap. 20,
sec. 10, in McNeill, *Institutes*, 2:1497-99.

24. Peter Riedemann, *Account of Our Religion, Doctrine and Faith*
(London: Hodder and Stoughton, 1950), pp. 107, 108, 110,
112-20.

25. See ibid., pp. 229-66, for a listing of Riedemann's biblical
references. The Old Testament texts that are used to support
arguments are often those which stress the separation of the
people of Israel from the "heathen"; see, for example, pp.
143-44.

26. Doctrines of the church can be correlated with these views of
morality and faith. Troeltsch's discussions remain insightful;
Ernst Troeltsch, *The Social Teaching of the Christian Churches*,
2 vols. (Glencoe, Ill.: The Free Press, 1949), 1:331-43. For a
treatise on the Anabaptists, see Franklin H. Littell, *The Origins
of Sectarian Protestantism* (New York: Macmillan, 1964).

27. For discussions of banning, see Riedemann, "Account," pp.
131-33, and Menno Simons, "A Clear Account of Excommunication" (1550) in the *Complete Works of Menno Simons*
(Scottdale, Pa.: Herald Press, 1966), pp. 457-85.

28. See Calvin, *The Institutes*, bk. 4, chap. 12, secs. 6-15. See especially bk. 4, chap. 12, sec. 10, on excommunication, and bk. 4,
chap. 12, sec. 12, in which he accuses the Anabaptists of disrup-

tive severity such as Augustine had confronted in the Donatists (in McNeill, *Institutes,* 2:1234-41).

The Northford, Connecticut, Congregational Church, which I served as minister, recorded in the eighteenth century two cases of discipline in a long, detailed, and interesting manner. One was on a charge of blasphemy; one farmer had said to another, "By God, I will put this pitchfork into your very bowels." The accused repented, and could again receive the "seals of the covenant." The other was a charge of adultery. The alleged act was apparently committed shortly before the woman's (it was always the woman who had to bear the blame) husband died. That charge was brought by two deacons (a descendant of both was a deacon two centuries later), but pleas for confession of guilt and repentance were of no avail. After some months a meeting of the New Haven East Consociation was held, with members of neighboring congregations gathered to hear the evidence. In the end, they decided that while the deacons had evidence that the woman was "adulterously in bed with another man" they did not have evidence of adultery! The woman apparently moved from Northford.

29. For Calvin on the first two uses, see *Institutes,* bk. 2, chap. 7, secs. 6-10, in McNeill, *Institutes,* 1:354-60. Melanchthon's discussion is in "Loci Communes," 1555; see Clyde L. Manschreck, trans. and ed., *Melanchthon on Christian Doctrine* (New York: Oxford University Press, 1965), pp. 122-28. For him the "second use," "preaching the wrath of God" is, in Lutheran fashion, the "more important," but he is explicit about the third use: "The third use of the preaching of the law is concerned with those saints who are now believers, who have been born again through God's word and the Holy Spirit" (p. 127).

30. Calvin, *Institutes,* bk. 2, chap. 7, sec. 12, in McNeill, *Institutes,* 1:360-61.

31. For a persuasive thesis about this development, see David Little, *Religion, Order, and Law* (New York: Harper and Row, 1969), chap. 3, "The New Order of John Calvin," and chap. 4, "The Elite of the New Order: The Puritans."

32. Calvin, *Institutes,* bk. 3, chaps. 7-8, in McNeill, *Institutes,* 1:689-712.

33. *Institutes,* bk. 2, chap. 8, sec. 6, in ibid., p. 373.

34. *Institutes,* bk. 2, chap. 8, sec. 7, in ibid., p. 374.

35. Ibid., n. 5, pp. 367-68. The quotation is from p. 368.

36. Ibid. McNeill's footnote makes the case for the inward and natural law having the same reference.

37. *Institutes,* bk. 3, chap. 8, sec. 1, in McNeil, *Institutes,* 1:367-68. That the "first table" of religious duties is included is worth noting, though for the purpose of this section not necessary to

develop. For the continuity of this in Puritan ethics, see Perry Miller, *The New England Mind: The Seventeenth Century* (Cambridge, Mass.: Harvard University Press, 1954), pp. 196–200. Miller quotes William Ames, "The moral law of God revealed through Moses is completely the same with that which is said to be inscribed in the hearts of men" (p. 196). Like Calvin, the Puritans believed that God's commands are not good by virtue of his commanding them, but that he commands them because they are good. The congruence between Scripture and reason was stressed to the point that Thomas Shepard argued that even Sabbath-keeping is "according to the light of nature, even corrupt nature" (p. 199).

38. *Institutes,* bk. 3, chap. 8, sec. 2, in McNeill, *Institutes,* 1:369.

39. See Spurrier, *Natural Law and the Ethics of Love.* I have not expounded the theme of love in the Catholic tradition, where it is far from peripheral though complex and distinguishable from very radical Protestant views of agape. For an informative account of St. Thomas, see Gerard Gilleman, S.J., *The Primacy of Charity in Moral Theology* (Westminster, Md.: The Newman Press, 1959). Spurrier grossly underestimates the importance of love in that tradition. He uses also the symbols of "Rome" and "Geneva"; for the historically minded, Wittenberg would have been a better (but not fully appropriate) choice since Geneva evokes memories of Calvin and not of the World Council of Churches, and Calvin, as I have indicated, continues the natural law tradition.

40. I have previously published some analyses of the roles of Scripture in Christian ethics, but I believe it is important to introduce the problem again for this book.

41. John A. Ryan, *A Living Wage* (New York: Macmillan, 1906); *Distributive Justice* (New York: Macmillan, 1916). Both books were printed several times, and the second was newly edited a number of times. For a fascinating biography, see Francis L. Broderick, *Right Reverend New Dealer, John A. Ryan* (New York: Macmillan, 1963).

42. Walter Rauschenbusch, *Christianity and the Social Crisis* (New York: Macmillan, 1907); *Christianizing the Social Order* (New York: Macmillan, 1912); secondary literature on Rauschenbusch is voluminous.

43. *Christianizing,* p. 29.

44. Ryan, *A Living Wage,* quotations from pp. 43, 44, 45, 46. Ryan, like Leo XIII on whom he relies, can be interpreted as more individualistic in his views than the tradition warrants, with its stress on the "common good." In his case it may be that the classic natural law tradition has been influenced by the tradition of the Enlightenment. For a brief but cogent account of the changes the Enlightenment brought, see A. P. d'En-

treves, *Natural Law* (London: Hutchinson University Library, 1951), chap. 3.

45. Ryan, *A Living Wage*, p. xii.

46. Ibid., pp. 49-50.

47. Rauschenbusch, *Christianity*, p. xiii.

48. Ryan, *A Living Wage*, p. 149. The calculation is based on the studies he uses earlier in the chapter.

49. Rauschenbusch, *Christianity*, pp. 232-33.

50. Arthur Preuss, *A Handbook of Moral Theology Based on the "Lehrbuch der Moraltheologie" of the Late Antony Koch*, 5 vols. (St. Louis: B. Herder, 3d ed., 1925). Koch was a Tübingen theologian; at that university Catholic moral theology was developed in much closer relation to the Bible than in many other places. "Catholic moral theology, broadly speaking, is the scientific exposition of the ethical teaching of the Gospel, or more definitely, that theological discipline which sets forth the laws, rules, and precepts man must know and obey in order to attain his supernatural destiny" (1:1). For a brief account of modern German moral theology, see Bernard Häring, *The Law of Christ*, 3 vols. (Westminster, Md.; The Newman Press, 1961-66), 1:22-33.

51. Koch-Preuss, *Handbook*, 1:7. The other differences noted are that Catholic moral theology is "based on the dogmatic teaching of the one true Church" while "Protestant ethics rests on arbitrary doctrinal assumptions," that is, differences in views of the fall, free will, justification, and Christian liberty. With certitude characteristic of the time, the author states, after listing Protestant criticisms of Catholic ethics, "All these charges will be refuted in the course of this treatise" (p. 9).

52. Thomas Slater, S.J., *A Manual of Moral Theology for English-Speaking Countries*, 3d ed., 2 vols., (New York: Benziger, 1908), 1:311. One cannot help but note that the readers of this manual need to know Latin if they are to understand the text on certain sins committed against nature!

53. In Koch-Preuss, the outline of chapter 7, "The Sources of Moral Theology," is worth noting. The lead sentence indicates two sources, reason and revelation. Thus: I. Reason; II. Revelation; II.1. Scripture; II.2. Ecclesiastical tradition (indicated as "the third source" but under revelation); II.3. The lives of the saints (indicated as "another source"); II.4. The teaching of Catholic moralists (Koch-Preuss, *Handbook*, pp. 26-35).

54. Fuller treatment of the history would have to take special note of the Anglican tradition. For example, the "Christendom movement" in the Church of England and in North America which generated a steady flow of literature from the first World War until after the second, developed a view of "natural orders"

which was in the Catholic tradition. For examples of the writings of this movement, see V. A. Demant, *God, Man, and Society* (Milwaukee: Morehouse, 1934); idem, *Theology of Society* (London: Faber and Faber, 1947); and Maurice B. Reckitt, ed., *Prospect for Christendom* (London: Faber and Faber, 1945). For an example of how seriously the "natural order" was taken: "In agriculture, as in all other occupations, where machinery can be shown to relieve men of laborious and unprofitable drudgery . . . , its advent should surely be welcomed; on the other hand, where it can be proved that machinery has actually displaced human labour to the extent of driving men off the land into the towns or unemployment, and that its speed and rhythm have seriously disturbed the natural temper of the earth and vegetation, its use should be called in question and its practice made explicitly dependent upon a proper observance of these natural priorities" (Patrick McLaughlin, in Reckitt, *Prospect,* p. 107).

55. For an account of how these texts and other texts are used in the Jewish legal tradition, see Gerald J. Blidstein, "Capital Punishment—The Classic Jewish Discussion," *Judaism* 14 (1965):159–71.

56. Jacob J. Vallenga, "Is Capital Punishment Wrong?" *Christianity Today* 4 (1959):7–9, quotations from p. 8. The brackets are in Vallenga's text. The article is reprinted in Hugo Adam Bedeau, *The Death Penalty in America* (New York: Doubleday Anchor Books, 1964), pp. 123–30. Cf. Thomas Aquinas, *Summa Theologica,* II-II, Q. 64, art. 2, where the argument for capital punishment is that it preserves the common good.

57. Since I have dealt with these matters in previous publications, I do not elaborate on them more here. See James M. Gustafson, *Christ and the Moral Life* (New York: Harper and Row, 1968), and *Can Ethics Be Christian?* (Chicago: University of Chicago Press, 1975), especially chap. 5.

2   **Practical Moral Reasoning**

1. My own crucial differences with Ramsey are noted in my Pere Marquette Lecture, 1975, *The Contributions of Theology to Medical Ethics* (Milwaukee: Marquette University, Department of Theology, 1975), pp. 40–45.

2. See Paul Lehmann, *The Politics of Transfiguration* (New York: Harper and Row, 1975). For example, Lehmann removes the question of the use of violence in revolutions from a moral context by placing it in an apocalyptic one. "At the level of revolutionary politics, violence is unveiled not as the endemic nemesis of revolution but as a sign that politics has arrived at an apocalyptic moment of truth and point of no return. . . . In

short, the apocalyptic significance of violence is the talisman of its transfiguration." "The shift is the recognition and assessment of violence not in primarily ethical (moral), or legal, or even sociological terms; but as an apocalyptic phenomenon" (pp. 261–62). Within the range of materials I am considering, the use of violence would always require ethical justification.

3. The most extensive American "evangelical" book on ethics is Carl F. H. Henry, *Christian Personal Ethics* (Grand Rapids: Eerdmans, 1957); Henry's principal aim is to assert a biblical authority over against all forms of relativism in ethics—Christian and philosophical. See also, from a similar viewpoint but more subtly written, Millard J. Erickson, *Relativism in Contemporary Christian Ethics* (Grand Rapids: Baker, 1974). In Carl F. H. Henry, ed., *Baker's Dictionary of Christian Ethics* (Grand Rapids: Baker, 1973), the movement most frequently referred to critically is "situational ethics," which epitomizes relativism.

4. Joseph Fletcher, *Situation Ethics: A New Morality* (Philadelphia: Westminster, 1966). For Roman Catholic literature on the situation ethics movement in that Church, see nn. 26 and 27 below.

5. Paul Ramsey, *War and the Christian Conscience* (Durham, N.C.: Duke University Press, 1961), p. 6. Note must be taken of the Boston University tradition, beginning with Edgar S. Brightman, *Moral Law* (New York: Abingdon, 1933), and continuing, for example, in Walter G. Muelder, *Moral Law in Christian Social Ethics* (Richmond: John Knox Press, 1966).

6. That Ramsey has maintained that interest is amply clear from almost all of his subsequent publications. See, for example, Ramsey, *The Just War: Force and Public Responsibility* (New York: Scribner's, 1968); idem, *The Patient as Person* (New Haven: Yale University Press, 1970); idem, *The Fabricated Man: The Ethics of Genetic Control* (New Haven: Yale University Press, 1970); idem, *The Ethics of Fetal Research* (New Haven: Yale University Press, 1975), and numerous articles. For discussions of Ramsey's work, see James T. Johnson and David H. Smith, eds., *Love and Society: Essays in the Ethics of Paul Ramsey* (Missoula, Mont.: Scholars Press, 1974).

In my judgment, in recent years Ramsey has so concentrated on the methods and substance of practical moral choices that he has lost sight of questions of more general philosophical and theological importance.

There is a distinctively different tone to writings of many Protestants beginning in the late 1960s. Many of the authors were graduate students at that time; others took a new interest in moral philosophy. Among the persons I have in mind are Frederick S. Carney, David Little, Ralph Potter, Arthur Dyck, Gene Outka, John P. Reeder, James F. Childress, Charles W. Powers, LeRoy B. Walters, Merle Longwood, Sumner B. Twiss,

Theodore R. Weber, David H. Smith, Stanley M. Hauerwas, James T. Johnson, Charles Reynolds, Karen Lebacqz, and Robert M. Veatch. I suspect that each of these persons would admit some influence by Ramsey and critical admiration for his work.

Professor Ragnar Holte of Uppsala University and his students are among the few European Protestants who clearly reflect similar philosophical concerns; see, for example, Carl-Henric Grenholm, *Christian Social Ethics in a Revolutionary Age: An Analysis of the Social Ethics of John C. Bennett, Heinz-Dietrich Wendland and Richard Shaull* (Uppsala: Verbum, 1973).

7. Paul Ramsey, *Basic Christian Ethics* (New York: Scribner's, 1950), p. 116. William K. Frankena correctly doubts that deontological theories can avoid judgments of good and evil. See Frankena, *Ethics,* 2d ed. (Englewood Cliffs, N.J.: Prentice-Hall, 1973), p. 44.

8. For one discussion of promise keeping, and also of the wider issues, see W. D. Ross, *The Right and the Good* (Oxford: The Clarendon Press, 1930). See especially chap. 2, "What Makes Right Acts Right?"; the discussion of promises is on pp. 37–40. An essay frequently cited to indicate the issues sharply is Kant, "On a Supposed Right to Lie from Altruistic Motives." See I. Kant, *Critique of Practical Reason, and Other Writings on Moral Philosophy* (Chicago: University of Chicago Press, 1949), pp. 346–50.

9. See Joseph F. Fletcher, "Indicators of Humanhood: A Tentative Profile of Man," *The Hastings Center Report* 2, no. 5 (November 1972):1, 4, and idem, "Four Indicators of Humanhood— The Enquiry Matures," ibid., 4, no. 6 (December 1974):4, 7.

10. Fletcher, *Situation Ethics.* William K. Frankena classifies Fletcher's ethics as utilitarian in *Ethics,* p. 36.

11. Fletcher, *Situation Ethics,* p. 126.

12. Fletcher, "Indicators of Humanhood," p. 1. Fletcher was a serious student of Roman Catholic casuistry at a time when the most prominent Protestant theologians writing ethics dismissed the whole movement with sweeping theological and philosophical judgments.

13. Maurice Mandelbaum, *The Phenomenology of Moral Experience* (Glencoe, Ill.: The Free Press, 1955), p. 93. See the whole of chap. 2, "Direct Moral Judgments."

14. H. Richard Niebuhr, *The Responsible Self* (New York: Harper and Row, 1963), especially pp. 55ff. See Richard E. Coulter, "H. Richard Niebuhr and Stoicism," *Journal of Religious Ethics* 2 (1974):129–44.

15. Rudolph Bultmann, *Existence and Faith* (New York: Meridian Books, 1960), p. 145.

16. Barth, *Church Dogmatics,* II/2, pp. 522–23.

17. Ibid., p. 663; the whole of sect. 38 deals with the definiteness of the divine command.

18. Paul Tillich, *Morality and Beyond* (New York: Harper and Row, 1963), pp. 24–25.

19. Ibid., pp. 27–28.

20. Paul Lehmann, *Ethics in a Christian Context* (New York: Harper and Row, 1963), p. 358.

21. Ibid., pp. 116, 117.

22. Ibid., p. 55.

23. In a public discussion of this book in 1964 at Yale University after I had elaborated my criticisms more than I have here, I asked Professor Lehmann, "What is the meaning of the human?" His immediate response was, "Jim, if you don't know I can't tell you."

24. John C. Ford, S.J., "The Morality of Obliteration Bombing," *Theological Studies* 5 (1944):261–309.

25. Paul Ramsey, "Two Concepts of Rules in Christian Ethics," in Ramsey, *Deeds and Rules in Christian Ethics* (New York: Scribner's, 1967), pp. 123–44. Rawls' essay is frequently found in anthologies; one is Philippa Foot, ed., *Theories of Ethics* (London: Oxford University Press, 1967), pp. 144–67.

26. Karl Rahner, S.J., *Nature and Grace* (London: Sheed and Ward, 1963), pp. 84–111. Joseph Fuchs, S.J., *Situation und Entscheidung* (Frankfurt: Joseph Knecht, 1952). John C. Ford, S.J., and Gerald Kelly, S.J., *Contemporary Moral Theology,* 2 vols. (Westminster, Md.: The Newman Press, 1958), 1, especially pp. 104–40; an account of the response of Pius XII and the Holy Office is found on pp. 104–23. Robert W. Gleason, "Situational Morality," *Thought* 32 (1957): 533–58.

27. Walter Dirks, "How Can I Know What God Wants of Me?" *Cross Currents* 5 (1955):76–92, quotation from p. 80. Dirks is responding to Rahner's article cited above.

28. Ibid., p. 81.

29. Ibid., pp. 82, 83.

30. Ibid., p. 90.

31. Quoted in full in Ford and Kelly, *Contemporary Moral Theology,* 1:120–23.

32. Louis Dupré, "Situation Ethics and Objective Morality," *Theological Studies* 28 (1967):245–57.

33. See Peter Knauer, S.J., "The Hermeneutic Function of the Principle of Double Effect," *Natural Law Forum* 12 (1967):132–62; Bruno Schüller, S.J., "Zur Problematik allgemein verbindlicher ethischer Grundsätze," *Theologie und Philosophie* 45 (1970):1–23; Josef Fuchs, S.J., "The Absoluteness of Moral

Terms," *Gregorianum* 52 (1971):415–57; Richard A. McCormick, S.J., *Ambiguity in Moral Choice* (Milwaukee: Marquette University, 1973), and Charles E. Curran, "The Principle of Double Effect," in his *Ongoing Revision: Studies in Moral Theology* (Notre Dame, Ind.: Fides, 1975), pp. 173–209. For a critical analysis of the Catholic ethics of consequences that is made in the light of problems in utilitarianism, see John R. Connery, S.J., "Morality of Consequences: A Critical Appraisal," *Theological Studies* 34 (1967):396–414.

34. Philipp Schmitz, S.J., makes the inductive approach to moral norms the central theme of his study of writings of Harvey Cox, Joseph Fletcher, and J. A. T. Robinson. See Philipp Schmitz, *Die Wirklichkeit Fassen.*

35. Charles E. Curran, *Contemporary Problems in Moral Theology* (Notre Dame, Ind.: Fides, 1970), pp. 175–76.

36. Ibid., pp. 176–77.

37. John Giles Milhaven, *Toward a New Catholic Morality* (Garden City, N.Y.: Doubleday, 1970), pp. 59–68; quotations from pp. 62, 63, 67.

38. John Giles Milhaven, "The Abortion Debate: An Epistemological Interpretation," *Theological Studies* 31 (1970):106–24, quotation from p. 121. This article is reprinted in slightly altered form in Milhaven, *Toward a New Catholic Morality,* pp. 69–84.

39. Milhaven, "Towards an Epistemology of Ethics," *Theological Studies* 27 (1966):228–41, quotation from p. 235. See also Milhaven, "Objective Moral Evaluation of Consequences," *Theological Studies* 32 (1971):407–30, and idem, *Toward a New Catholic Morality,* especially "The Behavioral Sciences," pp. 113–26. Robert H. Springer, S.J., is another writer very open to the behavioral sciences both for knowing consequences and for understanding the moral agent. See Springer, "Conscience, Behavioral Science and Absolutes," in Charles E. Curran, ed., *Absolutes in Moral Theology?* (Washington: Corpus Books, 1968), pp. 19–56. Charles E. Curran, by establishing a stance of "dialogue" with various empirical sciences, usually maintains a more critical attitude in his uses of them; see, for example, among many others, his essays, *Catholic Moral Theology in Dialogue* (Notre Dame, Ind.: Fides, 1972).

40. Connery, "Morality of Consequences."

41. Richard A. McCormick, S.J., "Notes on Moral Theology," *Theological Studies* 26 (1965):603–8, for a critique of Knauer; 27 (1966):617–20, for a critique of Milhaven; 32 (1971):86–95 for a critique of Knauer and Schüller; 33 (1972):68–90, for a critique of Schüller, Fuchs, Knauer, Milhaven, Curran, Nicholas Crotty and others; 36 (1975):93–99, for a response to Connery; *Ambiguity in Moral Choice* for a critical analysis of some of the above-named and others.

42. McCormick, *Ambiguity*, p. 1.

43. Ibid., p. 93.

44. Connery, "Morality of Consequences," p. 413.

45. Connery introduces the principle of justice, citing William Frankena and others, as one consideration that will hold the line (ibid., pp. 412-13).

46. See, for example, Thomas Dubay, S.M., "The State of Moral Theology: A Critical Appraisal," *Theological Studies* 35 (1974): 482-506, which is a conservative response to Curran, "Moral Theology: The Present State of the Discipline."

47. Paul VI, *Humanae Vitae* (1968), par. 11. Among other places, this can be found in Joseph Gremillion, ed., *The Gospel of Peace and Justice: Catholic Social Teachings since Pope John* (Maryknoll, N.Y.: Orbis Books, 1976), pp. 387-41. The quotation is on p. 433.

48. Pius XI, *Casti Connubii*, 1930. This can be found in, among other places, Terence P. McLaughlin, C.S.B., ed., *The Church and the Reconstruction of the Modern World: The Social Encyclicals of Pius XI* (Garden City: Doubleday Image Books, 1957), pp. 118-65.

49. John T. Noonan, Jr., *Contraception: A History of Its Treatment by the Catholic Theologians and Canonists* (Cambridge, Mass.: Harvard University Press, 1965). For a summary account of how the tradition might have been different if greater weight had been given to "counter elements" in the medieval period, see pp. 299-300.

50. See LeRoy B. Walters, "Five Classic Just War Theories: A Study in the Thought of Thomas Aquinas, Victoria, Suarez, Gentile, and Grotius" (Ph.D. diss., Yale University, 1971). See also Walters, "Historical Applications of the Just War Theory: Four Case Studies in Normative Ethics," in Johnson and Smith, *Love and Society*, pp. 115-38.

3   **Philosophical Bases**

1. Paul Ramsey is not untypical of Protestants who borrow concepts developed in the natural law tradition but engraft them onto an ethical theory that eschews the natural law in its ontological or metaphysical formulations.

2. Walter Rauschenbusch, *The Social Principles of Jesus* (New York: Association Press, 1917), p. 128.

3. See Reinhold Niebuhr, *An Interpretation of Christian Ethics* (New York: Harper, 1935), for stress on Jesus' teachings; *The Nature and Destiny of Man*, 2 vols. (New York: Scribner's, 1945), 2:75, 81-90, for the centrality of the cross; *Faith and History* (New York: Scribner's, 1949), pp. 174ff., for an exposition of love as the law of life.

4. John Howard Yoder, *The Politics of Jesus* (Grand Rapids: Eerdmans, 1972), p. 14.

5. Ibid., p. 24, n. 14. Yoder does not undertake an argument for biblical authority as he uses it, but he quite properly distinguishes it from verbal inspiration theories and engages other biblical exegetes in debate over the proper interpretation of texts that are crucial to his view.

6. H. Richard Niebuhr, *The Responsible Self*, p. 126.

7. Barth, *Church Dogmatics* II/2, pp. 509–781. Barth's favorite descriptive language for the relation of God to man is covenant partners, which introduces a social metaphor rather than one drawn from nature; his dominant ethical language is command-obedience, which emphasizes a voluntaristic note backed by God's freedom rather than moral laws imbedded in nature which are the source of rational prescriptions. H. Richard Niebuhr, in *The Responsible Self*, uses an action-response model as basic to both the God-man relation and human relationship. Paul Lehmann, in *Ethics in a Christian Context*, has as his central theme God's "humanizing" action in history. Since I have discussed these theologians in previous publications, I do not elaborate on these themes here. These theologians are reliant upon various studies of the Bible, for example, of writings of Gerhard von Rad, *Old Testament Theology*, 2 vols. (Edinburgh: Oliver and Boyd, 1962 and 1965), George Ernest Wright, *The God Who Acts* (London: SCM Press, 1952), and others. For an account of the status of the "biblical theology" movement, see Brevard Childs, *Biblical Theology in Crisis* (Philadelphia: Westminster Press, 1970).

8. No authors who exemplify the options stated in this paragraph and the previous one are cited; specific authors could be named, including myself. The only two options that do not have contemporary proponents are the view of God as absolutely free (not even self-restrained) and absolutely determinative.

9. See Chapter 2, p. 47.

10. Rudolph Bultmann, *Jesus and the Word* (New York: Scribner's, 1934), p. 87. See also, Knud Løgstrup, *The Ethical Demand* (Philadelphia: Fortress, 1971), pp. 156–72. For a critical analysis of Bultmann's ethics, see Thomas Oden, *Radical Obedience: The Ethics of Rudolph Bultmann* (Philadelphia: Westminster, 1964), and Dorothee Soelle, *Political Theology* (Philadelphia: Fortress, 1974). For a critical interpretation of Løgstrup's theology, see Lars-Olle Armgard, *Antropologi: Problem i K. E. Løgstrups Författarskap* (Lund: Gleerups, 1971), especially pp. 21–59.

11. Barth, *Church Dogmatics*, II/2, pp. 663–64.

12. Ibid., p. 663.

13. Bultmann, *Existence and Faith*, pp. 222–23; Løgstrup, *The Ethical Demand*, pp. 8–29.

14. Barth discusses this literature in an incisive passage in *Church Dogmatics*, III/4, pp. 19-23.
15. Løgstrup, *The Ethical Demand*, p. 9.
16. Ibid., p. 18.
17. "All life has the character of responsiveness, I maintain" (H. Richard Niebuhr, *The Responsible Self*, p. 46).
18. Paul Ramsey, *Christian Ethics and the Sit-in* (New York: Association Press, 1961), pp. 22-24, for one place among several in which Barth's views are cited.
19. Gibson Winter, *Elements for a Social Ethic* (New York: Macmillan, 1966), p. 227.
20. David Little, "Calvin and the Prospects for a Christian Theory of Natural Law," in Gene H. Outka and Paul Ramsey, eds., *Norm and Context in Christian Ethics* (New York: Scribner's, 1968), p. 176.
21. Ibid., p. 188.
22. Ibid., p. 189.
23. Stanley M. Hauerwas, *Character and the Christian Life: A Study in Theological Ethics* (San Antonio: Trinity University Press, 1975).
24. Ibid., p. 4.
25. Ibid., p. 11.
26. The person as agent is receiving attention by Protestant thinkers who are not as persuaded by the British and American action theorists as is Hauerwas. An interesting and promising proposal has been ventured which comes from the phenomenological tradition; see Howard L. Harrod, "Interpreting and Projecting: Two Elements of the Self as Moral Agent," *Journal of the American Academy of Religion* 41 (1973): 18-29. Another comes from a study in recent personality theories, and argues that the best prospects are emerging from the work of Erik Erikson; see Don Browning, *Generative Man* (Philadelphia: Westminster Press, 1973).
27. Gene Outka, *Agape: An Ethical Analysis* (New Haven: Yale University Press, 1972).
28. Anders Nygren, *Agape and Eros* (London: SPCK, 1953), p. 210.
29. Outka, *Agape*, p. 2.
30. Ibid., p. 9.
31. Ibid., p. 279.
32. John T. Noonan, Jr., *The Scholastic Analysis of Usury* (Cambridge: Harvard University Press, 1957); "An Absolute Value in History," in John T. Noonan, ed., *The Morality of Abortion* (Cambridge: Harvard University Press, 1970), pp. 1-59; Noonan, *Contraception*.

33. Noonan, *Contraception*, pp. 299–300. For another illuminating account of the history of marriage doctrine, see E. Schille-beeckx, O.P., *Marriage: Secular Reality and Saving Mystery*, 2 vols. (London: Sheed and Ward, 1965), vol. 2. Charles E. Curran traces the history of the development of the "physical-ist" bias and its significance in natural law theory in "Abso-lute Norms and Medical Ethics," in Curran, *Absolutes in Moral Theology?* pp. 115–20. He sees its source in Roman law, particularly in the influence of Ulpian (third century A.D.). Jus-tinian's *Digest* attributes to Ulpian the following: "Natural law is that which nature has taught all animals; this law is not peculiar to the human race, but belongs to all animals" (quoted in Columba Ryan, O.P., "The Traditional Concept of Natural Law: An Interpretation," in Illtud Evans, O.P., *Light on Natural Law* [Dublin: Helicon, 1965], p. 15).

34. Thomas Aquinas, *Summa Theologica*, I-II, Q. 94, art. 4.

35. Ryan, "The Traditional Concept," p. 19.

36. Ibid., p. 30.

37. Ibid., p. 23, italics added.

38. Bruno Schüller, "Wieweit kann die Moral theologie das Natur-recht entbehren?" *Lebendiges Zeugnis* 1/2 (March 1965): 41–65. A more recent article by Schüller which deals with the rela-tions of natural law to Christian ethics is "Die Bedeutung des naturlichen Sittengesetzes für den Christen," in Georg Teicht-weier and Wilhelm Dreier, eds., *Herausforderung und Kritik des Moraltheologie* (Würzburg: Echtes Verlag, 1971), pp. 105–30. (This entire symposium is of importance to the study of developments in Catholic moral theology.)

39. Richard A. McCormick, S.J., "Human Significance and Chris-tian Significance," in Outka and Ramsey, *Norm and Context*, p. 239, quoting Louis Monden, S.J., *Sin, Liberty and Law* (New York: Sheed and Ward, 1965).

40. Ibid., p. 247.

41. Bernard Häring, "Dynamism and Continuity in a Personalistic Approach to Natural Law," in Outka and Ramsey, *Norm and Context*, p. 200.

42. Ibid., p. 202.

43. Ibid., p. 203.

44. Häring, *The Law of Christ*, 3 vols. (Westminster, Md.: The Newman Press, 1961–66).

45. Curran, *Contemporary Problems in Moral Theology*, p. 135.

46. William A. Luijpen, *Phenomenology of Natural Law* (Pitts-burgh: Duquesne University Press, 1967).

47. Ibid., pp. 98–100.

48. Ibid., pp. 100–101.

49. Ibid., p. 101.

50. Ibid., p. 103.

51. Ibid., p. 145.

52. Ibid., pp. 180-81.

53. Ibid., pp. 204-5.

54. Van Der Marck, *Toward a Christian Ethic* (Westminster, Md.: The Newman Press, 1967), p. 25, p. 27. The publication of this book was the occasion for my extensive review of it and other trends in Catholic moral theology in Gustafson, "New Directions in Moral Theology," *Commonweal* 87 (1968): 617-23 (a significant deletion from the article is noted on p. 727).

55. Van Der Marck, *Toward a Christian Ethic*, p. 25, p. 27.

56. Ibid., p. 21.

57. Ibid., p. 35.

58. Ibid., p. 50.

59. Ibid., p. 92. The discussion of *habitus* is found on pp. 81-92.

60. Robert O. Johann, *Building the Human* (New York: Herder and Herder, 1968). See John MacMurray, *The Self as Agent* (New York: Harper and Row, 1957), and idem, *Persons in Relation* (New York: Harper and Row, 1961).

61. Johann, *Building the Human*, pp. 27-28.

62. Ibid., p. 22.

63. Ibid., p. 66.

64. Ibid., p. 79.

65. Ibid., p. 84. I reviewed Johann's book more extensively in *Thought* 44 (1969): 309-12.

66. See Robert O. Johann, *The Pragmatic Meaning of God* (Milwaukee: Marquette University Press, 1966).

67. The implications of Rahner's philosophical anthropology for ethics is developed most fundamentally in "On the Question of a Formal Existential Ethics," in Karl Rahner, *Theological Investigations*, vol. 2 (Baltimore: Helicon, 1963), pp. 217-34. The other important essays for ethics are, "Concerning the Relationships between Nature and Grace," in Rahner, *Theological Investigations*, vol. 1 (Baltimore: Helicon, 1961), pp. 297-317; "The Theological Concept of Concupiscentia," ibid., pp. 347-82; "Some Thoughts on 'A Good Intention,'" in Rahner, *Theological Investigations*, vol. 3 (Baltimore: Helicon, 1967), pp. 105-28; "Theology of Freedom," in Rahner, *Theological Investigations*, vol. 6 (Baltimore: Helicon, 1969), pp. 178-96; and "Reflection on the Unity of Love of Neighbor and the Love of God," ibid., pp. 231-49. For Rahner's own reflections on practical problems, see "Theological Remarks on the Problem of Leisure," in Rahner, *Theological Investigations*,

vol. 4 (Baltimore: Helicon, 1966), pp. 368–90; "The Theology of Power," ibid., pp. 391–409; "The Experiment with Man," in Rahner, *Theological Investigations*, vol. 9 (New York: Herder and Herder, 1972), pp. 205–24; and "The Problem of Genetic Manipulation," ibid., pp. 225–52. For my understanding of Rahner's ethics I am deeply indebted to James F. Bresnahan, S.J., for a decade of intellectual discourse. For a brief synopsis of Rahner's work, see James F. Bresnahan, "Rahner's Christian Ethics," *America* 123 (1970): 351–54; for a more extensive treatment, see Bresnahan, "Rahner's Ethics: Critical Natural Law in Relation to Contemporary Ethical Methodology," *Journal of Religion* 56 (1976): 36–60; for the most extensive, see Bresnahan, "The Methodology of 'Natural Law' Ethical Reasoning in the Theology of Karl Rahner" (Ph.D. diss., Yale University, 1972).

68. Rahner, "Formal Existential Ethics," p. 226.

69. Ramsey, *Fabricated Man*, pp. 139–42.

70. Rahner, *Investigations*, 9: 205–24.

71. Ibid., p. 231.

72. A major statement coming out of the tradition which Rahner represents came to my attention as I was completing this book. It is Klaus Demmer, *Sein und Gebot: Die Bedeutsamkeit des Transzendentalphilosophischen Denkansatzes in der Scholastik der Gegenwart für den formalen aufriss der Fundamentalmoral* (Munich: Verlag Ferdinand Schöningh, 1971). No better reasons than expediency can be offered for not mastering its argument for inclusion in this and the next chapter. Fellow scholars, I hope, will understand, though to be excused for this omission is more than my conscience permits me to ask.

4   **Theological Bases**

1. See Ernest Sandeen, *The Roots of Fundamentalism* (Chicago: University of Chicago Press, 1970), for evidence of the multi-denominational character of Darbyite dispensationalism.

2. I agree with Van A. Harvey's eloquent criticism of this in *Religious Studies Review* 1 (1975):13–14, contained in his review of Anders Nygren, *Meaning and Method*.

3. Friedrich D. E. Schleiermacher, *The Christian Faith* (Edinburgh: T. and T. Clark, 1928), p. 524. The lectures on morals were published as *Die Christliche Sitte* (Berlin: Reimar, 1843).

4. I. A. Dorner, *System of Christian Ethics* (New York: Scribner and Welford, 1887); H. Martensen, *Christian Ethics*, 2 vols. (Edinburgh: T. and T. Clark, 1891, 1882).

5. Bernard Häring, *The Law of Christ*. It was upon reading Häring's *Das Gesetz Christi* in 1959 that I began to see

the possibilities of a new ecumenical rapprochement in theological ethics. To sense the innovative character of that work one needs only to compare it with articles and books in moral theology from the United States published during the 1950s.

Two essays by distinguished Catholic theologians are of special significance for examining the renewed exchange between moral and dogmatic theology. M. D. Chenu, O.P., "The Renewal of Moral Theology: The New Law," *The Thomist* 34 (1970):1-12, while brief, is sensitive and profound, and shows that the "return to the Gospel," while not novel in Catholic history, is of transforming significance for moral theology. Joseph Fuchs, S.J., "Moral Theology and Dogmatic Theology," in Fuchs, *Human Values and Christian Morality* (Dublin: Gill and Macmillan, 1970), pp. 148-77, states basic principles on which the two separate disciplines complement each other. Enda McDonagh's essays deal with these matters as well; see his *Invitation and Response: Essays in Christian Moral Theology* (Dublin: Gill and Macmillan, 1972).

6. Karl Rahner, *Theological Investigations*, 2:217-34.

7. See Bresnahan, "The Methodology of 'Natural Law' Ethical Reasoning in the Theology of Karl Rahner." See also, Bresnahan, "Rahner's Ethics."

8. For examples, Johannes B. Metz, "The Church's Social Function in the Light of Political Theology," *Concilium* 36 (1968):2-18; Edward Schillebeeckx, O.P., "The Magisterium and the World of Politics," in ibid., pp. 19-39; idem, *God and Man* (New York: Sheed and Ward, 1969), pp. 257-303; idem, *Marriage: Secular Reality and Saving Mystery*; Bernard Lonergan, *Insight* (London: Longmans, Green, 1957), pp. 595-633 and passim; idem, *Method in Theology* (New York: Herder and Herder, 1972), pp. 27-55; Michael Novak, "Bernard Lonergan: A New Approach to Natural Law," *Proceedings of the American Catholic Philosophical Association* (Washington, D.C.: Catholic University Press, 1967), pp. 246-49.

9. For a summary of some of these trends, and a critical and constructive response to them, see Charles E. Curran, "Dialogue with the Scriptures: The Role and Function of the Scriptures in Moral Theology," in Curran, *Catholic Moral Theology in Dialogue*, pp. 24-64.

Both Roman Catholics and Protestants can benefit from a careful study by David H. Kelsey, *The Uses of Scripture in Recent Theology* (Philadelphia: Fortress Press, 1975). Kelsey has provided an apparatus for sophisticated critical analysis of the many ways in which Scripture is used in theology, based in part on Stephen Toulmin, *The Uses of Argument* (Cambridge: Cambridge University Press, 1963). My discussion here could be refined in the light of Kelsey's work, but I have chosen not to do so because the explanation of it that would be required to make its use intelligible would also take a disproportionate amount of space. Incidentally, all the materials Kelsey uses to demonstrate his procedures are Protestant; a number of interesting inferences can be drawn from this!

10. See, for example, Gustavo Gutierrez, *A Theology of Liberation.*

11. Fuchs, *Natural Law,* p. 14.

12. Ibid., p. 17.

13. Ibid., p. 31.

14. Ibid., p. 60.

15. Ibid., p. 61.

16. Ibid., p. 67.

17. See Gordon D. Kaufmann, "The *Imago Dei* as Man's Historicity," *Journal of Religion* 36 (1956):157–68.

18. Fuchs, *Natural Law,* p. 74.

19. See James M. Gustafson, *Christ and the Moral Life,* chap. 2, for extensive discussion of how Christologies based on these texts affect ethics. Fuchs discusses Barth's Christological ground of human rights in *Natural Law,* pp. 79–84.

20. See Fuchs, *Natural Law,* pp. 74–78; idem, "Gibt es eine spezifisch christliche Moral?" *Stimmen der Zeit* 185 (1970):99–112; idem, "The Law of Christ," in Fuchs, *Human Values and Christian Morality,* esp. pp. 87–91; idem, "Human, Humanist, and Christian Morality," ibid., pp. 112–47. This last article is essentially a less technical version of the argument published in *Stimmen der Zeit.* For my resolution of the issues under discussion, see James M. Gustafson, *Can Ethics Be Christian?*

21. Fuchs, "Gibt es," pp. 100–104; "Human, Humanist," pp. 123–26.

22. "Human, Humanist," p. 120.

23. Ibid., pp. 122–23.

24. Milhaven, "Moral Absolutes and Thomas Aquinas," in Curran, ed., *Absolutes in Moral Theology?* pp. 154–85.

25. Thomas Aquinas, *Summa Theologica,* II–II, Q. 64, art. 5. The quotation from Augustine is in Reply to Obj. 5, and is from *The City of God,* Bk. I, Ch. 21.

26. Bruno Schüller, "Zur Problematik," pp. 1–23. The discussion of suicide is on pp. 13–18, the quotation, p. 15.

27. For other discussions of this general issue, see Richard A. McCormick, S.J., *Theological Studies* 32 (1971):71–78; Charles E. Curran, "Is There a Distinctively Christian Social Ethics?" in Philip D. Morris, ed., *Metropolis: Christian Presence and Responsibility* (Notre Dame: Fides, 1970), pp. 92–120; idem, "Is There a Catholic and/or Christian Ethic?" in *Proceedings of the Catholic Theological Society of America* 29 (1974):125–54 (with responses by Gustafson and McCormick, pp. 155–60, 161–64).

28. Fuchs, *Natural Law*, pp. 75–76, n. 20. The entire footnote is a condensed summary of Fuch's argument for the unity of the natural law and the law of Christ.

29. Ibid., p. 78.

30. Fuchs, "Gibt es," p. 101.

31. Fuchs, "Human Humanist," p. 124. For a more elaborate discussion see "Gibt es," pp. 100–104.

32. "Human, Humanist," p. 124.

33. Charles E. Curran, *A New Look at Christian Morality* (Notre Dame: Fides, 1968), p. 156.

34. Fritz Tillmann, *Die Idee der Nachfolge Christi*, 4th ed. (Düsseldorf: Patmos Verlag, 1953), and idem, *Die Verwirklichung der Nachfolge Christi*, 2 vols., 4th ed. (Düsseldorf: Patmos Verlag, 1950). The traditional structure of Catholic moral theology is kept largely intact in *Die Verwirklichung*. I have had occasion to use these volumes over the past sixteen years when working in a number of libraries associated with strong centers of Protestant theological scholarship. An indication of the state of Protestant work in Catholic ethics is the absence of these volumes in a number of libraries; in most of those in which I have found them I have been the first person to withdraw them. Tillmann's biblical studies are found more frequently.

35. Bernard Häring, *The Law of Christ*, 1:vii. These themes are developed in many of the addresses Häring has published; see especially those found in *This Time of Salvation* (New York: Herder and Herder, 1966), and *Christian Maturity* (New York: Herder and Herder, 1967).

36. Häring, *This Time of Salvation*, p. 44.

37. Häring, *The Law of Christ*, 1:35.

38. Ibid., pp. 43–44.

39. Particularly comprehensive are C. Spicq, *Théologie Morale du Nouveau Testament*, 2 vols. (Paris: J. Gabalda, 1964, 1965), and Rudolph Schnackenburg, *Die Sittliche Botschaft des Neuen Testamentes* (Munich: Max Hueber, 1962), Eng. trans., *The Moral Teaching of the New Testament* (New York: Herder and Herder, 1965). Schnackenburg takes much more account of problems of historical and literary criticism than does Spicq. Spicq has an interesting popular book, *The Trinity and Our Moral Life according to St. Paul* (Westminster, Md.: The Newman Press, 1963).

40. H. Richard Niebuhr, *Christ and Culture* (New York: Harper, 1951).

41. Ernst Troeltsch, *The Social Teaching of the Christian Churches*, 1:331–43. Sociologists of religion who use Troeltsch forget that this is a typology of Christologies and ethics. John C. Bennett developed a pattern similar to Niebuhr's refinement of

Troeltsch's in *Christian Ethics and Social Policy* (New York: Scribner's, 1946), pp. 32-57.

42. One can also set the polarity of love and justice in this way.

43. In principle one could also describe a relation of culture above Christ (nature above grace) and culture transforming Christ (nature transforming grace). Theologians are normative thinkers, and tend for reasons of religious convictions not to develop these two possibilities; as indications of actual historical developments, however, they may be very accurate, indeed painfully accurate for the theologian.

44. See a less well-known but equally insightful contribution, H. Richard Niebuhr, "The Doctrine of the Trinity and the Unity of the Church," *Theology Today* 3 (1946):371-84.

45. For discussion of these matters more fully, see Gustafson, *Christ and the Moral Life.*

46. An initial effort indicating a direction I would personally defend can be found in Gustafson, *The Contribution of Theology to Medical Ethics,* especially pp. 47-52.

47. Karl Rahner, S.J., "The Order of Redemption within the Order of Creation," in *The Christian Commitment* (New York: Sheed and Ward, 1963), pp. 38-74; quotation from pp. 38-39.

48. Ibid., p. 41.

49. This theological theme is almost omnipresent in Rahner's systematic theological essays. The principal texts I am relying upon are Karl Rahner, "Concerning the Relationship between Nature and Grace," *Theological Investigations* 1:297-318; idem, "The Order of Redemption"; idem, "Nature and Grace," in *Theological Investigations* 4:165-88 (also published in a different translation in *Nature and Grace*). Other articles, some cited in Chapter 3, are important. In addition to the writings of James Bresnahan, I am especially indebted to Gerald A. McCool, S.J., for his "Introduction: Rahner's Philosophical Theology," in McCool, ed., *A Rahner Reader* (New York: Seabury, 1975), pp. xiii-xxviii, and his introductions to the readings he has selected; and to Anne Carr, "Theology and Experience in the Thought of Karl Rahner," *Journal of Religion* 53 (1973):359-76.

50. McCool, in *A Rahner Reader,* p. 173.

51. Karl Rahner, "Anonymous Christians," in *Theological Investigations* 6:390-98.

52. Karl Rahner, "Reflections on the Unity of the Love of Neighbor and the Love of God," in ibid., pp. 231-49.

53. See above, Josef Fuchs' discussion of the distinctive element in the morality of Christians; Fuchs is one moral theologian who is developing Rahner's perspective.

54. I believe this is clear even from the brief discussion of Calvin in

Chapter 1; the literature on Calvin and natural law would be an access route to further elaboration.

55. See Niebuhr, *Christ and Culture*, pp. 220–29. See also Gustafson, *Christ and the Moral Life*, Chapter 2.

56. Hans Küng, *Justification: The Doctrine of Karl Barth and a Catholic Reflection* (London: Burns and Oates, 1964); Hans Urs Von Balthasar, *The Theology of Karl Barth* (New York: Holt, Rinehart and Winston, 1971) (German ed., 1962).

57. See Gustafson, "Introduction," in H. Richard Niebuhr, *The Responsible Self*, pp. 25–40.

58. Joseph Sittler, *Essays on Nature and Grace* (Philadelphia: Fortress, 1972). One of the very few significant aspects of the World Council of Churches' Faith and Order Conference in Montreal, 1963, was a Sunday afternoon informal discussion of the need to rethink the relations of creation and redemption, of nature and grace for theological ethics. The meeting was called and led by Sittler and Professor Gustaf Wingren of Lund University.

59. Allan Galloway, *The Cosmic Christ* (London: Nisbet, 1951).

60. Sittler, *Essays*, p. 14.

61. Ibid., p. 17.

62. Ibid., p. 82.

63. Ibid., p. 83.

64. Ibid., pp. 88, 89.

65. Ibid., p. 115.

66. Since I have previously published an interpretation of Barth's theology and ethics in *Christ and the Moral Life*, chap. 2, my discussion here can be brief.

67. Karl Barth, *Church Dogmatics*, II/2, p. 509.

68. Ibid., p. 511.

69. Ibid., p. 576.

70. Ibid., p. 526.

71. Ibid., p. 541.

72. Barth, *Church Dogmatics*, IV/2, p. 275. For further discussion of these points see Robert E. Willis, *The Ethics of Karl Barth* (Leiden: E. J. Brill, 1971), pp. 102, 144–45.

73. For Barth's discussion of Catholic ethics, see *Church Dogmatics*, II/2, pp. 528–35.

74. Ibid., IV/2, pp. 499–613.

75. Ibid., III/4; see the discussion of the protection of life, pp. 397–470.

76. See Gustaf Wingren, *Theology in Conflict* (Philadelphia: Muhlenberg, 1958), p. 25. "There is in Barth's theology no active

power of sin, no tyrannical, demonic power that subjects man to slavery and which God destroys in his work of redemption. There is no devil in Barth's theology. This is a constant feature of his theological production."

77. Walter M. Abbott, S.J., ed., *The Documents of Vatican II* (New York: Guild Press, 1966), pp. 199–308.

78. Charles Curran, in his catholicity of concerns, made a creative foray into some of these matters in "Dialogue with a Theology of the Church: The Meaning of Coresponsibility," in Curran, *Catholic Moral Theology in Dialogue,* pp. 179–83.

79. Paul Ramsey, *Who Speaks for the Church?* (Nashville: Abingdon Press, 1967).

80. See Paul Ramsey's polemic against a Methodist statement on abortion, "Feticide/Infanticide upon Request," *Religion in Life* 39 (1970):170–86.

81. See for example, Jeffrey K. Hadden, *The Gathering Storm in the Churches: A Sociologist's View of the Widening Gap between Clergy and Laity* (Garden City: Doubleday, 1969).

82. In the field of ethics one thinks, among others, of two recently retired leaders who have devoted a large portion of their energy to denominational and ecumenical bodies: Walter G. Mueldur, for many years dean of the Boston University School of Theology (Methodist), and John C. Bennett of Union Theological Seminary, New York. Bennett's participation is reflected clearly in his recent book, *The Radical Imperative* (Philadelphia: Westminster, 1975).

83. That efforts are being made to answer these questions is clear. I have made some general proposals in "The Church: A Community of Moral Discourse," in James M. Gustafson, *The Church as Moral Decision-Maker* (Philadelphia: Pilgrim, 1970), pp. 83–95. Also at a general level see James B. Nelson, *Moral Nexus* (Philadelphia: Westminster, 1971). For more practical responses that are occurring, one would have to cite denominational literature and various programs conducted by churches and ecumenical agencies.

84. Pius XI, *Casti Connubii* (On Christian Marriage), 1930; *Quadragesimo Anno* (On Reconstructing the Social Order) 1931; these are available in many editions; among others, McLaughlin, ed., *The Church and the Reconstruction of the Modern World,* pp. 118–65, 219–74.

85. Paul VI, *Populorum Progressio* (On the Development of Peoples) 1967; *Humanae Vitae* (On the Regulation of Birth) 1968. These can be found in Gremillion, ed., *The Gospel of Peace and Justice,* pp. 387–413, 427–43.

86. For a summary and evaluation of literature on this matter, see Richard A. McCormick, S.J., "Notes on Moral Theology,"

Theological Studies 29 (1968):707–41. McCormick updates the discussion in ibid., 30 (1969):653–68, and ibid., 36 (1975):77–83.

87. Bruno Schüller, S.J., "Bemerkungen zur authentischen Verkündigung des kirchlichen Lehramtes," in *Theologie und Philosophie* 42 (1967):534–51. For translated excerpts, see *Theology Digest* 16 (1968):328–43.

88. Dubay, "The State of Moral Theology."

89. McCormick, "Notes," *Theological Studies* 36 (1975):81.

90. For fuller discussion see ibid., pp. 81–83.

91. I have not discussed, or even cited, the growing body of literature on ecclesiology that has been written by Catholic theologians in recent years. Avery Dulles, S.J., *Models of the Church* (Garden City: Doubleday, 1974), is only the most recent of major publications, and one can be certain that more will follow. It is hoped that detailed attention will be given by some author to the implications of various views of the church for moral theology and moral life.

5   Basic Issues and Prospects for the Future

1. Although I do not develop the following in a way that explicitly follows the work of David Tracy, a similarity of purpose and of vocabulary is evident. Tracy's *Blessed Rage for Order: The New Pluralism in Theology* (New York: Seabury, 1975), was a great stimulant in many ways to the final version of this chapter. I acknowledge this with gratitude.

2. This has been a recurring theme in my publications and was first systematically stated in "Context vs. Principles: A Misplaced Debate in Christian Ethics," *Harvard Theological Review* 58 (1965):171–202. I have not self-consciously attempted to use these points in subsequent publications but in retrospect observe their frequent appearance in different formulations and combinations.

3. Thomas Aquinas, *Summa Theologica,* II-II, Q. 64, art. 5.

4. Other illustrations could be given. A study of the theology and ethics of Jonathan Edwards, for example, can revolve around his favorite ascription to the glory of God, 1 Timothy 1:17, "Now unto the King eternal, immortal, invisible, the only wise God, be honor and glory forever and ever." A doctrine of the sovereignty of God (*a*) is the decisive point in determining what he has to say about moral agents—their limited freedom and the new life in those who are converted (*c*), his view of ethics as "consent to being" (*d*), and his highly causal-determinist view of history and nature (*b*).

5. Specific materials used in previous chapters are not cited again

here; I believe the index provides the means to find the materials for those who wish to do so.

6. An influential American Protestant theologian remarked to me, after he read James Childress, *Civil Disobedience and Political Obligation: A Study in Christian Social Ethics* (New Haven: Yale University Press, 1971), "It reads like a legal brief." This dismissed the book as unimportant.

7. I have also developed the thesis in *The Contributions of Theology to Medical Ethics*. For more elaborate analysis, see Lisa Cahill, "Euthanasia: A Catholic and a Protestant Perspective" (Ph.D. diss., University of Chicago, 1976). See also Charles E. Curran, "Paul Ramsey and Traditional Roman Catholic Natural Law Theory," in Johnson and Smith, *Love and Society*, pp. 47-65, and Charles E. Curran, *Politics, Medicine and Christian Ethics: A Dialogue with Paul Ramsey* (Philadelphia: Fortress, 1973).

8. Roger Mehl's *Catholic Ethics and Protestant Ethics*, and Franz Böckle's *Laws and Conscience* both go to the basic theological issues immediately and in some depth. I believe they do not sufficiently develop the complexity of theological ethics. While they have the merit of exposing theological controversies, the approach to these controversies is more direct; I am attempting to show that the traditional "theological" issues must be addressed in their complex relations to moral theory. Indeed disputes about moral theory are as problematic in the discussions as are more technically theological aspects.

The only book I know which is apparently integrally co-authored by a Catholic and a Protestant ethician proposes some levels of consensus in a response to the 1960s discussion of situation ethics. It is Johannes Gründel and Hendrik van Oyen, *Ethik ohne Normen?: zu den Weisungen des Evangelium* (Freiburg: Herder, 1970). The first part is brief but comprehensive; indeed, its subtitle is "Zur Begründung und Struktur christlicher Ethik." The second part uses the golden rule to develop a normative practical principle and takes into account American Protestants Joseph Fletcher and Paul Lehmann.

9. Many theologians have recently discovered that the critical apparatus of the sociology of knowledge is applicable to theology. This discovery is applied with cogency to unmask all sorts of theological enterprises, especially the theology that comes from universities and seminaries. The apparatus is a knife that cuts many ways, and can lead to the regress of the sociology of the sociology of knowledge.

Surely the imperative of this thesis can be subjected to the critique: what interests does it represent implicitly? and so forth. I would respond to a challenge in part autobiographically. My graduate studies concentrated a great deal on the literature that existed in the field at that time; I continue to believe that some additional clarity could be gained if theologians examined Robert K. Merton's "paradigm" for the sociology of knowledge in his *Social Theory and Social Structure* (Glencoe, Ill.: The Free Press, 1949), pp. 221-22. The direction of my intellectual quest has been from an acceptance of certain primary assumptions of that field toward ways of correcting the partialities and distortions implied, both among different groups within the historic Christian community and in Christian outlooks in relation to other communities. To do so is not to surrender distinctiveness, or to fault distinctiveness as only a distorting factor. Distinctiveness can lead to qualitatively important perceptions, relevant to particular historic conditions and to more general matters. But distinctiveness is different from claims to exclusivity; to acknowledge partiality requires for me its correction in interaction with other communities, and thus to finding more common or general principles (not only moral ones).

That this book can have little immediate influence on the choices and actions of Catholics and Protestants in struggles for liberation, in discussion about support for nuclear energy or whether the guidelines for research in recombinant DNA should be stronger or weaker, is clear. I only desire to make the claim that from one intellectual point of view the work this book attempts to further is necessary, but not sufficient, for the intellectual and also practical health of the Christian community.

10. Dorothee Soelle, *Political Theology*, p. 59.

Index

ref of. Maguire p. 39